Edward II

ARDEN EARLY MODERN DRAMA GUIDES

Series Editors:
Andrew Hiscock, University of Wales, Bangor, UK and Lisa Hopkins, Sheffield Hallam University, UK

Arden Early Modern Drama Guides offer practical and accessible introductions to the critical and performative contexts of key Elizabethan and Jacobean plays. Each guide introduces the text's critical and performance history, but also provides students with an invaluable insight into the landscape of current scholarly research, through a keynote essay on the state of the art and newly commissioned essays of fresh research from different critical perspectives.

A Midsummer Night's Dream edited by Regina Buccola
Doctor Faustus edited by Sarah Munson Deats
King Lear edited by Andrew Hiscock and Lisa Hopkins
1 Henry IV edited by Stephen Longstaffe
'Tis Pity She's a Whore edited by Lisa Hopkins
Women Beware Women edited by Andrew Hiscock
Volpone edited by Matthew Steggle
The Duchess of Malfi edited by Christina Luckyj
The Alchemist edited by Erin Julian and Helen Ostovich
The Jew of Malta edited by Robert A Logan
Macbeth edited by John Drakakis and Dale Townshend
Richard III edited by Annaliese Connolly
Twelfth Night edited by Alison Findlay and Liz Oakley-Brown
The Tempest edited by Alden T. Vaughan and Virginia Mason Vaughan

Romeo and Juliet: A Critical Reader, edited by
Julia Reinhard Lupton
Julius Caesar: A Critical Reader, edited by
Andrew James Hartley
The Revenger's Tragedy: A Critical Reader, edited by
Brian Walsh
The White Devil, edited by Paul Frazer and Adam Hansen
Further titles are in preparation

Edward II

A Critical Reader

Kirk Melnikoff

Bloomsbury Arden Shakespeare
An imprint of Bloomsbury Publishing Plc

B L O O M S B U R Y
LONDON • OXFORD • NEW YORK • NEW DELHI • SYDNEY

Bloomsbury Arden Shakespeare
An imprint of Bloomsbury Publishing Plc

Imprint previously known as Arden Shakespeare

50 Bedford Square	1385 Broadway
London	New York
WC1B 3DP	NY 10018
UK	USA

www.bloomsbury.com

BLOOMSBURY, THE ARDEN SHAKESPEARE and the Diana logo are trademarks of Bloomsbury Publishing Plc

First published 2017

© Kirk Melnikoff, 2017

Kirk Melnikoff has asserted his right under the Copyright, Designs and Patents Act, 1988, to be identified as author of this work.

All rights reserved. No part of this publication may be reproduced or transmitted in any form or by any means, electronic or mechanical, including photocopying, recording, or any information storage or retrieval system, without prior permission in writing from the publishers.

No responsibility for loss caused to any individual or organization acting on or refraining from action as a result of the material in this publication can be accepted by Bloomsbury or the author.

British Library Cataloguing-in-Publication Data
A catalogue record for this book is available from the British Library.

ISBN: HB: 978-1-4725-8404-5
       PB: 978-1-4725-8403-8
       ePDF: 978-1-4725-8406-9
       ePub: 978-1-4725-8405-2

Library of Congress Cataloging-in-Publication Data
A catalog record for this book is available from the Library of Congress.

Series: Arden Early Modern Drama Guides

Cover image taken from the 1615 title page of *The Spanish Tragedy* by Thomas Kyd

Typeset by Fakenham Prepress Solutions, Fakenham, Norfolk NR21 8NN

CONTENTS

Series Introduction ix
Acknowledgements x
Notes on Contributors xi
Timeline xv

    Introduction   *Kirk Melnikoff* 1
1 The Critical Backstory: *Edward II's* Critics in History to 1990   *Darlene Farabee* 21
2 *Edward II*: A Stage History   *Andrea Stevens* 43
3 The State of the Art: Desire, History and the Theatre   *Judith Haber* 73
4 Edoüard et Gaverston: New Ways of Looking at an English History Play   *Alan Stewart* 97
5 *Edward II* in Repertory   *Roslyn L. Knutson* 119
6 'Overpeered' and Understated: Conforming Transgressions and *Edward II*   *James Siemon* 145

7 'My Life, My Company': Amity, Enmity and Vitality in *Edward II*
   Garrett A. Sullivan, Jr. 175
8 A Survey of Resources: Teaching *Edward II*
   Edward Gieskes 195

Notes 221
Select Bibliography 281
Index 285

SERIES INTRODUCTION

The drama of Shakespeare and his contemporaries has remained at the very heart of English curricula internationally and the pedagogic needs surrounding this body of literature have grown increasingly complex as more sophisticated resources become available to scholars, tutors and students. This series aims to offer a clear picture of the critical and performative contexts of a range of chosen texts. In addition, each volume furnishes readers with invaluable insights into the landscape of current scholarly research as well as including new pieces of research by leading critics.

This series is designed to respond to the clearly identified needs of scholars, tutors and students for volumes which will bridge the gap between accounts of previous critical developments and performance history and an acquaintance with new research initiatives related to the chosen plays. Thus, our ambition is to offer innovative and challenging guides that will provide practical, accessible and thought-provoking analyses of early modern drama. Each volume is organized according to a progressive reading strategy involving introductory discussion, critical review and cutting-edge scholarly debate. It has been an enormous pleasure to work with so many dedicated scholars of early modern drama and we are sure that this series will encourage you to read 400-year-old play texts with fresh eyes.

Andrew Hiscock and Lisa Hopkins

ACKNOWLEDGEMENTS

This volume is in many ways a product of my work with the Marlowe Society of America (MSA) over the past two decades, first as a member, then as Treasurer and now as President. During these years, the Society's international conferences, newsletter, Roma Gill Prize and MLA panels have together helped ensure that Marlowe – his times, his contemporaries and his work – has remained front and centre in my thinking about early modern England. It is not an overstatement to say that without the MSA, my editorial work on *Edward II: A Critical Reader* would not have happened.

Since I began this project, I have accumulated numerous debts. For their camaraderie and support, I owe many thanks to fellow MSA members Claire Bourne, Bruce Brandt, Robert Darcy, Sara M. Deats, Brett Foster, Pierre Hecker, Robert A. Logan, David McInnis, Paul Menzer, Lucy Munro, Tom Rutter, Sarah K. Scott and Michael Stapleton. For their input and interest, I owe more than a few drinks to Sonya Brockman, Andrew J. Hartley, Helen Hull, Jeremy Lopez, Genny Love, Jennifer A. Munroe, James Siemon, Adam Smyth and Garrett Sullivan. I am particularly grateful to Edward Gieskes for reading an early version of the introduction and to Roslyn L. Knutson for her wit, mentorship and wisdom about all things Marlowe. And I would be remiss not to mention series editors Lisa Hopkins and Andrew Hiscock, and assistant editor Emily Hockley. Their support and guidance have been essential throughout the process of putting this volume together.

Two years ago, I was lucky to see a production of *Edward II* with my daughter Finley. She hated it, with good reason. Her insightful comments made this editor, this father proud. I'll close by thanking my partner, Lara Vetter. She continues to be my most important adviser and advocate. She is, has been and always will be an inspiration.

NOTES ON CONTRIBUTORS

Darlene Farabee is Associate Professor and Chair of the English Department at the University of South Dakota. Her book *Shakespeare's Staged Spaces and Playgoers' Perceptions* was published by Palgrave Macmillan in 2014, and she was co-editor of and contributor to the essay collection *Early Modern Drama in Performance* (Delaware, 2015). Farabee has a chapter in *Macbeth: The State of Play* (Arden, 2014) and has published several pieces in *Shakespeare Bulletin*. Her current book project explores the language of travel, navigation and proprioception in early modern drama.

Edward Gieskes is Associate Professor of English at the University of South Carolina, where he teaches courses on Shakespeare and early modern drama. His book *Representing the Professions* was published in 2006; he is the co-editor (with Kirk Melnikoff) of *Writing Robert Greene* (Ashgate, 2008); he has an essay on genre in the *Women Beware Women* volume in this series, and most recently a chapter on Bakhtin's genre theory and Thomas Kyd in the essay collection *Bakhtin and His Others* (Anthem, 2013). He has published essays in *ELH*, *Medieval and Renaissance Drama in England*, and *Renaissance Papers*. He is currently at work on a book-length study of genre and generic change.

Judith Haber is Professor of English at Tufts University. She is the author of *Desire and Dramatic Form in Early Modern Drama* (Cambridge, 2009) and *Pastoral and the Poetics of Self-Contradiction*: *Theocritus to Marvell* (Cambridge,

1994). She has published articles on Marlowe and other early modern writers in numerous anthologies and journals, including *Renaissance Drama*, *English Literary Renaissance*, *Representations* and *Shakespeare Studies*. She is currently working on a book tentatively entitled *Adoptive Strategies: Imagining Paternity in Early Modern England,* which will include an essay titled 'Marlowe's Queer Jew'.

Roslyn L. Knutson, Emerita Professor of English at the University of Arkansas at Little Rock, is the author of *Playing Companies and Commerce in Shakespeare's Time* (Cambridge, 2001) and *The Repertory of Shakespeare's Company, 1594–1613* (Arkansas, 1991) A pioneer in the field of repertory studies, she has published essays on playhouse commerce in numerous journals and collections including *Acts of Criticism* (2005); *Locating the Queen's Men* (2009); *Thunder at a Playhouse* (2010); *Shakespeare Quarterly* (2010); *Thomas Middleton in Context* (2011); and *Richard II: New Critical Essays* (2012). Her work on Marlowe's plays includes the following: 'Marlowe Reruns', in *Marlowe's Empery* (2002); co-editor of 'Marlowe the Play-maker', *Shakespeare Bulletin* (special issue, 2009); '*The Jew of Malta* in Repertory', in *The Jew of Malta: A Critical Guide* (2013); and 'Marlowe in Repertory', in *Marlowe, Theatrical Commerce, and the Book Trade* (forthcoming, Cambridge, 2017). An ongoing project is the wiki-style database, *Lost Plays* Database, which she co-edits with David McInnis (University of Melbourne).

Kirk Melnikoff is an associate professor in the Department of English at the University of North Carolina at Charlotte. He is a 2013 winner of the Hoffman Prize for Distinguished Publication on Marlowe and has edited two collections: *Writing Robert Greene* (with Gieskes, Ashgate, 2008) and *Robert Greene* (Ashgate, 2011). His essays have appeared in *Mosaic*, *Medieval and Renaissance Drama in England*, *Studies in Philology*, *The Library*, *The Continuum Handbook to Shakespeare Studies* (2009), *Shakespeare's Stationers* (2013), and *The Jew of Malta: A Critical Guide* (2013). He is currently co-editing (with Roslyn L. Knutson) the volume *Marlowe, Theatrical Commerce, and the Book Trade* for Cambridge University Press.

James Siemon is Professor of English at Boston University. He is the author of *Shakespearean Iconoclasm* (California, 1986) and *Word Against Word: Shakespearean Utterance* (Massachusetts, 2002); he has edited Christopher Marlowe's *Jew of Malta* (New Mermaids, 1994; rev. 2009), Shakespeare's *Richard III* (Arden, 2009) and *Julius Caesar* (Norton, 2013); and he has written numerous articles on early modern English drama and culture. He is currently editing *Shakespeare Studies*, and he is working on a monograph on social distinction in early modern English drama.

Andrea Stevens is Associate Professor of English, Theatre, and Medieval Studies at the University of Illinois at Urbana-Champaign, specializing in Shakespeare and early modern drama. Her research appears in such journals as *ELR*, *Theatre Notebook* and *Shakespeare Bulletin*, and in the essay collections *Thunder at a Playhouse* and *The Effects of Performance in the Theatres of Shakespeare and His Contemporaries*. Her book *Inventions of the Skin: The Painted Body in Early English Drama 1400–1642* (Edinburgh, 2013) examines the painted body of the actor on the early modern stage.

Alan Stewart is Professor of English and Comparative Literature at Columbia University, and International Director of the Centre for Editing Lives and Letters in London. He is the author, most recently, of *Shakespeare's Letters* (Oxford, 2008), editor of volume 1 of the *Oxford Francis Bacon* (Oxford, 2012), and co-editor, with Garrett Sullivan, of the three-volume *Encyclopedia of English Renaissance Literature* (Blackwell, 2012). He is currently working on editing volume 2 of the *Oxford Francis Bacon*; a student anthology of Tudor drama for Broadview; and a monograph on early modern life-writing for Oxford University Press. His chapter here is related to his project on *French Shakespeare*, for which he was awarded a John Simon Guggenheim Foundation Fellowship in 2011–12.

Garrett A. Sullivan, Jr., Liberal Arts Research Professor of English at Penn State University, is the author of three books: *The Drama of Landscape: Land, Property, and Social Relations on the Early Modern Stage* (Stanford, 1998); *Memory and Forgetting in English Renaissance Drama: Shakespeare, Marlowe, Webster* (Cambridge, 2005); and most recently *Sleep, Romance and Human Embodiment: Vitality from Spenser to Milton* (Cambridge, 2012). He has edited numerous volumes including *Environment and Embodiment in Early Modern England* (with Mary Floyd-Wilson, Palgrave Macmillan, 2007); *The Cambridge Companion of English Renaissance Tragedy* (with Emma Smith, Cambridge University Press, 2010); and *The Encyclopedia of English Renaissance Literature* (with Alan Stewart, Blackwell, 2012).

TIMELINE

1284, 25 April: Edward II born in Caernarfon Castle in Northern Wales.

1307, 26 February: Piers Gaveston ordered into exile by Edward I, Edward II's father.

1307, 7 July: Edward I dies in the northern village of Burgh by Sands, England.

1307, 20 July: Edward II proclaimed King of England. Days later, Gaveston returns from exile.

1308, 25 January: Edward II marries Isabella, the French King's daughter in Boulogne, France.

1312, 19 June: Piers Gaveston executed near Warwick Castle.

1312, 13 November: Edward III born at Windsor Castle.

1314, 24 June: English forces led by Edward II routed in the Battle of Bannockburn in Scotland.

1326, 27 October: Hugh le Despenser, the elder, executed in the city of Bristol.

1326, 24 November: Hugh le Despenser, the younger, executed in the city of Hereford.

1327, January: Edward II resigns crown at Kenilworth Castle.

1327, 1 February: Edward III crowned King of England at Westminster Abbey.

1327, 28 May: Robert Baldock dies in Newgate Prison.

1327, 21 September: Edward II dies at Berkeley Castle.

1330, 29 November: Roger Mortimer hanged at Tyburn.

1358, 23 August: Isabella of France, Edward II's widow, dies at Hertford Castle.

1564, February: Christopher Marlowe born, the first son of John (a Canterbury shoemaker) and Katherine Marlowe. He is the second of what will be nine children.

1564, 26 February: Christening of Marlowe at St George's Church in Canterbury.

1578, December: Marlowe receives scholarship for the Queen's (now 'King's') School in Canterbury. He likely had attended another Canterbury petty school and grammar school from as early as 1570.

1580, December: Marlowe arrives at Corpus Christi College in Cambridge University.

1581, 17 March: Marlowe matriculates at Cambridge University.

1581, 7 May: Marlowe formally awarded Archbishop Parker Scholarship at Cambridge University. The scholarship was endowed for Canterbury Queen's School students to attend Corpus Christi College.

1582, 13 October: Thomas Nashe, co-author of *Dido Queen of Carthage* with Marlowe, matriculates at St John's College in Cambridge University. Nashe would leave Cambridge in 1588.

1584, July: Marlowe formally receives BA. Around this time, he is also admitted to Corpus Christ College to pursue his MA.

1585, November: Marlowe is in Canterbury where he signs the will of Katherine Benchkin with his father, uncle and brother-in-law. This document contains the only extant signature of Marlowe.

1587: Marlowe is writing plays for the professional playing companies. The first part of *Tamburlaine* probably staged by the Admiral's Men; the second part is staged the following year.

1587: The second edition of Raphael Holinshed's *Chronicles*, Marlowe's primary source for *Edward II*, is published in London.

1587, March: Marlowe leaves Cambridge for the final time.

1587, 29 June: Elizabeth's Privy Council requests that Marlowe 'be furthered in the degree he was to take this next commencement: Because it was not her Majesties pleasure that anie one emploied as he had been in matters touching the benefitt of his countrie should be defamed by those that are ignorant in th'affaires he went about'.

1587, July: Marlowe receives MA.

1588: The first edition of the anonymous libel *Histoire tragique et memorable de Pierre de Gauerston* published in France.

1588, August: The English defeat the Spanish Armada at the Battle of Graveslines.

1589, 2 August: French King Henry III assassinated in Saint-Cloud, France.

1589, 18 September: Marlowe incarcerated in Newgate prison with the poet Thomas Watson for the murder of the innkeeper's son William Bradley. That afternoon, Watson had killed Bradley in London's Hog Lane after intervening in a fight between him and Marlowe. After a few weeks, Marlowe is released on bail and, with Watson, ultimately acquitted of Bradley's murder.

1590: The London printer Richard Jones publishes the two parts of *Tamburlaine* without an author attribution. These are the first works by Marlowe to appear in print. Jones will reprint the titles in 1593 and 1597.

1591: Marlowe shares a writing room with the dramatist Thomas Kyd.

1591, 26 February: First recorded performance of *The Jew of Malta* in Philip Henslowe's diary.

1592, January: Marlowe arrested with the goldsmith Gifford Gilbert for counterfeiting in Flushing, Netherlands after being accused by their roommate Richard Baines. The two are eventually sent back to England and released.

1592, 9 May: Marlowe is required by the Middlesex Justice of the Peace to 'keep the peace' after threatening two constables. He is also bound to appear at the next session in October.

1592, 15 September: Marlowe fights with the tailor William Corkine in the streets of Canterbury. Corkine's suit for damages is later settled out of court.

1592, 26 December: First record and recorded performance of Pembroke's Men, one of the first playing companies to own *Edward II*.

1593, 30 January: First recorded performance of *The Massacre at Paris* in Philip Henslowe's diary. Henslowe marks it as a new play.

1593, February: Serious outbreak of the plague in London; professional theatres are closed for most of the remaining year.

1593, 12 May: Thomas Kyd arrested on suspicion of libel. After heretical papers are found in his room, Kyd, upon being tortured, attributes these to Marlowe.

1593, 20 May: Marlowe appears before Elizabeth's Privy Council and is ordered to give 'his daily attendance'.

1593, 30 May: Marlowe dies at the Deptford house of the widow Eleanor Bull, killed by Ingram Frizer after a dispute over the 'reckoning' (the bill). A day later, the coroner's inquest finds that Frizer acted in self-defence. Frizer is later pardoned.

1593, 1 June: Marlowe buried at St Nicholas's Church in Deptford.

1593, 6 July: *Edward II* entered by the London bookseller William Jones into the Stationers' Register.

1594: The first edition of *Edward II* published by William Jones and printed by the London printer Robert Robinson with the full title *The Troublesome Reign and Lamentable Death of Edward II, King of England, with the Tragic Fall of Proud Mortimer*. The octavo's title page advertises that the play 'was sundrie times publiquely acted … *by the* right honourable the Earle of Pem*brooke his seruants*' and written by 'Chri. Marlow *Gent.*'. This information will appear in the play's second, third and fourth editions.

1594: The first edition of Michael Drayton's poem *Piers Gaveston Earl of Cornwall. His Life, Death, and Fortune* is published. Subsequent editions (some revised) appear in 1595, 1596, 1605, 1608, 1610, 1613, 1616, 1619, 1630 and 1637.

1594: *Dido Queen of Carthage* is published and is attributed to 'Christopher Marlowe, and *Thomas Nash. Gent.*'. *Edward II* and *Dido* are the first print titles that are attributed to Marlowe.

1594, 30 September: First recorded performance of *Doctor Faustus* in Philip Henslowe's diary.

1596: The first edition of Michael Drayton's poem *Mortimeriados. The Lamentable Civil Wars of Edward II and the Barons* is published. Subsequent editions (some revised) appear in 1603, 1605, 1608, 1610, 1613, 1616, 1619, 1630, and 1637.

1598: The second edition of *Edward II* published by William Jones and printed by the London printer Richard Bradock. In this and subsequent editions, the original print title is expanded to include *the Life and Death of Piers Gaveston, the Great Earl of Cornwall and Mighty Favorite of King Edward II.*

1610: Richard Niccols's 'The Woeful Life and Death of King Edward II' printed as part of *The Mirror for Magistrates*.

1611, 16 December: Right to copy *Edward II* transferred from William Jones to the London bookseller Roger Barnes.

1612: The third edition of *Edward II* published by Barnes and printed by the London printer William Jaggard.

1612–22: *Edward II* is at some point possibly revived by the Queen Anna's Men at the Red Bull Theatre.

1617, 17 April: Right to copy *Edward II* transferred from Barnes to the London bookseller Henry Bell.

1622: The fourth edition of *Edward II* published by Bell at Eliot's Court Press. A variant strand of the edition advertises that the play 'was publikely Acted by the late Queenes *Maiesties Seruants at the* Red Bull *in* S. Iohns *streete*'.

1626: Elizabeth Cary finishes *The History of the Life, Reign, and Death of Edward II*.

1638, 4 September: Right to copy *Edward II* transferred from Bell to the London printer John Haviland and to the London bookseller John Wright.

Introduction

Kirk Melnikoff

Edward II has long been considered Christopher Marlowe's most mature drama. Masterful in its adaptation of chronicle source material, relentless in its ambiguities and inversions and deeply unsettling in its tragic conclusion, the play offers an equivocal portrait of an ardent king amid the internecine politics of a feudal court.[1] Infamously, Edward II's murder is staged in the penultimate scene, the assassin Lightborne penetrating the tortured monarch with a 'red hot' spit. With Shakespeare's *King Henry VI Part 1* and *2*, *Edward II* has been identified as one of our first surviving examples of an English history play, and in its earliest manifestations on stage and in print it appears to have been well received for a number of decades. Since the 1980s, Marlowe's history has stood at the centre of scholarship concerned with the intersections of identity, power and sexuality in the early modern period. During this time, it also has inspired a number of provocative revivals, from Nicholas Hytner's production at the Royal Exchange in 1986 to Gerald Murphy's Royal Shakespeare Company (RSC) production starring Simon Russell Beale in 1990 to Derek Jarman's film version in 1991. As Joe Hill-Gibbins's multimedia staging at London's National Theatre in 2013 suggests, the play's characters and themes continue to hold appeal for audiences in the twenty-first century.

§

Like the entirety of Marlowe's oeuvre, *Edward II* has proven almost impossible to date with any certainty. Most commentators have settled on late 1591 or early 1592 as the *terminus ad quo*, cautiously citing the artistic maturity of the play and/or passages that echo phrases or lines from Shakespeare's first tetralogy (possibly completed by 1591), George Peele's *Edward I* (possibly composed between 1590 and 1591), the anonymous *Thomas of Woodstock* (possibly composed as early as 1591), and the anonymous *The Troublesome Reign of King John* (printed in 1591). The year 1592 has been identified as the play's *terminus ad quem* both because *Edward II* has commonly been assumed to precede Marlowe's *The Massacre at Paris* which was first staged in January 1593 and because the anonymous *Arden of Faversham* (possibly composed in early 1592) and Thomas Kyd's *Soliman and Perseda* (possibly composed in 1592) contain echoing passages.[2]

While its date of composition remains elusive, evidence of *Edward II*'s early fortunes on the stage and on the page does exist. On 6 July 1593, the London bookseller William Jones paid the clerk at Stationers' Hall six pence to register ownership of a 'booke' entitled 'The troublesom Reign and Lamentable Death of Edward the Second, king of England, with the tragicall fall of proud Mortymer'.[3] When Jones distributed the play the next year under this title, his title page also advertised both that it 'was sundrie times publiquely acted *in the honourable citie of London, by the* right honourable the Earle of Pembrooke his seruants' and written by 'Chri. Marlow *Gent.*'.[4] In naming Pembroke's Men as a professional playing company that owned the play, Jones's playtext suggested a range of recent performance dates: from 1594 back to late 1592 when, as Knutson's chapter in this volume suggests, the company likely came into existence. As possibly the first printed text to bear his name, the 'quarto' announced Marlowe as a professional playwright of the day even as it – likely printed less than a year after his death – memorialized his name.[5]

Jones's decision to pursue an edition in the summer of 1593 also put *Edward II* at the centre of significant developments in

London's book trade. Between 1576 and 1592, only fourteen different adult professional plays made it to the bookstalls of St Paul's, and of these, only *Common Conditions* (1576, *after* 1576), Robert Wilson's *The Three Ladies of London* (1584, 1592) and possibly Thomas Kyd's *The Spanish Tragedy* (1592, 1592) had been successful enough to reach a second edition.[6] Even after sixteen years of amphitheatre playhouses, playwrights, players and playgoing, London in 1592 had still not mustered a vibrant print market for adult professional drama. The year 1593 marked the very beginnings of a significant change. That year, not only would first editions of *Edward I* and *The Life and Death of Jack Straw* be published by Abel Jeffes and John Danter respectively, but the ubiquitous printer Richard Jones would bring out a second edition of his two-part unascribed *Tamburlaine*. While it is impossible to know whether these new editions inspired William Jones's registration of *Edward II* in July, it does seem probable that the 1592 second editions of *The Three Ladies of London* and *The Spanish Tragedy* did. Thus, sometime during 1594 Jones distributed his first edition of *Edward II*, and by the end of the year it was one of as many as fifteen newly printed adult professional playbooks available on London's bookstalls.[7] This 1594 'boomlet' would lead to what was the first extended publishing boom in adult professional plays between 1598 and 1613.[8] The year 1598 witnessed the publication of eleven professional play titles, and Jones's second edition of *Edward II* was one of them.[9]

Marlowe's history play would be published two more times by booksellers before 1640, once in 1612 by Roger Barnes and then again in 1622 by Henry Bell.[10] In this, gauged according to reprint rates, *Edward II* proved to be one of the more popular professional plays to be printed before 1640. What drove such success is unclear.[11] It is conceivable that book buyers were drawn by the new currency of Marlowe's name, the beginnings of a 'Marlowe moment' in London's sphere of print.[12] This seems especially probable at the opening of the seventeenth century when the bookseller Thomas Thorpe could estimate that Marlowe's 'ghoast or *Genius* is to be seene walke the *Churchyard* in (at the least) three of foure sheets' (*Lucan*, sig. A2ʳ). *Edward II*'s popularity in print might also have been linked to the play's continued presence on the professional stage. Though it has commonly been assumed that late 1593 marked the endpoint of *Edward II*'s first short-lived theatrical run that started in 1592, Knutson's chapter in this volume suggests an earlier stage life in 1591 possibly with the Admiral's Men; she also outlines three possible paths of playing-company ownership and transmission between 1593 and 1622.[13] This early theatrical vitality appears to be documented by the 1622 edition's new advertisement that the play had been 'publikely Acted by the late Queenes *Maiesties Seruants at the* Red Bull *in* S. Iohns *streete*'.

It is also possible to imagine that Marlowe's play – riding a new wave of professional drama in print – came to stand as a successful historical narrative in its own right, a host of readers drawn to Marlowe's rendition of feudal politics, tragic love, civil war and deposition in fourteenth-century England. Indeed, this topic – England under Edward II – continued to be popular in London's book markets long after Marlowe was initially inspired by the chronicle histories of Fabyan, Grafton, Stow and especially Holinshed.[14] Shortly after Marlowe's death, Michael Drayton produced the bestselling poems *The Legend of Piers Gaveston* (1595?) and *Mortimeriados* (1596) along with *England's Heroicall Epistles* (1597).[15] In the earliest of these, Drayton points to much contemporary 'confusion' surrounding Edward II's companion Gaveston: 'Diuers haue been the opinions, of the byrth and first rysing of *Gaveston*, (amongst the Writers of these latter times:) some omiting things worthy of memory, some inferring thinges without probabilitie, disagreeing in many particulars, and caueling in the circumstances of his sundry banishments' (sig. G1ʳ). A few years later in 1602, the first of two editions of Thomas Deloney's *Strange Histories* was published with long poems on Edward II's imprisonment; on Edward II's torture and murder; and on the exile of Maltravers and Gourney. A new edition of *The Mirror for Magistrates*, was published in 1610, expanded by Richard Niccols to include among other things his tragic *Woeful Life and Death of King Edward II* told from the perspective of the deposed and murdered king. The decade also witnessed the publication of three new chronicle histories of England: John Speed's *The History of Great Britain* in 1611; William Martyn's *The History and Lives of the Kings of England* in 1615; and Samuel Daniel's *The Collection of the History of England* in 1618. Each recounts with much energy and detail the events and personages of Edward II's tumultuous reign. Together, these works attest both to a heightened interest in Edward II's story during the late Elizabethan and Jacobean periods. Reprinted and staged through these years, Marlowe's play likely benefited from and contributed to this currency.

Whether part of a larger Marlowe moment, offshoot of a theatrical mainstay, and/or contribution to a larger cultural obsession with historical narratives of civil war and deposition, *Edward II* was eagerly read in the decades following Marlowe's death. However, if the play's early readers were looking for commanding poetic language in the vein of *Tamburlaine*, they most certainly would have been disappointed. Marlowe's English history play affords only fleeting traces of these 'mighty lines' – blank verse, first-person addresses characterized by ambitious 'wills' and 'shalls'; exotic imagery; and classical allusion.[16] In fits and starts, the play's most aspirational characters Gaveston – 'And there hard by, / One like Actaeon peeping through the grove, / Shall by the angry goddess be transformed' (1.65–7) – and Mortimer Junior – 'I stand as Jove's huge tree, / and others are but shrubs compared to me' (25.11–12) – deliver such lines. Edward II too, in his frequent moments of frustration and anger, speaks with the striking language of Marlowe's overreaching heroes. Responding to the threat of Gaveston's banishment in the fourth scene, he may promise that 'Ere my sweet Gaveston shall from me, / This isle shall fleet upon the ocean / And wander to the unfrequented Inde', but such assertive flights of fancy are still rare in the play and always abbreviated.

Instead, what the play gives us – aside from Gaveston's opening soliloquies and Edward II's moving late complaints (e.g. in scenes 19, 20 and 22) – is language that is for the most part 'prosaic' (Guy-Bray, xxiv), even 'stifle[d]' (Siemon, 146).[17] This is especially noticeable not only in the Barons' dialogue but also during some of the most charged moments of the play. All that Gaveston is made to muster before being carted off to execution is 'Treacherous Earl, shall I not see the king?' (10.15). Edward II's second favourite may have more lines at his final moment on stage, but other than a compound trio of short cosmic commands, Spencer Junior can only mouth redundant questions and observations: 'O, is he gone? Is noble Edward gone, / Parted from hence, never to see us more? / Rend, sphere of heaven, and fire forsake thy orb! / Earth melt to air! Gone is my sovereign, / Gone, gone, alas, never to make return' (19.99–103). As some commentators have observed, this dearth of heightened expression is appropriate in this 'harsh, gray' (Wiggins, xxii) political world where 'sweet speeches … and pleasing shows' (1.55) are suspect, aligned by the Barons with upstart ambition and misrule.[18] One wonders too whether Marlowe might have been looking to modify his dramatic idiom as his career progressed. Even if we admit the likelihood that *Tamburlaine* was the inspiration for an explosion of 'weak-son' imitations, it also is true that what was likely Marlowe's first efforts on the adult professional stage provoked much derision from his contemporaries.[19] Robert Greene, in his *Perimedes the Black Smith* (1588), was quick to deride 'verses [that] iet vpon the stage in tragicall buskins, euerie worde filling the mouth like the faburden of Bo-Bell, daring God out of heaven with that Atheist *Tamburlan*' (sig. A3r). A year later, Marlowe's collaborator Thomas Nashe, in his epistle prefacing Greene's *Menaphon* (1589), would double down on this critique, condemning those 'idiote art-masters, that intrude themselues to our eares as the alcumists of eloquence; who (mounted on the stage of arrogance) think to outbraue better pens with the swelling bumbast of a bragging blanke verse' (sig. **1r).

Whatever its motivation, Marlowe's turn away from the mighty line was accompanied by a strong turn toward English history. As was recognized by its earliest commentators, *Edward II* owes a heavy debt to Raphael Holinshed's *Chronicles of England, Scotland, and Ireland* (1577, rev. 1587).[20] There, Marlowe found a rich albeit 'clotted' (Forker, 44) chronological account, and from it he took many of the play's places, personages and episodes.[21] From Holinshed too, Marlowe took such details as Mortimer Junior's derisive description of what in the play is represented as Edward II's only Scottish campaign (6.179–84); Spencer Junior's plan to elude Isabella's army by escaping to Ireland (18.3); and Winchester's entreaty to Edward II that 'it is for England's good / and princely Edward's right we crave the crown (20.38–9)'. The chronicle also provided much creative stimulation. From it, Marlowe appears to have taken inspiration for the second half of Gaveston's opening soliloquy (1.49–70). On the opening page of its account, the chronicle describes how, at the encouragement of Gaveston, the newly crowned Edward II 'furnished his court with companies of iesters, ruffians, flattering parasites, musicians, and other vile and naughtie ribalds, that the king might spend both daies and nights in iesting, plaieng, banketing, and in such other filthie and dishonorable exercises' (6.318).[22] Marlowe seems to have been similarly inspired by Holinshed's description of Edward II's holding dungeon at Berkeley Castle, by the chronicle's sketch of its stench and filth. This led to the penultimate scene's moving depiction of Edward II's emotional and physical suffering in a 'mire and puddle,' a place that 'stifle[s] for the savour' (24.58–9).

Nonetheless, as much as he was influenced by Holinshed, Marlowe shaped his dramatic rendering of *Edward II* in ways that were original and as such telling. To begin with, Marlowe barely mentions Edward II's inept management of an inherited northern war with Robert Bruce and Scotland that lasted for more than two thirds of his reign. In the play, we hear of Mortimer Senior's commission to Scotland (4.360–4) and

then of his capture in Edward II's 'wars' (6.113–17). With
Mortimer Junior's ridicule of Edward II's Scottish campaign,
Lancaster makes reference to the Scots coming to 'the walls
of York ... unresisted', to violence at the northern border and
to 'England's high disgrace' at Bannockburn (6.163–4, 176–7,
186). In Holinshed, however, episodes from this conflict
constitute a substantial part of its account of Edward II's reign,
recurring again and again. These include lengthy descriptions
of Bruce's many destructive raids across the border along with
Edward II's stumbling campaigns around Berwick in 1311 and
1319, his devastating defeat at Bannockburn in 1314 and his
narrow escape from capture near Yorkshire's Byland Abbey
in 1322. Taking stock of much of this, the chronicle laments
that 'all the kings exploits by one means or other quailed,
and came but to euill successe, so that the English nation
began to grow in contempt by the infortunate gouernment
of the prince, the which as one out of the right waie, rashlie
and with no good aduisement ordered his dooings' (6.325).
Of course, the muting of these 'exploits' in *Edward II* helps
streamline what is still a complicated narrative, but it also
helps sustain what is the play's ambiguous portrait of Edward
II's stewardship of the realm.[23] Marlowe's Edward II may be
accused in the sixth scene of offering weak mettle at home and
of avoiding confrontation abroad, but from the start what we
actually see is a king quick to succumb to fits of anger and
swift to move to a fight.[24] This is readily apparent even as
early as his first exchange with the Barons when he turns to
Kent and complains, 'I cannot brook these haughty menaces:
/ Am I a king and must be overruled? / Brother, display my
ensigns in the field' (1.134–5). What may appear in the first
half of the play to be Mycetes-like bravado, however, is shown
to be potentially in earnest by Edward II's actions in the play's
two battles where he proves a zealous soldier and forthright
leader. With the 'evil successe' of his northern war essentially
veiled, Edward II's courage both in defeating the barons –
'Why do we sound retreat? Upon them lords! / This day I shall
pour vengeance with my sword / On those proud rebels that

are up in arms' (12.1–3) – and in being defeated by Isabella – 'Give me my horse, and let's r'enforce our troops. / And in this bed of honour die with fame' (18.6–7) – stands out.[25]

Even as he curbed Holinshed's description of England's ill-fated encounters with Scotland under Edward II, Marlowe reimagined the social status of Edward II's three favourites: Gaveston is reduced from 'an esquire of Gascoine' (Holinshed, 6.313) to 'base and obscure' (1.100) and a 'peasant' (2.30); Baldock is converted from a 'master' (Holinshed, 6.332) or gentleman to Lady Margaret de Clare's tutor (5.29–30); and Spencer Junior is downgraded from a nobly appointed Lord Chamberlain (Holinshed, 6.331) to a 'base upstart' (12.21), a servant in the Earl of Gloucester's household.[26] With this version of history, Marlowe, as more than one commentator has noted, transformed Edward II's favourites into surrogates, each of these characters experiencing, as he did as the ambitious son of a shoemaker, the love and scorn of his social superiors. In this, Marlowe's *Edward II* presents an account of deposition deeply infused with social mobility as both recurring anxiety and theme.[27] Such a concoction, as James Siemon tracks in his contribution to this volume, is both complex and essentially unique among similar professional plays of the period. A drama of proto-class antagonism through and through, Marlowe's *Edward II* gives us a larger plot entirely motivated by conflict between ranks, and it continually stages scenes where labels of position – 'king', 'lord', 'prince', 'knight', etc. – are deployed in such a way that they are recognized but continually compromised in their authority.

As much as tensions surrounding social distinction drive the play, questions regarding the sexuality of Edward II and his favourite Gaveston have driven the play's more recent critical tradition. In the chronicle, Edward II is often accused of being unduly influenced by what is vaguely described as his 'feruent affection' (6.319) for Gaveston. This affection leads the new king to 'burst out into most heinous vices; … so that within a while, he gaue himselfe to wantonnes, passing his time in voluptuous pleasure, and riotous excesse' (6.318). In Marlowe's play, images and literary allusions along with tender exchanges in the first, fourth and sixth scenes together make it clear that Edward II's relationship with Gaveston is as sexual as it is intimate. Newly returned from exile at the play's opening, Gaveston imagines himself as Leander crossing the Hellespont to rejoin his lover Hero. Briefly interrupted from his reverie by three poor men, he then dreams of presenting an erotic pageant to Edward II, one which includes 'a lovely boy in Dian's shape, / With hair that gilds the water as it glides, / Crownets of naked pearl about his naked arms / And in his sportful hands an olive tree / To hide those parts which men delight to see' (1.60–4). Later on, Edward II's queen and rivals also conceive of his relationship with Gaveston in sexually suggestive terms. Lamenting her abandonment, Isabella complains that 'never doted Jove on Ganymede / So much as [Edward] on cursèd Gaviston' (4.180–1). Likewise, counseling patience in the face of Edward II's private dotage, Mortimer Senior advises his nephew 'to let [the king] without controlment have his will', invoking the examples of Alexander, Hercules, Achilles, Tully and Socrates as powerful men who all 'have had their minions' (6.391–8). As Alan Stewart tracks in his contribution to this volume, Marlowe appears to have initially derived this sexual sense of 'minion' from the anonymous French libel *Histoire tragique et memorable de Pierre de Gauerston* (1588), a tract that compares the bond between Edward II and Gaveston to that between the French King Henry III and his favourite the Duc d'Espernon.

Most commentators have concurred that *Edward II* sexualizes Edward II's 'feruent affection'; they have not agreed about the significance of this.[28] Before the 1980s, it was often argued that the play gives us a homosexual king whose actions are symbolically punished – in the dramatic style of a moral interlude – by Lightborne's red-hot spit.[29] To this, some countered that the brutality and symbolism of Edward II's staged murder in fact works to confound, even indict the homophobia that the play's first half so provokes.[30] Inspired by the work of Foucault in the late 1970s and Eve Sedgwick in the 1980s, more recent commentators have attempted to read the play's engagement with desire and sex historically. For some of these critics, *Edward II* opens a space for a form of sexual subjectivity during the period, showing sodomy – vaguely associated in the 1500s with buggery, criminality and social deviance – literally being written onto Edward II's body. The play's penultimate scene then becomes a crucial moment in what was the early modern period's emergent epistemology of sexuality.[31] Arguing against such a history, other critics have maintained that sodomy is in fact not limited to homosexuality by the play, that Mortimer Junior and Isabella's sexual relationship in proving politically disruptive to the state would have qualified too as sodomitical.[32] In this, Marlowe juxtaposes two pairs of monarchs and minions, ultimately indicting heterosexual desire as potentially more destructive – given the play's apparent empathy with its deposed king – than homosexual desire.

Key to all of these readings is the play's penultimate scene, the onstage murder of Edward II. Much of this sequence's detail Marlowe derived from Holinshed, including what in the play is described as the intended means – 'a spit ... red hot' along with a 'table and featherbed' (24.30, 33) – and the method – 'lay the table down and stamp on it; / But not too hard, lest that you bruise the body' (24.111–12).[33] Lightborne, however, stands as a clear interpolation by Marlowe. Reminiscent of Barabas and of stage devils from an earlier mystery-play tradition and from *Doctor Faustus* ('Lightborne' being an Englished 'Lucifer'), this Vice-like, Machiavellian character helps enable the didacticism of the scene while at the same time reprising the 'savage streak' (Wiggins, xxxiii) present throughout and affording an opportunity for suggestive casting – the actor playing Gaveston free to double as Lightborne.[34]

As arguably 'the most sodomitical character in the play' (Guy-Bray, xviii), it is Mortimer Junior who is made to provide consistent and virulent opposition to Edward II. At the beginning, he not only reminds the king that it was he and his uncle who had 'sworn to [Edward II's] father at his death, / That [Gaveston] should ne'er return into the realm' (1.82–3), but he also threatens violent rebellion with his departing 'let us leave the brainsick King, / And henceforth parley with our naked swords' (1.124–5). After a staged private conversation between him and Isabella, Mortimer Junior pleads for Gaveston's repeal. Two scenes later, awaiting Gaveston's imminent return from Ireland, he again incenses Edward II with his irreverent device of a cankered cedar tree (6.59–63); once Gaveston enters, Mortimer Junior then wounds Edward II's favourite, thus inciting the first of two civil wars. None of these particular details is to be found in Holinshed or in any of Marlowe's other sources. In fact, neither Mortimer plays a significant role in these accounts until Gaveston had been dead for many years. Invented entirely by Marlowe, Mortimer Junior's early impulsive and imperious actions establish not simply the early grounds for what the printed playtexts will describe as 'the tragicall fall of proud Mortimer', but they also provide a compelling foil for the actions of Edward II.[35] Indeed, both identified during the course of the play as young men, Mortimer Junior and Edward II confront the audience with differing expressions of youthful vitality.[36] For Mortimer Junior, such energy is defined by untrammelled will and ambition, so much so that he can muse in facing death that 'seeing there was no place to mount up higher, / Why should I grieve at my declining fall?' (25.62–3). For England's deposed king, as Garrett Sullivan's chapter in this volume well demonstrates, this vigor is directed toward forms of 'corporate vitality', and it is defined in particular against the dynastic logic of hereditary monarchy.

Unlike his actions in the first half, Mortimer Junior's adulterous relationship with Isabella in the play's second half was at least suggested by Marlowe's sources. Holinshed, however, does not mention the affair until its account of Edward III's reign. There in a long paragraph preceding the accusation that Mortimer Junior had 'procured Edward of Carnaruan the kings father to be murthered', it reports not simply that Isabella 'loued [Mortimer Junior] more (as the fame went) than stood well with hir honour' but that 'their manner of dealing, tending to such euill purposes as they continuallie thought vpon, ... was so much the more heinous, bicause they were persons of an extraordinarie degree' (6.349).[37] Marlowe may have been inspired by Holinshed's elusive suggestion of 'evill purposes', making his Mortimer Junior not just patently guilty of plotting Edward II's murder but responsible for Spencer Senior being sent 'to the block' (18.78); for the deposed king being '[r]emove[d] ... from place to place by night' (21.58), for the commissioning and double crossing of Lightborne and for the execution of Kent. In this, the play counterbalances the pathos of Edward II's demise and murder with the unsettling displays of Mortimer Junior's cresting power.

Also the product of Marlowe's imagination, Mortimer Junior's deeds at the end of Edward II's reign provide the final ingredients of his tragic fall; they put the finishing touches as well on what is Marlowe's complicated portrait of Isabella, Edward II's infamous queen.[38] In Holinshed, Isabella is represented consistently as the confident prime mover of Edward's defeat in 1326 and of his deposition in 1327, this even as the chronicle suggests at one point that 'without [Mortimer Junior] the queene in all these matters did nothing' (6.339) and identifies the Bishop of Hereford as one of the Queen's main collaborators in Edward II's murder. In the play, Marlowe's Isabella may be as politically motivated as her male counterparts, but her agency is shown throughout to be defined and ultimately delimited by her gender. At the start, to garner notice from the male barons and to protect her privileged position, Isabella moves between modes of female complaint – 'Like frantic Juno will I fill the earth / With ghastly murmur of my sighs and cries' (4.178–9) – and maternal sympathy – 'Ah me, poor soul, when these begin to jar' (6.72). Upon gathering an army in France, though, she re-enters England triumphantly and in a speech to 'lords, our loving friends and countrymen' invokes both her commanding alter ego in Holinshed and, as a number of commentators have pointed out, Elizabeth I at Tilbury. This, however, does not last long. Advising 'if you be a warrior, / Ye must not grow so passionate in speeches' (17.14–15), Mortimer Junior interrupts Isabella midline with a pointed reminder of gender, him observing that her passions have marked her as woman. From this moment on, Isabella plays the surrogate wife (Callaghan, 288) to Mortimer's general – 'Be ruled by me,' he tells her after learning of Edward II's deposition – 'and we will rule the realm' (21.5). It should be said that Mortimer Junior's offer here is paradoxical, and its promise comes to a fitting conclusion in the final scene when a judgement on Isabella's agency in the death of Edward II is deferred by the newly crowned Edward III: 'Mother, you are suspected for his death, / And therefore we commit you to the Tower / Till further trial may be made thereof' (25.81–2).[39]

On the face of it, Edward III at the play's close stands as the embodiment of a new order and, as he himself casts it, 'innocency' (25.102). Here, the play vaguely echoes Holinshed's providential description of England after Edward III's accession to the throne: 'in the beginning of this kings reigne the land trulie séemed to be blessed of God: for the earth became fruitfull, the aire temperate, and the sea calme and quiet' (6.345). As many commentators have observed, though, Marlowe's ending comes with strong ironic undercurrents. While the new king may present himself as grieving son and agent of political justice – 'Could I have ruled thee then, as I do now, / Thou hadst not hatched this monstrous treachery' (25.96–7) – his final action of offering up Mortimer Junior's decapitated head to his dead father's hearse is profoundly unsettling. In this closing tableau, Marlowe gives us a gruesome spectacle portending more violence as part and parcel of continued dynastic authority.[40] Portentous too, given Edward II's own destructive failure to disentangle his private affections from his public duties, is Edward III's command toward the end of the scene that his mother be immediately taken 'away' lest 'her words enforce these tears, / And I shall pity her if she speak again' (25.85–6). We are thus left to wonder about Edward III's 'tears, distilling from mine eyes' (25.101) as the play closes and what for England these may portend.[41]

Edward III in the play's final scene may thrice accuse Mortimer Junior of acting the 'traitor' in murdering his father and England's rightful king, but in doing so he never once invokes God as warrant for Mortimer Junior's execution or Isabella's arrest. Indeed, in this charged moment, not one of the assembled characters attempts to suggest about the last turn of Mortimer Junior's wheel of 'Base fortune' (25.59) that now 'the land trulie séemed to be blessed of God.' The absence here of any mention of providence does not come as a surprise. Throughout the play, the actions that shape history are shown to be profoundly human, worldly, predictably driven by greed, affection, ambition and pride. In *Tamburlaine*, Marlowe's title protagonist proclaimed his sole ambition to be 'That perfect bliss and sole felicity, / the sweet fruition of an earthly crown' only to be finally and ironically thwarted by his heretical treatment of the Qu'ran; in *Edward II* the desire for earthly power is omnipresent, so ubiquitous that a heavenly spiritual alternative is barely voiced by a desperate Edward II in his final scenes.[42] Before this, Edward II may warn 'Proud Rome,' threaten to 'fire thy crazèd buildings and enforce / The papal towers to kiss the lowly ground (4.97–101), but at this point there is little evidence that he is motivated by religious sentiment, and there is even less that the surrounding cosmos is capable of offence. This, of course, is very different from what Shakespeare gives us in his own earliest English history plays. There, in his tetralogy recounting England's fifteenth-century War of the Roses, the movement of history is shown to be mysterious and providential, divinely working toward the Tudor monarchal line and Elizabeth I. When Henry VII then, at the conclusion of *Richard III*, confidently proclaims that he will 'unite the white rose and the red,' we have little reason to doubt that heaven will smile 'upon this fair conjunction, / That long have frowned upon their enmity!'[43] In *Edward II*, no similar expectation of divine good will is to be had at play's end. All that we are made to look forward to is Isabella's trial, where Edward III has promised not to be 'slack or pitiful' if she be found guilty.

§

Presenting extremes of egotism, ambition, conflict and human fraility amid a narrative drawn from chronicle sources, *Edward II* effectively proffers tragedy in the guise of history. As Darlene Farabee shows in this volume's opening chapter 'The Critical Backstory: *Edward II*'s Critics in History to 1990', this potent mix has long inspired critical deliberations over the play's true generic identity and effects. It at the same time has led early critics actively to debate the play's place in Marlowe's canon and in the larger canon of early modern dramatic literature. By the second half of the twentieth century, *Edward II*'s workings as tragedy precipitated some of what are still the play's most 'revelatory' critical investigations. Complementing Farabee's overview, Judith Haber's third chapter 'The State of the Art: Desire, History, and the Theatre' surveys *Edward II* criticism from its 'tremendous upsurge' after the 1980s to the present. Not surprisingly, it finds that the most 'groundbreaking' scholarship on the play was produced in the 1990s when a multitude of critics were influenced by the work of Foucault and Sedgwick on sexuality and gender. After the turn of the century, criticism mostly 'refined and rehearsed' this scholarship, though notable exceptions explored the play's engagement with early modern understandings of aesthetics, friendship, history and government. Haber ends her chapter with the observation that still 'there remains much to be said about *Edward II*'; and she looks forward to seeing innovative 'ways of contextualizing ... Marlowe's play [that] can provide new perspectives and transform earlier critical views' (95).

An essential complement to these chronological surveys of criticism, Andrea Stevens' second chapter '*Edward II*: A Stage History' offers a rich and selectively detailed overview of the play's theatrical fortunes from the early 1590s up until the present day. Her chapter considers the probable elements of *Edward II*'s earliest enactments; Brecht's groundbreaking twentieth-century adaptation (first staged in Munich in 1924); the rise of gay Edward productions from Tony Robertson's in 1958 to Gerard Murphy's in 1990; Derek Jarman's 1991 film adaptation; and recent stagings since 2000. As Stevens well tracks, dramatizations of *Edward II* over the past century have generally moved from embarrassed mufflings of homoerotic themes at the beginning of the twentieth century to ever increasing amplification in and after the 1950s. The past fifteen years have witnessed continued amplification along with tendencies toward enlarging the play's contexts.

Expanding upon J. A. Nicklin's 1895 essay 'Marlowe's "Gaveston"', Chapter 4 'Edoüard et Gaverston: New Ways of Looking at an English History Play' makes the case that – counter to the received critical wisdom that sees Marlowe's drama as based narrowly on the chronicles of Holinshed, Fabyan and Stow – *Edward II* was profoundly influenced by contemporary developments in the French Wars of Religion. Here, Alan Stewart tracks the various workings and considerable sway of the much-reprinted 1588 French libel *Histoire tragique et memorable de Pierre de Gauerston*, an attack on the then French king Henri III's favourite, the duc d'Épernon. Unlike traditional sources studies by Bullough (Shakespeare) and by Thomas and Tydeman (Marlowe), Stewart's chapter recovers what was a subtle yet pervasive 'discursive air' that infused the moment of *Edward II*'s composition. It ultimately demonstrates how Marlowe's play is shaped by the *Histoire tragique*'s telescoped retelling of Gaveston's and Edward II's story, and it shows how Marlowe, by 'thread[ing] anachronisms' throughout, 'produces a medieval English chronicle history that resonates with the libel-drenched culture of contemporary French politics' (117).

This volume's fifth chapter, Roslyn L. Knutson's '*Edward II* in Repertory', offers the most thorough, the most erudite account of *Edward II*'s early fortunes in repertory written to date. The chapter also identifies a number of unfounded critical orthodoxies about *Edward II*'s early stage history and about the lifespan, repertory and venues of Pembroke's Men. Revising previous accounts that have given the play an unsuccessful, short-lived debut along with a mostly unremarkable revival in the early seventeenth century, Knutson envisions an initial propitious tour (in all likelihood with Ned Alleyn and the Admiral's Men) followed by a healthy spate with Pembroke's Men and then runs possibly with the Chamberlain's Men or Worcester's Men until the play was being performed by Queen Anna's Men up to 1622. This healthy early run was both invigorated and sustained by its repertorial contexts which over the years included plays such as Shakespeare's Peele's *Edward I*, Shakespeare's *Richard II*, and the lost plays 'The Spencers' and 'Mortimer'. '*Edward II*', avers Knutson, 'enjoyed a long career in the hands of skilled professionals; it was therefore a more significant contributor to the industry of early modern theatre than a brief tenure with Pembroke's Men in 1592–3 has implied' (120).

Like Stewart's chapter, Chapters 6 and 7 well answer Haber's call for 'new ways of contextualizing' the play. James Siemon, in '"Overpeered" and Understated: Conforming Transgressions and *Edward II*', draws upon Pierre Bourdieu's notion of 'conforming transgression' in order to analyse the play's treatment of rank and degree. Distinguishing it from other English history plays of the period, Siemon identifies an idiosyncratic tendency in *Edward II* not simply to deploy non-restrictive, collective designations of rank (e.g. 'kings', 'peers', 'earls', 'nobles', 'lords' and 'barons') but also for such designations to be consistently wielded in an over determined fashion. '[I]dentities and relationships', he argues, are 'phrased and defined in relation to traditional terms and schemata of rank and deference; but ... the terms and uses [are] sometimes subtly, often brutally, and many times ironically invoked in ways that recognize them but also compromise or complicate their nature and authority' (153). Continually staging multivalent struggles over status, then, the play invokes but ultimately works to destabilize orthodox assumptions about hereditary nobility. Siemon associates this bipolar trajectory with Marlowe's own experiences with a late-Elizabethan system of distinction as both the son of a relatively prominent assistant Churchwarden and a 'gentleman' by academic degree.

In Chapter 7, '"My Life, My Company": Amity, Enmity and Vitality in *Edward II*', Garrett A. Sullivan, Jr. provocatively builds both upon Lee Edelman's groundbreaking *No Future: Queer Theory and the Death Drive* and recent early modern scholarship concerned with sexuality, friendship and the body. Here, Sullivan considers the play's 'profound engagement' with different conceptions of life and vitality, concluding that what Marlowe ultimately fashions in the face of patriarchal dynastic power and reproductive futurity is a '*concept* of life that is untethered from the demands of past and future' (176). Associated primarily with Edward II and his corporate relations first with Gaveston and then with Spenser Junior and Baldock, this, argues Sullivan, is a non-teleological notion that reverses logics associated with life and death; destabilizes early modern assumptions about the King's two bodies; embraces the sodomitical; and idealizes pointless play as a mode of existence. In *Edward II*, then, Marlowe diagnoses the alignment between selfhood and paternity that Shakespeare so famously later gives us in his Young Man sonnets. To Sonnet 13's diachronic 'then you were / Yourself again after yourself's decease / when your sweet issue your sweet form should bear', the play instead prescribes with phrases like Edward II's 'my life, my company' (19.65) a synchronic conception of shared existence.

The final chapter in this volume, Edward Gieskes's "A Survey of Resources: Teaching *Edward II*', describes a number of approaches to the play that can be successfully adopted in upper-level secondary, undergraduate and graduate classrooms. Drawing on his own experiences as a professor at a public university, Gieskes in his chapter considers how Marlowe's only English history play can be used both to introduce students to Marlowe's penchants with verse and rhetoric and to anchor broad classroom discussions about dramatic genre, history, politics, gender and sexuality, and career during Marlowe's day. He concludes with an invaluable annotated catalogue of resources now available for instructors interested in teaching the play, including available editions, useful criticism for the classroom and digital tools.

1

The Critical Backstory: *Edward II*'s Critics in History to 1990

Darlene Farabee

In January of 1940 in Wimbledon, England, Frederick S. Boas closed the preface to his book on Christopher Marlowe by thanking the Delegates of the Oxford Press 'for proceeding with the publication of this work amidst war's alarms'. He continued to say,

> Yet it is perhaps not inappropriate that this study of Marlowe should appear at a time when we are witnesses of double-crossing and megalomaniac fury as rampant as in *The Jew of Malta* and *Tamburlaine*. Will they be material for some Marlowe of the future?[1]

Although Boas does not mention it here, *Edward II* was affected by the war more immediately than most other Marlowe plays and in ways no one predicted. In 1940, only two copies of the 1594 octavo first printing of *Edward II* were known, and only one of those two copies remains, held by the Zentralbibliothek in Zürich, Switzerland. The other copy of the same octavo, held by the Landesbibliothek in Kassel, Germany, was destroyed by bombing (or looted in the aftermath) in 1944.[2] It is apt that Marlowe's only play depicting a series of troubling and difficult shifts in the control of power in England would be the one affected by the war. The oblique interactions between this play and historical circumstance seem to mirror the balancing act of the play itself as it combines the frameworks of tragedy with the representation of an historical figure.

Categorizing the play has proved difficult and has led to much disagreement over its value and meaning. As scholars developed new ways of understanding power relationships, readings of the play shifted; as they developed critical vocabularies, this complex, multifaceted play continued to be reread. This chapter traces such critical engagements with the play, from its appearance to 1990. *Edward II* evoked responses on stage and in print in the sixteenth and seventeenth century, was recovered by the antiquarian interests of the late eighteenth century, became a point of contention in discussions of canon formation, was extolled and edited in the nineteenth century and emerged in the twentieth century as the provocative outlier in Marlowe's dramatic canon.

Sixteenth and seventeenth centuries

Other plays of the early modern period, particularly history plays by Shakespeare and his contemporaries, can be considered to be in a critical dialogue with Marlowe's *Edward II*. Charles Forker notes that it 'would be astonishing if Marlowe's grim tragedy of failed kingship had not influenced Shakespeare's play on a similar subject'.[3] Both *Edward II* and *Richard II* show a youthful, capricious king surrounded by upstart followers who lead the king into situations of civil unrest followed by his capture, imprisonment and assassination. Sympathy for the main character can shift in similar ways in both plays, resting finally with the usurped king. Despite these similarities, the differences in tone and depictions of violence are distinctive. Shakespeare's two earliest history plays (*Henry VI, Part Two* and *Henry VI, Part Three*) might have been responding to and reinterpreting the historical representations in *Tamburlaine* by depicting what could happen after the death of a strong warrior leader. *Edward II* in turn may have been responding to those history plays.[4] Developing materials from Holinshed's *Chronicles* in such a way as to telescope the passage of time between historical events and explore the possibilities of dispersed power structures, Marlowe's combination of history and tragedy probably influenced later English history plays.[5]

The title page of *Edward II*'s first printing asserts that the play was 'sundrie times' acted by Pembroke's Men in London, and scholars have compellingly argued that it may have played in the provinces.[6] While it has been difficult to trace the effects the play had on playing companies' staging decisions, two early readers' responses to the play do exist. Interpretations are frequently inflected by readers' immediate historical surroundings, and *Edward II* seems especially prone to this. In 1601, John Newdigate II wrote notes as he read a copy of the play, describing some of the major events in the narrative and copying out passages mostly 'from speeches made by Edward or Mortimer'. Siobhan Keenan suggests that these speeches may have been chosen 'because their stories of misused and usurped power were more topical in the aftermath of the Essex rebellion and/or because he thought their tales offered the more significant moral lessons for contemporary readers, demonstrating the dangers of excessive or misdirected passion and ambition, respectively'.[7] The recently located Erlangen copy of the play was bound in 1612 with two other texts of the period: a 1584 Italian Protestant treatise in favour of religious toleration and Joachim Vaget's 1611 examination of Turkish rule and religion. Looking at this early seventeenth-century amalgamation of different titles, Jeffrey Masten concluded that 'the theological, juridical, and sexual meanings around this text may be more complexly interleaved for Marlowe's readers in sixteenth- and seventeenth-century northern Europe than we have yet imagined' (19).

In the late sixteenth and early seventeenth centuries, Marlowe's presence persevered even as *Edward II*'s for a time waned. Lisa Hopkins traces echoes of Marlowe's plays in other drama of the late 1590s, but most of these are echoes of plays other than *Edward II*. *Edward II* resurfaced, though, when, in the Civil War years, 'Gaveston' was used as short-hand for overly influential court favourites in a 1648 playlet called *Crafty Cromwell*.[8] Despite scattered references to Marlowe's plays in the 1640s and 1650s, 'Marlowe's name is notably absent from many contexts where one might expect to find a writer of importance' (Potter, 73). Lois Potter suggests that in these years plays 'probably did matter more than playwrights in the popular consciousness' (74).

In the later seventeenth-century, references to *Edward II* established the play as an important one in English literary history and mark out several areas that continue to interest scholars, including the play's links to Shakespeare, biographical concerns and generic make-up. In 1675, Edward Phillips included Marlowe in his *Theatrum Poetarum*, an attempt to catalogue, as his subtitle claims, 'A compleat collection of the poets'. Phillips's descriptions are important both because they were made available to a wide readership and because they were reprinted freely by other authors engaged in later, similar cataloguing projects. Phillips describes Marlowe as 'a kind of second' Shakespeare, who similarly 'rose from an Actor to be a maker of Plays'.[9] He also includes a vague description of how Marlowe 'in some riotous Fray came to an untimely and violent End' (sig. Bb1r). Phillips's listing of Marlowe's plays describes the generic categories to which the plays can be relegated:

> [O]f all that he hath written to the Stage his Dr. *Faustus* hath made the greatest noise with its Devils and such like

Tragical sport, nor are his other 2 Tragedies to be forgotten, namely his *Edw.*the II. and *Massacre at Paris*, besides his *Jew of Malta* a Tragecomedie, and his Tragedy of *Dido*, in which he was joyned with *Nash*. (sig. Bb1ʳ)

Phillips considers *Edward II* to be a tragedy rather than a history play, although he does use 'historical Drama' (sig. Hh12ʳ) to describe, for example, some of Sir William Davenant's work, showing that the history play as a generic category was not unknown to Phillips. In his descriptions and comments, Phillips values tragedy more highly than other genres. Thus, his categorization of *Edward II* as a tragedy valorizes the play. William Winstanley, when he published *The Lives of the Most Famous English Poets* in 1687, revisited Phillips's cataloguing of poets and borrowed many of his descriptions. Winstanley wrongly attributed *Lust's Dominion* to Marlowe and averred that Marlowe's 'Pen was chiefly employ'd in tragedies'.[10] Winstanley lists *Edward II* after *Tamburlaine*, keeping *Edward II*'s role as a history play second to its tragic elements.

Eighteenth century

The mid-eighteenth-century antiquarian interest in early modern plays brought *Edward II* back into print in Robert Dodsley's 1744 *Select Collection of Old Plays*. Importantly, this inclusion marked the 'first publication of any authentic work by Marlowe since the last edition of *Hero and Leander* in 1637'.[11] *Edward II* was the only Marlowe play chosen by Dodsley for inclusion. In his work on canon formation, Jeremy Lopez has shown that:

> *Edward II* is the only play to appear in every anthology of early modern drama published since 1911. It was also printed in Keltie's anthology of 1870 and was the sole

representative of Marlowe's work in Dodsley's original *Select Collection* of 1744. This distinguished lineage is explained by, or explains, the modern editorial consensus that *Edward II* is Marlowe's greatest play.[12]

Although Dodsley may have meant to incorporate *The Jew of Malta* instead of *Edward II*, Dodsley's inclusion of *Edward II* helped establish it as *the* Marlowe tragedy to reprint.[13] Dodsley's editorial decisions might not be generally read as critical commentary, but the print availability of *Edward II* expanded and altered its critical reception.

When Thomas Warton in *The History of English Poetry, from the Close of the Eleventh to the Commencement of the Eighteenth Century* (1781) calls *Edward II* a 'forgotten tragedy' he quotes from the 1780 second edition of Dodsley, at which point the play was less forgotten than it had been previously.[14] In this 1781 work, Warton suggests that he might be recovering a critical appreciation for Marlowe, and he initiates a conversation about how past critics had read Marlowe. To begin his engagement with previous scholarly work, Warton selectively quotes from Phillips's 1675 description of Marlowe as 'A second Shakespeare, not only because he rose like him from an actor to be a maker of plays, though inferior both in fame and merit, but also, because in his begun poem of Hero and Leander, he seems to have a resemblance of that clear unsophisticated wit, which is natural to that incomparable poet' (440). Having thus emphasized the recognition of Marlowe's wit, Warton continues on to assert: 'Criticisms of this kind were not common, after the national taste had been just corrupted by the false and capricious refinements of the court of Charles the second' (440). Warton thus raises another concern that follows criticism of Marlowe into the twentieth and twenty-first centuries: the assertion that previous generations, particularly through their own corruptions and misjudgement, have misunderstood the meaning and value of the plays. The only Marlowe passage Warton includes comes from *Edward II*, Gaveston's opening 'I must have wanton poets, pleasant wits, / Musicians, that with touching of a string / May draw the pliant King which way I please' (1.50–2).[15] This establishes the play as a synecdoche for Marlowe; Gaveston's words would become the most frequently quoted from the play. Warton's quotation includes a series of asterisks in place of the line 'To hide those parts which men delight to see', indicating discomfort with the possible same-sex attractions of the 'lovely boy in Dian's shape' as one of 'Such things as [...] best please his majesty' (1.64, 60, 70). According to Warton, 'It must be allowed that these lines are in Marlowe's best manner. His chief fault in description is an indulgence of the florid style, and an accumulation of conceits, yet resulting from a warm and brilliant fancy' (439). This kind of selective reading helped to establish this play as the one to attend to if choosing from among Marlowe's plays.

Not only did Warton's book provide readers with an accessible version of early poetry, but it also encouraged interest in literature of the past.[16] One reason to attend closely to Warton is that his contemporaries did. At least one response was not commendatory. In 1782, Joseph Ritson published his sixty-page *Observations* on Warton's book, within which he included a transcription of the manuscript 'Baines' letter of 1593.[17] This document records accusations against Marlowe given by Richard Baines to Queen Elizabeth's Privy Council, and it attributes to Marlowe many extreme ideas and comments, including: 'all thei that love not tobacco and boyes are fooles', 'That Christ was a bastard, and his mother dishonest', and that Marlowe actively 'perswadeth men to Athiesme'.[18] The document was given the title 'Damnable Opinions and Judgment of Relygion and Scorne of Gods Worde', and contains much of the fuel that enflames biographical considerations of Marlowe. Thus, in 1782, the reading public could read for itself what had previously been an inaccessible manuscript version of Marlowe's alleged personal opinions.

Ritson describes his publication of the transcription of the Baines letter as furthering the cause of literary 'truth and justice', and claims he has:

a great respect for Marlowe as an ingenious poet, but I have a much higher regard for the truth and justice; and will now take the liberty to produce the strangest (if not the whole) proof that now remains of his diabolical tenets and debauched morals; and if you Mr Warton still choose to think him innocent of the charge, I shall be very glad to see him thoroughly whitewashed in your next edition. (40)

Taken out of context, the commentary seems vituperative about Marlowe. However, Ritson's main interest in publishing his *Observations* (and the transcription of the Baine's letter) was not Marlowe, but to refute the kind of literary criticism Warton was doing, which relied heavily on descriptions already in print. The tone of Ritson's commentary makes clear that he considered Warton's work as riddled with inexcusable misrepresentations.[19] Ritson attempted to correct errors in Warton's description of Marlowe's death, but Ritson's information is no better than Warton's. Ritson's argument has the merit of pleading for consistency:

Your propensity to corruption and falsehood seems so natural, that I have been sometimes tempted to believe, you often substitute a lye in the place of a fact without knowing it. How else you came to tell us that Marlow was stabbed in the bosom I cannot conceive. It could not, surely, be for the *smoothness of the paragraph?* All former writers, and Wood, amongst the rest, whom you expressly quote, and (which does not always follow) by a slight peculiarity in your expression, I think you must have consulted, say it was in his head. (42)

In the fray between Warton and Ritson, Marlowe becomes one of many weapons drawn and the inclusion of the Baines letter encourages the larger controversy over what is literary history – a controversy that had very little to do with Marlowe's texts.

Nineteenth century

Questions about which authors ought to be included in the history of English literature obviously did not end with the eighteenth century. In different ways, Charles Lamb and William Hazlitt both attempted to reclaim the imaginative excitements of Marlowe's drama. Lamb offered readers an accessible print version of the play through his excerpts and Hazlitt encouraged contextualizing Marlowe's work through broader reading of early modern authors and attending to the circumstances within which those authors were writing.

At the beginning of the nineteenth century, *Edward II* appeared in Charles Lamb's *Specimens of English Dramatic Poets Who Lived About the Time of Shakespeare* (1808), a collection of passages from a range of plays, chosen from various print sources (including Dodsley's anthology) and from manuscripts in the British Museum.[20] *Edward II* is one of several Marlowe plays Lamb includes in *Specimens*. Lamb describes his editorial precepts by explaining that he has had 'no hesitation in leaving [a] line or passage out' if it had confused meaning or introduced too many plot complications, and he has 'expunged, without ceremony, all that which the writers had better never have written' (iii). Lamb does not explain how he imagines his readers using these passages, but he describes having chosen them 'to illustrate what may be called the moral sense of our ancestors' (iv). He goes on to suggest that the excerpts will 'show in what manner they felt, when they place themselves by the power of imagination in trying situations, in the conflicts of duty and passion, or the strife of contending duties; what sort of loves and enmities theirs were; how their griefs were tempered, and their full-swoln joys abated' (iv). These criteria illustrate Lamb's interest in the human condition and readers' identification with characters' situations. Lamb's commentaries on the plays are brief and idiosyncratic; as George Saintsbury says, they 'pretend to no method, and fulfill their pretence very strictly'.[21] About *Edward II*, Lamb says,

> *Edward II* is in a very different style from 'mighty Tamburlaine'. The reluctant pangs of abdicating Royalty in Edward furnished hints which Shakespeare scarce improved on in his Richard the Second; and the death-scene of Marlowe's king moves pity and terror beyond any scene, ancient or modern with which I am acquainted. (25–6)

Excerpts from *Tamburlaine* appear immediately before the passages from *Edward II*, an ordering that might help explain the initial comparison here. This judgement about the final scene of the play is one that gets adopted by other critics after Lamb, and it added weight to the belief that it is Marlowe's best play.

The chosen passages from *Edward II* offer a necessarily truncated, but interestingly slanted version of the play for a reading public, and this version had subsequent reach since Lamb's *Specimens* was reprinted multiple times in the nineteenth century. This abbreviated version of the play smooths some of the narrative difficulties and increases pity for Edward at the end of the play. Lamb includes a total of five passages, taken from scenes 1, 4, 6, 20 and 24.[22] The passage from the first scene is the one abbreviated earlier by Warton; however, Lamb prints it with the line Warton omitted. Lamb includes, from scene 4, Mortimer Senior advising his nephew to allow the king to have his way since 'The mightiest kings have had their minions' (4.392) and 'riper years will wean him from such toys' (4.402). Mortimer junior responds, 'Uncle, his wanton humour grieves not me' (4.403); instead, he says, his complaint rests on Gaveston's actions and conspicuous attire, especially that Gaveston has 'in his Tuscan cap / A jewel of more value than the crown' (4.415–16). These inclusions emphasize Edward's irresponsibility in giving lavish gifts and treatment of his favourites that encouraged flouting of conventions of appropriate attire. Lamb's next selection, from scene 6 again emphasizes Mortimer's complaints that,

> The idle triumphs, masks, lascivious shows,
> And prodigal gifts bestow'd on Gaveston,
> Have drawn thy treasure dry, and made thee weak;
> The murmuring commons, overstretched, break.[23]

This excerpt also includes Mortimer's description of Edward's lack of martial skills, which returns to the question of clothing and self-presentation.

The two remaining scenes included by Lamb focus attention and pity on the king. The final excerpt from the play begins with Edward calling out, 'Who's there?' (24.41) and includes the moving descriptions of the tortures he has endured while imprisoned. By presenting the play through these passages, Lamb does several things. He essentially removes any suggestion that Edward's mistreatment of Isabella drives her into an adulterous relationship (since Isabella does not appear), and he removes the back and forth over Gaveston's banishment in the first part of the play. Lamb as well omits Gaveston and Edward interacting with one another. These and other omissions smooth the structural difficulties caused by the death of Gaveston part-way into the play. Lamb's choices increase pity for Edward, as he grapples with Lightborne's murderous intent, and also remove any necessity for imagining the actualities of the murder of Edward. Lamb's selections reflect and encourage a particular critical reading of the play, a less troubled and less troubling presentation of a king's tragic downfall.[24]

Shortly after Lamb's *Specimens* was printed, Samuel Taylor Coleridge made a tantalizing series of notes in his journals contemplating 'Historical Drama'. He describes how it 'would be desirable that some man of dramatic Genius, (to which I have no pretensions,) should dramatize all those omitted by Shakespeare', and notes that 'A few scenes of Marlow's Edward the second might be preserved'.[25] Coleridge uses this moment to think about history and how the genre of historical drama functions:

> the History of our ancient Kings, the Events of them,

I mean, are like stars in the Sky—whatever the real Interspaces may be & however great, they seem close to each other—the Stars, the Events, strike us & remain in our Eye, little modified by the difference of their Dates. An historical Drama is therefore a collection of Events borrowed from History, but connected together in respect to cause & time poetically by dramatic Fiction.

Although Coleridge did not write any formal lectures specifically on *Edward II*, his comments show that in 1809 he considered parts of it a compelling representation of England's history, and he recognized its history-shaping possibilities.[26]

In late 1819, William Hazlitt gave a series of lectures that were disseminated as *The Dramatic Literature of the Age of Elizabeth* in 1820. These lectures followed on the heels of his successful series of *Lectures on the English Poets* (1818) and *Lectures on the English Comic Writers* (late 1818), both of which had been published after delivery. Through these various projects, Hazlitt encouraged sustained attention to earlier English writers. In his opening lecture of the series, Hazlitt argued that discussions should be broadened to include many of the writers of the period, rather than 'singl[ing] out one or two striking instances'. He adds that Dr Johnson was mistaken when he claimed the reasonableness of the subsequent obscurity of many earlier authors, and that the 'nature of our academic institutions [...] estranges the mind from the history of our own literature'.[27] In other words, part of Hazlitt's project in the lectures was to effect a change in the ways the British understood their own literary tradition.[28] In his discussion of *Edward II*, Hazlitt confirms and extends earlier judgements about the ending of the play, but he quarrels with some received opinions about how well the play succeeds in larger terms. He begins his discussion by explaining that it is 'according to the modern standard of composition, Marlowe's best play' (211). He had already claimed that *Doctor Faustus*, 'though an imperfect and unequal performance, is his greatest work' (202). Since Hazlitt reads Marlowe as a writer with 'a lust of power in his writings, a hunger and thirst after unrighteousness, a glow of the imagination, unhallowed by any thing but his own energies' (202), it stands to reason that he would prefer the excitements and torments of *Doctor Faustus* over the surfaces and equivocations of *Edward II*. Hazlitt says that *Edward II* 'is written with few offences against the common rules, and in a succession of smooth and flowing lines', but he continues on to describe what he sees as faults in the play:

> The poet however succeeds less in the voluptuous and effeminate descriptions which he here attempts, than in the more dreadful and violent bursts of passion. Edward II is drawn with historic truth, but without much dramatic effect. The management of the plot is feeble and desultory; little interest is excited in the various turns of fate; the characters are too worthless, have too little energy, and their punishment is, in general, too well deserved, to excite our commiseration; so that this play will bear, on the whole, but a distant comparison with Shakespear's Richard II in conduct, power, or effect. But the death of Edward II in Marlow's tragedy, is certainly superior to that of Shakespear's King; and in heart-breaking distress, and the sense of human weakness, claiming pity from utter helplessness and conscious misery, is not surpassed by any writer whatever. (211)

Hazlitt's list of criticisms brings to light his own concerns and basis for aesthetic judgement, which were firmly rooted in his assumptions that earlier English writers lived in an age of unpredictability and excitement: 'We find that the ravages of the plague, the destructive rage of fire, the poisoned chalice, lean famine, the serpent's moral sting, and the fury of wild beasts, were the common topics of their poetry, as they were common occurrences in more remote periods of history' (189). Hazlitt wishes that all 'violent bursts of passion', energy and excitement in literature be driven by corresponding 'turns of fate'.

In keeping with a rise in interest in early modern plays and increased editorial activity, *Edward II* was published in six different single-play editions in the nineteenth century. This increased availability began with two editions published in 1818 and then continued in the 1870s and 1880s. In the interval between, Alexander Dyce produced his 1850 and 1858 editions of *The Works of Christopher Marlowe*. A. H. Bullen's *Works of Christopher Marlowe* followed in 1885. The availability of *Edward II* encouraged re-evaluation of the play, although in many instances attention focused on comparisons with Shakespeare's *Richard II* or on questions of prosody noting the differences between *Edward II* and other Marlowe plays. For example, in 1880, A. C. Bradley notes that the 'stately monotone of *Tamburlaine* ... gives place in *Edward II* to rhythms less suited to pure poetry, but far more rapid and flexible', and he asserts that, if a later play, *Edward II* shows 'the most decided advance both in construction and in the dialogue'.[29]

Twentieth century

In the early twentieth century, literary scholars continued to determine whether *Edward II* was Marlowe's best play. Obviously, this rested heavily on the criterion established for 'best'; in some instances, those criteria are not as clear as one might wish, but they are connected to the play's classification as either history play or tragedy. G. Gregory Smith, in 1910, asserted that the play's generic innovations keep it from attaining the full heights of either tragedy or history. Smith firmly asserts that the previous estimations of the play must be revised:

> The praise of *Edward II* has probably been extravagant. Because it is the first historical play of the stricter type, and because there is more characterisation and episode in

it than in his earlier plays, it is singled out as Marlowe's best dramatic effort. It is necessary to supplement this half-truth. Such improvement as it shows, in construction and in development of character, is less real than may seem.[30]

Smith goes on to claim that Marlowe's choice of a longer period of history to condense into the shorter time frame offered in the play necessitated the development of the '"fine restraint" for which *Edward II* has been admired' (173).

Although late eighteenth-century scholars such as Warton and Ritson were concerned with how literary history would be written, early twentieth-century interest in *Edward II* concentrated (in many instances) on questions of how history itself would be represented. Smith claims:

> the shackles of the chronicle keep it, on the one hand, from the imaginative range of *Tamburlaine* or *Faustus*, and, on the other, from the reach of great tragedy. Yet, as an effort to interpret history on the stage, it is the first of any account, and hardly inferior to what is reputed best in this genre. Independent of such merit as is individual to it as literature is the credit of having reformed the awkward manners of the 'true tragedies' to statelier bearing. ('Marlowe', 174)

This determinedly progressive notion of *Edward II* as an improvement over the other history plays of the period places a high value on the combination of history and tragedy and diminishes the possibility of the history chronicle successfully being combined with comedic modes. Felix Schelling, in 1914, similarly tried to separate out the strands of chronicle, history and tragedy. He offers a contextualizing description of pre-*Edward II* English chronicle history plays and remarks:

> The epic character, which imbues most of these [earlier history] plays, was not preserved by Marlowe in his *Edward II*, and it may be suspected that he wrote his play more for the tragic pathos which the story of the unkingly

and discrowned sovereign exhales than for any other reason. It is worth noting, however, that in this tragedy Marlowe raised the whole species of the chronicle play to a higher artistic level and reached the crown of his own dramatic art.[31]

Both Smith and Schelling are primarily interested in establishing worth through genre, although they essentially disagree about the value of *Edward II*. Presumably it is the active engagements of these and other scholars that led T. S. Eliot to pass over *Edward II* in his discussion of Christopher Marlowe's verse, saying, '*Edward II* has never lacked consideration.'[32]

Early in the twentieth century, Bertolt Brecht wrote a German translation of *Edward II* and directed it in 1924 as *Leben Eduards des Zweiten von England*. Brecht's enormous impact on the field of twentieth-century drama makes this production an important critical response to Marlowe's play. Brecht's version of the play diverges from Marlowe's in multiple ways.[33] It begins by making the conflict around Gaveston's banishment more pervasive in the first scene: 'The ink's not faded from the page on which / They wrote that I was Edward's whore and therefore / Banished.'[34] Ultimately, Brecht's version emphasizes class conflict, but it also forefronts sexuality, presciently predicting later critical responses to Marlowe's play.

As we have seen, Marlowe's biography has excited derision and interest since he was murdered on 30 May 1593. James Broughton's nineteenth-century investigations clarified some of the historical record, establishing that Marlowe was not an actor and bringing to light the correct name of Marlowe's murderer.[35] J. Leslie Hotson revisited the topic of Marlowe's biography with his investigations in the Public Record Office and sparked a revival of Marlowe biographies in the twentieth century.[36] The beginning of Hotson's book links Marlowe's biography with drama: 'The life and death of Christopher Marlowe make one of the few dramas in our history which satisfy Aristotle's definition of tragedy' (9). Comments ascribed to Marlowe in the Baines letter and representations of homoerotic love in *Edward II* (as well as in other plays) have been read as a demonstration of Marlowe's own sexual preferences. Ever increasing acceptance of sexual preference and decriminalization of sexual acts in the twentieth century led to a broader range of interpretations of *Edward II* and many of these have linked themselves to biographical readings of Marlowe's plays. Paul H. Kocher's *Christopher Marlowe: A Study of his Thought, Learning, and Character* (1946) considers much of the biographical evidence that can be gleaned from history and from Marlowe's plays: what books did Marlowe read? Which ideas did he study? Which beliefs did he uphold and which question? Kocher also argues, at length, that the Baines letter outlines Marlowe's own beliefs. He contextualizes the sexual imagery Marlowe employs and asserts that it surpasses others of the period:

> He and Gaveston use images of sexual love, like the Hero-Leander image in I, i, 6–8, and the Danae image in II, ii, 52–58 to describe their affection, and the Queen compares them to Jove and Ganymede (I, iv, 180), a notorious instance of the passion which Marlowe himself had already utilized in the opening scene of *Dido*. The physical endearments go far beyond those customary between Elizabethan friends exemplified in such plays as *Damon and Pithias*, Lyly's *Campaspe, The Taming of a Shrew,* and *Mucedorus*.[37]

Despite his interest in the biographical, Kocher's reading of *Edward II* depends on structural elements of the play and returns to the question of generic success. In his discussion of Marlowe's ability to control his audience's response, Kocher claims that the play depends on the 'political ethical judgments normal to an Elizabethan audience' and argues that:

> Thus he obtains in the first division of the play a dramatic clash between two parties, both of whom are half wrong

and half right, and in the second division a dramatic concentration on pity of the defeated. Whether this is a good method for tragedy may perhaps be open to question. (207)

Kocher emphasizes the balance the play achieves, contextualizing contemporary references in the play, while raising the question of generic effectiveness.

Edward II's unique concerns and characterizations have led to criticism that has tried to connect the play to other of Marlowe's plays. Some of these twentieth-century approaches point to overpowering main characters with a lust for power, or to political and moral degeneracy centred in a particular social structure. Harry Levin's *The Overreacher: A Study of Christopher Marlowe* (1952) takes *Edward II* on its own terms and combines this with a biographical study of Marlowe. Levin asserts that, in *Edward II*, Marlowe 'sets forth his discovery that tragic life needs no villains; that plots are spun by passions; that men betray themselves'.[38] His focus on structure in the plays revisits in profitable ways concerns raised much earlier.

Later twentieth-century developments in theatre history have greatly altered our understanding of many early modern plays. Michael Hattaway's *Elizabethan Popular Theatre: Plays in Performance* (1982) explores minutely what *Edward II* might have looked like on stage in its own period. Hattaway argues that *Edward II* is 'a demythologizing work, uncompromisingly realist' and he continues: 'It is therefore not surprising that this play calls for the use of only one stage level: no ghost need appear from below, no character, devil or god, appears above to submit the actions [of] the political antagonists to moral scrutiny.'[39] Examining stage imagery, playing positions, speed of scenic movement and the modes of possible delivery, Hattaway argues compellingly that 'Marlowe in this play sought to turn tragedy back towards history' (144).

Several twentieth-century scholars concentrated on tracing the structures of the play and have revealed the elements that probably gave rise to the nineteenth-century assertion that it is Marlowe's best constructed play. Explorations of plot structure show the echoing elements that occur in the play. For instance, Sara Munson Deats traces the duplications of scenes and actions in the play. As an example, Deats notes that 'the play opens and closes with two similar rituals, the funeral of an older Edward and the assumption of royal power by an heir of the same name'.[40] The reverse parallelisms between the scenes in the play have been carefully noted by David Bevington in *From Mankind to Marlowe* (1962) and by J. B. Steane who praises 'the symmetry' of the play.[41]

Some of the most revelatory interpretations of the play in the mid- to late-twentieth century have appeared in standalone essays rather than in monographs focused on Marlowe. Three of these essays bear particular mention, as they are exemplars of the work on *Edward II* in the later twentieth century. Clifford Leech's 'Marlowe's *Edward II:* Power and Suffering' argues that 'what Marlowe has done is to make us deeply conscious of a humanity that we share with this man who happened to be also a king'.[42] Leech asserts that, 'There is no theory here which Marlowe illustrates, no warning, or programme for reform, no affirmation of a faith in man. The playwright merely focuses attention on certain aspects of the human scene' (196). The experimental and absurdist drama of the late 1950s may have made it easier to see *Edward II* as a drama that offered no affirming theory or programmatic call to action. Stephen Greenblatt, in his 1977 essay 'Marlowe and Renaissance Self-Fashioning', says that the play does function as 'admonitory drama' and claims that this emblematic method is used to such devastating effect that the audience recoils from it in disgust. Edward's grisly execution is, as orthodox interpreters of the play have correctly insisted, iconographically 'appropriate', but this very appropriateness can only be established *at the expense of* every complex, sympathetic human feeling evoked by the play. The audience is forced to confront its insistence upon coherence, and the result is a profound questioning of the way audiences constitute meaning in plays and in life.[43]

Greenblatt's reading of the play stresses its effects as a tragedy, arguing that its emotional impact undermines any putative didacticism. Claude J. Summers' 'Sex, Politics, and Self-Realization in *Edward II*' re-evaluates the play and its homoeroticism to clarify that, 'It is difficult to overstate the significance of *Edward II* in the history of literary depictions of homosexuality, yet it is equally important not to regard the play as simply a liberal defense of sexual freedom.'[44] Summers argues compellingly that social identity is undermined by multiple aspects and actions of the play including: the normalization of homosexual liaisons, the undermining of structures of class (Gaveston's and the Spencers' social standing was reduced by Marlowe from the status given in his source Holinshed), the overemphasis on appearance ('seeming') as a means of marking class and the solipsism of the play. 'It is precisely because the world of *Edward II* is so unstable', Summers claims, 'that the language of the play so frequently rings hollow' (228). Summers' project focuses on how the play undermines and destabilizes identities, both socially imposed and internally composed, 'real' identities, and suggests that characters' desires to merge these incongruent social and real identities lead finally to the confinement and breakdown of the characters. All three of these essays, then, consider *Edward II* to illuminate different ways to imagine our humanness, a function of drama and particularly of Marlowe's drama.

As is always the case, critical responses arise from and exist within the world in which readers and audience members find themselves. Marlowe's biography, together with *Edward II* as history play, tragedy and love story, has encouraged an awareness of the world of the play and the contemporary world in unusual ways. In a 1937 biography of the American poet Hart Crane (1899–1932), Philip Horton claims that the young poet 'had often reeled down the dark streets of Little Italy shouting "I am Christopher Marlowe" with a defiance worthy of Tamburlaine confronted by death'.⁴⁵ In an anecdote about the poet's search for self, the biographer elides differences between Marlowe and one of his characters. Often Crane's identification with Marlowe has been read as part of Crane's homosexual identity. A later biography revises the story and quotes Katherine Anne Porter in Mexico describing Hart Crane near the end of his short life:

> 'He talked about Baudelaire and Marlowe, and Whitman and Melville and Blake – all the consoling examples he could call to mind of artists who had lived excessively in one way or another.' Drunk, he 'would weep and shout, shaking his fist, "I am Baudelaire, I am Whitman, I am Christopher Marlowe, I am Christ." But never once did I hear him say he was Hart Crane.'⁴⁶

In Katherine Anne Porter's version, the questions of identity and identification become even more tangled, and Marlowe becomes part of a different iteration of Crane's biography. Given the shifts in critical responses to *Edward II* and to Marlowe, it is fitting that, in this biographical incident, history is rewritten and the use of Marlowe's own biography is altered. Marlowe becomes, in the twentieth century, an identity palimpsest, rewritten, re-envisioned and reviewed as a dramatist for our time.

2

Edward II: A Stage History

Andrea Stevens

Written after his blockbusters *Tamburlaine the Great* and *Doctor Faustus*, *Edward II* (c. 1591–2) is Christopher Marlowe's lone English history play.[1] Critics generally have assumed that by 1592 Marlowe's reputation as a play-maker was firmly established, but J. A. Downie has recently argued that 'unequivocal contemporary evidence of Marlowe's reputation as a playwright is only extant subsequent to the publication of *Edward II*'.[2] Especially in comparison to *Doctor Faustus*, however, the play's stage history after the 1620s has been sparse, to say the least. It is only by 1903 that *Edward II* begins to find new audiences, from an Elizabethan Stage Society production staring Harley Granville-Barker to Bertolt Brecht's 1924 adaptation for German audiences. If Brecht's radical revision of his source emphasizes class conflict, productions from the late fifties and sixties explore – at times, to controversy – the love story between the King and his male favourite, Piers Gaveston. Explicitly invoking contemporary queer politics, Derek Jarman's 1991 film *Edward II* cements this understanding of the play as essentially 'about' the consequences of same-sex desire, a crown lost not through Edward's weakness but to homophobia – an apt topic for a writer such as Marlowe, himself rumoured to have preferred sex with men.

The play's full title reads *The Troublesome Reign and Lamentable Death of Edward II, King of England, with the Tragic Fall of Proud Mortimer*. As this suggests, the very structure of the play elicits complex shifts in response to its major figures, consistently advancing, as David Fuller puts it, 'jockeying points of view' on the play's action. Whether these subtleties of perspective emerge in performance is another matter. This chapter will focus on the play's stage history from the late sixteenth century to 2015, noting key productions and paying particular attention to how different productions represent the most lurid of the competing historical narratives about Edward's death: execution by red-hot poker thrust through the anus. So too will it demonstrate how the play's production history has moved from the elision of explicit homoerotic content to a closer consideration of the sexual and affective relationship between the King and his favourite – a focus that amplifies even further in the wake of Jarman's influential 1991 film.

As it was 'sundrie times' performed: *Edward II* c. 1592–1622

The title page of the 1594 quarto of *Edward II* claims that the Lord Pembroke's Men performed the play 'sundrie times' in London. In her essay in this volume, Ros Knutson deftly engages the play's complicated early history of performance, speculating that *Edward II* could have been performed as early as 1591, perhaps by the Admiral's Men, before the Lord Pembroke's Men took the play to the road when the plague worsened during the spring and summer of 1593 (125). A 1622 quarto attributes the play to Queen Anna's Servants at the Red Bull, indicating that the play was revived into the Jacobean period. What Glynne Wickham calls the 'economy' of the play's action suggests that it could handily have been staged in a variety of spaces – from London playhouses, to churches, to provincial town halls, to rooms in great houses – since it requires very little in terms of specific architectural features or fixed props to be realized.[3]

As was the case with all the plays performed during the early modern period, *Edward II* would not have used a changeable set or scenic backdrop to establish the different locations of the action; that was left to language. Props would be minimal, but richly symbolic: likely a throne, a crown, a bed, perhaps a brazier to 'heat' the spit Lightborne uses to kill Edward.[4] Turning to the only contemporary picture of an English playhouse – a copy of Johannes de Witt's 1596 drawing of the Swan Theatre – we should note the elevated platform stage that 'thrust' out into the audience and around which spectators could stand. Although this isn't clear from the de Witt drawing, other sixteenth-century playhouses featured a trap door in the middle of the stage, a device which could have evoked, in the execution scene, the sewers underneath Berkeley castle where Edward is held prisoner (24.2–3). Since plays were typically performed during the afternoon, actors and spectators alike shared the same universal pool of light. As Tiffany Stern notes, early modern audiences were thus 'part of the play': playgoers were 'as well-lit as the actors, as visible, and sometimes, as talkative'. Or, indeed, more boisterous still; Stern mentions a poem addressed to the audience of the notoriously rowdy Red Bull asking them to 'forbear' from throwing fruit at the actors onstage.[5]

Marlowe weaves into the play's more realistically represented action a series of symbolic stage pictures evocative of an earlier medieval playing tradition: Isabella beating her breast in frustration at her mistreatment; Edward's towering passion as '*the King rageth*' (4.188; 20.85). Indeed, as Patrick Ryan has argued, imagery redolent of medieval religious drama recurs throughout the play, from references to Christ's passion to the naming of the assassin 'Lightborne', an anglicized version of 'Lucifer' as well as the name of a devil in the

Chester cycle drama.[6] Ryan describes the scene of Edward's arrest – whereupon soldiers enter with 'Welsh hooks' and a Mower enters bearing a scythe – as 'an emblematic tableau' featuring 'stage properties signifying death, Christ's Passion, and the apocalypse'; he furthermore sees in Edward's violent death an image of the 'Paschal lamb' first shorn (as Edward's beard is shorn [19.45]) and then violently skewered (478). A further example of the play's indebtedness to pre-Reformation religious drama comes in the play's opening scene, which abruptly swerves from the main plot – Gaveston's return to England from his exile in France – into more allegorical territory when 'three poor men' appear seemingly out of nowhere to ask for Gaveston's help, which they, in turn, do not receive; such tests of charity recur throughout the mystery play tradition (1.23–48).

If contemporary productions since the 1960s tend to emphasize the personal over the political, David Fuller reminds us that Marlowe's earliest audience would have been attuned to 'the responsibilities that are the obverse of the king's rights – responsibilities to the Church, to the nobility, and to the commonwealth – without necessarily advocating that a king who failed in these duties should therefore be deposed.[7] Edward is a feudal, not an absolute, monarch, and must out of necessity share some degree of power with the nobility and with the Church. Edward knows this – at no point, for example, does he invoke his 'divine right' to rule – but he does chafe under these obligations when they threaten his personal desires, going so far as to 'lay violent hands' on the Bishop of Coventry for his role in the exile of Gaveston from England (1.187). Especially for Marlowe's Protestant audience, this scene might have elicited warring perspectives on the action: that is, if some spectators would have seen Edward's violence as proof of his inability to govern his passions, still others may have 'relished' the play's anti-Catholicism and consequently sympathized with Edward (Guy-Bray, xx).

So too is it difficult to determine how Marlowe's first audiences would have viewed the King's attachment to

Gaveston. Given early modern notions of 'sodomy' as a violation of norms of class distinction with the further implication of treason and not just codes of sexual behaviour, we might recall Mortimer Junior's view that the King's 'wanton humour' is not in itself necessarily objectionable. Moreover, as such historians of sexuality as Alan Bray remind us, in the Renaissance male friendship often found expression in passionate – and public – gestures like kissing and embracing.[8] Rather, what is 'troublesome' about Edward's reign is that in favouring his lower-born protégé, the King raises Gaveston above his station even as he ignores other claims to his patronage. *Edward II* was, of course, also performed into the Jacobean era – a time when a play about a sodomitical king with problematic male favourites would have resonated in newly provocative ways, especially given James I's controversial relationship to George Villiers, the upwardly mobile Duke of Buckingham who certainly enjoyed from James a lavish degree of royal favour.[9] In one of his many letters to Buckingham, James writes 'God bless you, my sweet child and wife, and grant that ye may ever be a comfort to your dear father and husband', the King's warmth of expression confirming Bray's point about the 'passionate' terms in which Renaissance men expressed their bonds to one another.[10] In thinking about early modern friendship and sexuality we are of course on tricky grounds: that male friends could, and did, express their platonic esteem using language and gestures we might consider romantic does not rule out the possibility that some such relationships were sexually, as well as emotionally, intimate.

One aspect of the play's earliest staging should be addressed: how did Lord Pembroke's Men (or Queen Anna's Men) represent Edward's death? Hired to kill the King, Lightborne does not tell Mortimer how he will carry out this charge – he simply assures Mortimer that, as a skilled assassin, he has 'yet ... a braver way' to kill than his usual methods of poison, quicksilver or quills (23.30–6). Although not all historical accounts of Edward's death agree, Marlowe's primary source,

Raphael Holinshed's *Chronicles of England* (1587), reported that Edward was first pressed down with a bed or 'table' and then thrust through the anus with a red-hot iron; this account is consistent with Lightborne's instructions to Maltravers to bring him 'a spit, and let it be red hot', and a 'table and a featherbed' (24.30, 33). In his 1593 occasional poem *The Honour of the Garter* – a dream-vison narrating the founding of the Knights of the Garter by Edward III – George Peele appears to refer to a performance of *Edward II*, describing the death scene as follows:

> And Mortimer a gentle trustie Lord,
> More loyall than that cruell Mortimer
> That plotted Edwards death at Killingworth.
> Edward II, father to this King,
> Whose tragicke cry even now me thinkes I heare,
> When gracelesse wretches murthered him by night. (220–4)[11]

The sensual immediacy of the recollection suggests that what is being remembered is a theatrical performance and not simply a historical narrative of Edward's death. Whether or not the actual thrust to the anus – 'a form of punishment that reenacts the sin it punishes' – was represented onstage is, however, unclear from the playscript.[12] If performed, such a grotesque mimicry of the act of anal sex would surely complicate the play's otherwise more ambiguous representation of the King's relationship to Gaveston; although of course those playgoers familiar with the Holinshed version of Edward's death would not necessarily need to 'see' that final thrust, to have it in mind.[13]

Later productions of *Edward II* become more graphically violent even as directors, actors and audiences come to embrace overtly 'queer' interpretations of the play, including the idea that it is homophobia, and not the inherent challenge of feudal kingship itself, that causes Edward to fall. Interestingly, if different political climates predictably give rise to different *Edwards*, some of the more successful twentieth and twenty-first century productions also attempt to recreate features of the play's original staging, pursuing a 'bare' or stripped-down aesthetic in order to highlight the play's language and focused action.

Early twentieth century: Brecht and 'Epic Theatre'

If *Edward II* was performed at all in the eighteenth century, no record survives. To be sure, when it came to early modern drama the nineteenth-century canon was limited to a small sampling of Shakespeare's plays heavily adapted for Victorian audiences; as Peter Womack remarks of the period, 'for theatrical purposes Renaissance drama did not exist'.[14] At the fin de siècle, however, avant-garde practitioners were rediscovering early English drama, finding in the plays of Marlowe, John Webster and John Ford fertile ground for challenging the illusionistic aesthetic of the proscenium-arch theatre. In 1903 William Poel revived *Edward II* in repertory alongside *Richard II* at the New Theatre, Oxford, for the Elizabethan Stage Society, a group who sought to perform early modern drama according to the 'original practices' of the Elizabethan period: on a thrust stage, with continuous action, no changeable painted scenery and with the actors surrounded on three sides by audience members. Poel made significant cuts to the text, eliminating the play's homoeroticism even as he minimized the violence of the King's death by having it take place in an interior discovery space behind a curtain.[15] In her analysis of Poel's cuts, Rima Hakim argues that Poel also tried to 'remove puzzling aspects of characterisation', eliminating, for example, Isabella's speeches in which she declares her love for Edward.[16] The play was well received, one reviewer declaring of Poel's staging that he 'could never hereafter tolerate seeing a play of this kind performed with modern conventional upholstery. Mr. Poel … has struck, after a long experiment, upon the true and right method of staging' (Hakim, 135).

That said, other critics found the play lacking when considered alongside the theatrical power of *Richard II*. In a personal letter to Granville-Barker, George Bernard Shaw, for instance, dismissed Marlowe's play as inferior source material next to Shakespeare: 'there is nothing in it – no possibility of success' (qtd in Geckle, 79). Several other productions of the play followed, for the most part within academic settings (Cambridge, Oxford, Birkbeck College at the University of London). These productions often met the same criticism levied by Shaw: that Marlowe shows poorly next to Shakespeare.

It is precisely for its non-Shakespearean quality, however, that in 1924 Bertolt Brecht adapts *Edward II* for German audiences as *Leben Eduards des Zweiten von England*, or 'the Life of Edward II of England, a history'. Attracted to the genre of the chronicle play, Brecht later asserted that he and his collaborator, Lion Feuchtwanger, together 'wanted to ... break with the Shakespearean tradition common to German theatres: that lumpy monumental style beloved of middle-class Philistines'.[17] Performed at the Kammerspiele theatre in Munich, this was Brecht's first experiment with what he later came to theorize as 'epic theatre', a model of theatrical production that rejected hyperemotional acting and a realistic mise-en-scène ('expressivism') in favour of a narrative or 'epic' mode performed in a directly presentational style; in striving for this mode of dramaturgy, Brecht was also adapting the techniques of the Soviet revolutionary theatre of the time.[18]

In his own words, Brecht radically 'vandalized' Marlowe's source play. Loosely hewing to the play's *de casibus* structure of the turning of Fortune's wheel, Brecht changes characters' names and biographies, reassigns speeches, distorts historical details and 'shatters' Marlowe's blank verse. The action clusters around the four main figures of Edward, Gaveston ('Danny, the son of an Irish Butcher'), Isabella (renamed 'Anne'), and Mortimer, whom Brecht first presents as a world-weary scholar, later a 'fascistic politician' and 'Man of Reason' against Edward's 'Man of Feeling'.[19] Brecht also introduces the character of an unnamed 'ballad peddler' who comments on the action, at one point singing scathingly that 'Eddy's concubine has hair on his chest / pray for us, pray for us' (9). Brecht eliminates the poker from the scene of Edward's death; Lightborne instead 'chokes' the king, Edward having been confined to a 'cesspool' where he stands in sewage water, covered in 'the offal of London' (86–9).

Scenes were organized around specific actions or 'gests', with captions on title-cards announcing the action; props were symbolic rather than representational; actors' movements were coached to be mechanical or puppet-like. In one battle scene often described as a pivotal moment for Brecht's conception of epic theatre, soldiers were heavily made up with chalky white face-paint to signify 'fear', this stylistic choice clearly embracing artifice over naturalism (Fuegi, 507). Peter Womack describes the totality of these effects as 'anti-illusionistic, sardonically misanthropic, dadaistically discontinuous' (81). Well received by the more forward-thinking critics during its limited run, the production established Brecht's reputation as a director even if it did not generate for the Kammerspiele a significant amount of revenue (Fuegi, 133).

Cutting Marlowe's more poetical passages along with references to masquing and revelry, Brecht does not aestheticize same-sex desire, but grounds it in physical presence: 'amid the deafness nothing remains except / bodily contact between men' (55). Notwithstanding the frank earthiness of such a sentiment, Eric Bentley attributes an overall 'puritanic' quality to the play as Edward moves from heterosexual partner to the Queen, to homosexual lover of Gaveston, to 'saint-like' and indeed 'asexual' tragic hero at the play's end.[20] John Fuegi argues that with this production Brecht 'both personally and professionally' begins to 'distance himself from the homoerotic' (132–3) that had characterized his earlier work.[21] Finally, Deborah Willis observes that even though issues related to sexual reform were being publicly debated in Germany in 1924, Brecht is less interested in sexual politics than he is concerned with larger issues of 'class conflict and abuses of state power'.[22] In Willis's reading, the king is no tragic figure but a poor leader and administrator whose mismanagement of the state results in civil war. To be sure, Brecht makes it clear that Edward's love for Gaveston comes at a significant cost: all the lives sacrificed during the 'thirteen-year war' that breaks out when Edward refuses to banish his favourite (16).

Brecht's *Life of Edward II* continues to be staged, typically by smaller, less commercial and more self-consciously experimental theatre companies who occasionally include more graphic sex than would have been possible in 1924, as the reviews below reveal. A 1987 production by the Absolute Theatre Company in Chicago (praised for its deft combination of 'the physical directness of the Elizabethan stage with Brecht's spare stage action') veered from Brecht's script by restoring the infamous red-hot poker to the death scene.[23] Panned in the London Evening Standard for its 'vulgar tricksiness', a 1999 production by the Cherub Theatre company depicted Edward abdicating 'over the naked bodies of Anne and Gaveston', Anne renouncing her husband 'while being frenziedly taken, doggy-style, by Mortimer'.[24] A 2000 off-Broadway production of the play by Jean Cocteau Repertory 'bluntly confront[ed] the sexual nature of the King's relationship to Gaveston'.[25] Taking the cue from Mortimer's description of Anne 'with [her] legs open and [her] eyelids closed', this production had the Queen wear 'a tiny black cocktail dress that shows off her cleavage. At one point she even spreads her legs for the audience. She is no queen; she is a whore' (68).[26] And finally, another 2005 off-Broadway production by the Creative Mechanics Theater Company included 'simulated sexual acts' and near-nudity set within a court animated by 'a kind of gang lust for sexual pleasure'.[27]

It has been said of Marlowe's play that the charge of sexual 'deviance' cannot be confined to Edward alone: as adulterous co-conspirators against a lawful king, both Isabella and Mortimer become themselves 'sodomites' who challenge England's social order.[28] If occasionally guilty of 'vulgar trick-siness', the foregoing productions surely capture some of the ambient sexual unruliness of the Elizabethan original. These contemporary productions of *The Life of Edward II*, however, perhaps fail to convey what Brecht saw in the form of the Elizabethan chronicle play: a larger vision of history itself understood as *de casibus* tragedy – a vision which Brecht's audience, living in interwar Germany, would surely have found sympathetic.

'People are frightened of this play. It is long, and there is homosexuality in it'

By the 1940s and 1950s *Edward II* gets staged with greater frequency, often by student actors; the earliest recorded performance of *Edward II* in the United States, for example, is an all-female production at Barnard College in 1943 (Forker, 104). Audiences begin to find in the play both poetry and tragic scope, one reviewer calling a 1951 performance by the Amateur Dramatic Club of Cambridge 'one of the most extraordinary productions' the university had ever seen (Forker, 104). In 1958, at the behest of the Marlowe Society of Cambridge, Toby Robertson directed a stripped-down version of the play starring Derek Jacobi at an open-air theatre at Stratford-upon-Avon, using an aesthetic of bareness better to highlight the play's language; as Robertson later put it, 'the whole thing came back to the words'.[29] Touring to London and airing on BBC radio, this successful production was celebrated for its 'neutrality' of perspective and for its careful attention to fleshing out even the minor characters.[30] Robertson's production was also the first major performance of *Edward II* to engage the question of the King's homosexuality with any frankness; for Robertson,

> *Edward II* is a play of great passion and great love. Homosexual love is treated here as love in the classical

sense. There is, in the imagery, a feeling of going back perpetually to the classical precedents. From this, a strength is drawn. They see themselves as a part of a great tradition. It is nothing to be ashamed of – or afraid of. (177)

The majority of critics who reviewed this play inevitably emphasize the production's treatment of the King's homosexuality, with mixed degrees of sensitivity. For example, even as the critic Harold Hobson celebrated the fact that the relationship between Edward and Gaveston is treated neither 'hypocritically or forensically or with a puritanic shudder', he still called their attraction 'unnatural' (qtd in Geckle, 82).

Robertson used costume to distinguish Edward's cohort from the barons, the King and Gaveston wearing Italianate Renaissance clothing and the barons dressing 'more Gothic, with fur and steel'; so too did the barons speak with contemporary regional accents. Introducing an element of sado-masochism to the scene of Edward's torture, Robertson directed Lightborne to approach Edward almost as a lover or a caregiver. Lightborne in the execution scene is thus described as 'crooning' to Edward and 'gently stroking his hair', with Edward 'like a child asking for love' falling asleep in his killer's lap (Geckle, 92). Later productions of *Edward II* from the 2000s similarly take up this conception of the killer as surrogate lover, a number of them making this connection even more explicit by having the actor who plays Gaveston also double the role of Lightborne.

Robertson returned to *Edward II* once again in 1969, directing Ian McKellen in a celebrated Prospect Theatre Company production of the play that debuted at the Edinburgh Theatre Festival, toured widely, and was eventually filmed for British and American television. Robertson staged the play in tandem with a new production of *Richard II*, also starring McKellen – making this the first time since 1903 that the same actor doubled these roles in repertory. Two years earlier, British Parliament passed the Sexual Offences Act decriminalizing private homosexual acts between consenting adults (in

England and Wales, if not in Scotland or Northern Ireland); in 1968, the passage of the Theatres Act abolished the office of the Lord Chamberlain, the arm of government that censored stage performance. Taken together, these changes to the law enabled Robertson to stage with the greatest openness to date the sexual intimacy between Edward and Gaveston. Accordingly, *Time* reported that,

> McKellen and Director Toby Robertson have confronted with stark candor the fact that *Edward II* is a play by a homosexual about a king who was a homosexual who indeed ruined himself for an infatuation ... . It is sensuous, unpleasant, funny, guilt-obsessed – and intensely masculine.[31]

Official language surrounding the passage of the Sexual Offences Act nevertheless continued to characterize homosexuality as somehow shameful, the peer who sponsored the act asking 'those [homosexuals] to show their thanks by comporting themselves quietly and with dignity ... any form of ostentatious behaviour now or in the future or any form of public flaunting would be utterly distasteful'.[32] A police officer was dispatched to vet Robertson's production when it opened at the Edinburgh Festival. If no official objection was later levied against the production, the press coverage gleefully reported upon the 'searching' kiss between the two lead actors. In his astute analysis of this production, David Fuller speculates that the historical changes in Britain around the issue of homosexuality meant that 'attention was focused on love and sexuality and deflected from politics', even though the production itself 'forcefully presented' political issues (91).

Watching the BBC recording of this play today, contemporary viewers might well wonder just what exactly it was that playgoers found so starkly candid about the representation of homosexual desire.[33] Similar to what had been his concept for the 1958 production, Robertson used clothing to set the flamboyant Edward and his male favourites apart from the more soberly clad barons, who wear medieval-style cloaks (with vaguely tie-dyed swirls) and military accents such as breast plates and spaulders. The costumes worn by Edward's cohort are at once recognizably 'medieval' but also evocative of the style of the 1960s: tight, low-slung pants; jewellery; noticeably low-cut shirts, especially for Gaveston; one ought also to mention Edward's gold wig and cracking metallic codpiece. But what McKellen in a later interview referred to as his 'Shock Kiss' with Gaveston is so brief it barely interrupts his speech of greeting upon Gaveston's return from exile ('Kiss not my hand; / Embrace me, Gaveston, as I do thee!' [1.139–40]).[34] To be sure, the only time Gaveston swoons with anything like ecstasy or desire is when Edward anoints him Lord High Chamberlain and Earl of Cornwall.

By multiple accounts a more 'histrionic' Edward than the more reserved Jacobi of the 1958 production, McKellen was praised for his 'exciting display of nervous energy'; for J. C. Trewin, McKellen was 'always within Edward, credibly the hysterically obsessed neurotic, and at the last a man whose suffering would have touched any heart' (Geckle, 87).[35] McKellen himself explained that he approached the transformation of Edward from 'very young man' to vengeful 'tyrant' to 'desiccated old shell crawling about waiting to die' through 'changes in make-up, costume, [and] the carriage of the body'; he also indicated that he thought the King turns into a tyrant because he is fundamentally 'thwarted' in his desires (qtd in Geckle, 87). McKellen spoke the play's blank verse in a distinctly stylized and formal fashion in order to emphasize the beat of the poetry:

> Actor McKellen burns in that fire – thin, lips taut, gleaming with royalty and nerve. He has the mighty breath for the Marlowe line. He has the control to make the relentless rhythms a hammer of pulse. His Edward jumps and flickers, a petulant youth who grows in viciousness yet retains sympathy, who dies stripped to a rag and a whimper yet retains tragedy. ('A Double Crown', 77)

This approach to the speaking of verse is in keeping with what Michael Billington described as the 'emblematic' quality of the production and its 'stylised' set designs (qtd in Geckle, 87–8).

Once imprisoned, Edward is 'brutally' and bloodily shaved by Maltravers and Gourney, later dragged from the 'castle cesspool, half mad and dripping with muck' by the sexually sadistic Lightborne, who approaches the execution as a scene of seduction: he washes, soothes and kisses Edward's near-naked body before crushing him beneath a table.[36] Then, with the assistance of Maltravers and Gourney, comes the death blow, which David Fuller describes as follows:

> For the murder Edward lay centre-stage, sideways to the audience; Gurney put the mattress and up-turned table on his body and stood on them; Mattrevis lifted Edward's legs apart; Gurney held them raised; Lightborne thrust in the spit. The effect of an assisted rape could not have been presented more graphically. (97)

Several more 'gay' *Edwards* succeeded this landmark production, most notably Gerard Murphy's 1990 revival for the Royal Shakespeare Company. If Robertson's *Edward II* was staged in the wake of the Sexual Offences Act, Murphy's production was performed at an especially fervent moment for gay, lesbian and AIDS activism both in England and the United States. Groups such as OutRage! in the UK and ACT UP and Queer Nation in the US sought to challenge homophobia with such strategically aggressive tactics as the distribution of flyers with polemical messages ('I Hate Straights', 'Bash Back') and mass public demonstrations of same-sex affection in stereotypically 'straight' venues (Ahlgren, 9).

In its press materials the RSC positioned Murphy's production as both invested in 'contemporary queer politics' and 'conservative in its faithfulness to Marlowe's text'. In other words, the RSC justified what might have been perceived as the play's sensationalist or anachronistic representation of homosexuality as fidelity to the text: it is Marlowe's play, and not the production, that is prescient in its representation of identifiably twentieth-century notions of homosexuality. Calling Edward 'the first modern Gay Lib man', Murphy acknowledged potential backlash against his approach: 'people are frightened of the play. It is long, and there is homosexuality in it. I don't intend to shy away from that at all' (qtd in Ahlgren, 12).

Some reviews praised the production for this bold approach: 'Not the mere kiss between Edward and Gaveston which caused a councillor's outrage at the 1969 Edinburgh Festival but unbridled expression of the sensual-lyrical between young men'; 'there is nothing half-hearted about Gerard Murphy's approach to *Edward II*. The homosexuality which grips the first half of the play is treated in a very upfront fashion indeed, with the King making no bones about his physical passion for Piers Gaveston.'[37] Immediately before Gaveston is exiled he and the King (played by Simon Russell Beale) kneel and exchange rings in a mock-marriage scene: Gaveston kneels first, then the King, the stage action suggesting both the 'abnegation of [Edward's] status' and a 'tender proposal and marriage ritual' (Ahlgren, 12–13). Other homoerotic scenes included the spectacle of 'muscular and scantily-clad men' dancing before the King; so too do Spencer and Baldock 'indulge in some fairly specific groping under the sheet' as they are shown cavorting in bed together.[38]

Initially performed at the Swan playhouse, the smaller and more intimate RSC theatre used for less canonical plays, the production was scored by a visible string trio whose 'neurotic skitterings and plinkings quickly established that ... the world of the play is a cheerless, vicious place'.[39] Although the production left him unconvinced that *Edward II* deserved 'a regular place in the repertoire', Benedict Nightingale found Russell Beale's 'campy' performance as Edward ultimately effective:

> There is no doubting the party to which Russell Beale belongs far more than McKellen, he emphasises Edward's

homosexuality, to the point of becoming camp. He prances forward on the line 'I am king and not to be overruled,' as if to say 'Don't mess with me, ducky' ... . When he inveighs against 'the rebels and their accomplices', he might be threatening them with a handbag so precious does he sound. On occasions he could almost be a giant jellybaby bounced out of *La Cage Aux Folles*. Yet this is precisely why Russell Beale is so daring, he ventures perilously near stereotype, only to stop at the brink, and shows us the tenderness, the need, and the embarrassing yet enslaving passion behind the half-visible rogue.[40]

Less positive reviews described the play as 'distinctly limp-wristed', with Russell Beale, better known for playing comic or 'fop' characters, 'catastrophically miscast' as Edward.[41] For Michael Billington, Murphy's production lacked 'political subtlety' and – as we have seen throughout the history of this play's reception – paled next to Shakespeare: 'But watching Gerard Murphy's noisy, rhetorical production of *Edward II* at The Swan, I came away convinced that Canterbury's Christopher was no match, in poetry, intellect or pathos, for Stratford's William ... . Mr. Murphy's production is full of people noisily shouting at each other with little suggestion that Marlowe's poetry has passed through their imagination.'[42]

The production's eclectic costume scheme blended medieval fashion to more contemporary accents signifying 'queerness' to 1990s audiences. Called by one reviewer a 'swanky leather boy', Grant Thatcher as Gaveston 'makes his first entrance as John Travolta in black leather, zips, and studs, and caps it later as Elvis Presley in white'.[43] The barons wore 'spangled shiny black tunics with high collars, and gloves and boots of almost darker hue'.[44] In the part of Mortimer, Ciaran Hinds struck several reviewers as a Hitleresque figure 'who only needs a moustache to add to his floppy hair and hectoring snarl to be hideously complete'.[45] Recalling Robertson's vision of him as a 'sexual sadist', Murphy also has Lightborne seduce his sacrificial victim before killing him:

> Passionately kissing and straddling this matted, worn-out figure, Lightborne feigns a lover's concern while merely preparing Edward's body for the final, deadly intercourse … . As he succumbs to his killer's twisted ministrations, Russell Beale superbly wavers between an appalled, clear-eyed view of what is about to happen and the dreadful, blind dependency of a child / lover. The sordid outcome, graphically presented here, gives a new meaning to the term poker-work.[46]

Angela Ahlgren saw in Edward's final death pose an image 'reminiscent of a crucifixion – or of other young men tied up and then beaten (Ahlgren, 14). The graphic scene shocked audience members, one review calling it 'the most horror-filled dramatization of the King's murder probably ever presented on the legitimate stage' (Geckle, 12–13).

Over the course of thirty-odd years we therefore can see the different productions of *Edward II* shift from more candid representations of the play's same-sex relationship that nonetheless do not necessarily dislodge, in the popular and critical imagination, the idea that homosexuality itself is indeed 'unnatural', to productions such as Murphy's that deliberately use Marlowe's narrative to further a broader pro-gay rights agenda. In the 1950s and 1960s it was innovative for Robertson simply to stage the play with any degree of candour at all, whereas the political landscape, especially in the wake of the AIDS crisis, was dramatically different by the late 1980s. The self-same year of Murphy's RSC production also saw the first film adaptation of *Edward II* – and the most emphatically political, redemptive, and romantic reading of the play to date.

'Find a dusty old play and violate it'

In 1991, the innovative avant-garde filmmaker Derek Jarman – himself an out gay man and vocal proponent of gay rights

– adapted *Edward II* for the screen. For Jarman, Marlowe's play 'is an outing of gay history. Edward was murdered for his sexuality, which was then denied by historians until very recently. This unacceptable development in our history must be confronted.' Elsewhere, Jarman remarks that,

> It is difficult enough to be queer, but to be a queer in the cinema is almost impossible. Heterosexuals have fucked up the screen so completely that there's hardly room for us to kiss there. Marlowe outs the past – why don't we out the present? That's really the only message this play has. Fuck poetry. The best lines in Marlowe sound like pop songs and the worst, well, we've tried to spare you them.[47]

Thus does Jarman turn to an Elizabethan play to show the cost of homophobia in the 1990s, taking an ahistorical or totalizing view of the homosexual experience as the 'same' across time – Edward, in essence, a gay martyr in his time and in ours. The printed script of the film (titled *Queer Edward II*) clearly establishes Jarman's vision of the play as an urgent political intervention, the much smaller text of the film's dialogue printed under huge slogans from the queer activist group OutRage!: 'open your mind *not* your big mouth'; 'gender is apartheid'; 'heterosexuality is cruel & kinky'. Poignantly, Jarman annotates the script with memories of what it was to direct the film while sick with AIDS and periodically hospitalized; Jarman died of an AIDS-related illness in 1994.

Jarman certainly streamlines Marlowe's narrative by significantly cutting the source text, but – for all his defiant 'fuck poetry' – he does so without breaking the Marlovian line. His film also remains theatrical rather than cinematographic: as Bert Cardullo observes, it '"plays" as if it were filmed theatre' (completely different from, say, Kenneth Branagh's sweepingly cinematic film *Henry V* from 1989).[48] Jarman kept the stationary camera focused on the actors, who typically were framed at the centre of each shot. The film's interior sets – signifying a dungeon, an empty room, a bedroom, a boardroom – were largely bare and evocative a black-box theatre, and throughout the film the lighting was self-consciously theatrical or artificial. The actors wore contemporary costumes rather than period clothing: for the barons, expensive business suits; for Mortimer, a buzz cut, toothbrush moustache, and military garb. In the role of Isabella, Tilda Swinton donned increasingly elaborate and expensive designer clothing and jewellery as the film progressed, with her red hair and impassive face of make-up coming to resemble an opulent, modern-day Elizabeth I done up as a film star from Hollywood's golden age.[49]

Jarman constructed the film as a flashback, opening with a shot of Edward in a dungeon along with his coal-blackened jailor, Lightborne; periodically, Jarman interrupted the narrative to return to this ambiguous 'present' moment. Consistent with his treatment of historical subjects in his other films, Jarman incorporated deliberate anachronisms throughout; for instance, in one scene the pop star Annie Lennox sings 'Every Time We Say Goodbye' as Edward reluctantly writes the order to banish Gaveston, and at the end of the film members of OutRage! appear as themselves during a climactic protest scene evocative of the Stonewall riots.

Multiple images established the queerness of Edward's world, from explicit same-sex encounters to more diffused spectacles of homoeroticism: a snake dance performed by a young man wearing only a jockstrap; a naked rugby scrum watched by a young Prince Edward from the sidelines; Kent delivering his speech 'the mightiest kings have had their minions' while in a sauna receiving a massage from a buff young man. Our first glimpse of Gaveston is in a bedroom: dressed in a white nightgown, he sits on an unmade bed talking to Spencer while two naked 'sailors' kiss and embrace behind them – Edward's postcard from England finds Gaveston in the middle of an anonymous sexual encounter (Spencer's own participation in the scene is unclear). At times, queerness took on more sinister or violent aspects. Gaveston in particular uses sex as a form of humiliation, stripping naked the bishop who calls for his banishment and then forcing the bishop's face to his crotch in a rough parody of oral sex. So too does Gaveston at one point appear to lean in to kiss Isabella, only to pull away at the last minute to mock her (Jarman's annotation to this scene reads 'not all gay men are attractive. I am not going to make this an easy ride. Marlowe didn't.') Interestingly, Jarman chose not to include any explicit sex scene between Edward and Gaveston, although the two tenderly kissed, embraced and danced at various points; this veil of privacy that appears to cover only the two of them underscores the emotional aspect of their attachment (including the possibility that if shown elsewhere to be a brute, Gaveston is different with the King).

Nor does Jarman confine himself to showing images of gay male sex. One scene finds Mortimer in bed with two 'wild girls' who kiss each other; this, however, is queerness repurposed for the straight male gaze. What we see of heterosexual sex is grim indeed, for example Edward rising from bed with Isabella only to repeatedly beat his head against a wall. The film also makes it clear that Isabella's partnership with Mortimer is driven by expedience rather than sexual attraction. When we see them in bed together the pair lie side-by-side fully clothed, she sporting a green face mask, he – on top of the covers – reading a copy of *Unholy Babylon*, an Arab journalist's account of the United States's complicity in the rise of Saddam Hussein.

Throughout the play's performance history reviewers have often reacted negatively to Isabella, and it is difficult to say whether this lack of satisfaction is due to the play itself or to individual performances. Isabella is a tricky role to make sympathetic. Certainly in performance, the more abject Edward becomes in his suffering, the more villainous seems Isabella. The formidable Swinton does indeed come across as appealingly vulnerable during her early scenes with Edward. But by the end of the film Isabella has turned into a literal monster: she kills Kent by shredding his jugular vein with her teeth, and it is explicitly she, and not Mortimer, who hires Lightborne to kill the King. Accordingly, Susan Bennett takes Jarman to task for his 'breathtakingly misogynistic' portrayal of the queen; against Bennett and other reviewers who make similar claims, Niall Richardson reads Isabella as an intentionally 'campy' character 'in the same vein as Tallulah Bankhead, Gloria Swanson, Raquel Welch and (the most revered camp icon of all) Mae West', women whose artificial, high-fashion exteriors 'interrogate the assumed stable continuum of sex, gender and sexuality, on which the heterosexual matrix is based'.[50] Continuing his Isabella-centric reading, Richardson also argues that while Isabella retains an 'icy' reserve throughout the film, it is Gaveston and Edward who demonstrate the 'hysterical' swings of emotion more often associated with women. In other words, Jarman did not intend to demonize Isabella per se, but rather to challenge the overall 'apartheid' of gender binaries, to return to the OutRage! slogan.

Apart from the anachronisms woven throughout, Jarman's most significant departure from his source is his hopeful rendering of the play's end. Because the movie begins with Edward in prison, throughout one anticipates the scene of Edward's death. The moment finally comes: thugs in studded leather jackets brutally pin Edward down while Lightborne, framed in glowing red light, thrusts the poker into his body. Screaming, Edward then wakes up from what we now discover was merely a dream. Back in the waking world Lightborne throws away the poker and tenderly kisses Edward on the lips, the action implying that the men then run off together. To be sure, some of the historical narratives repeat the rumour that the actual King Edward II does not in fact die in jail, but escapes to the continent. Of Edward's grave site in Gloucester, Jarman writes that 'a diviner who works for the Police looking for bodies wrote me a letter saying that the tomb was empty. So this is why we have a 'happier' ending'. The film's last image is of a young King Edward II resplendent in lipstick, gold earrings and sparkly silver high heels dancing on top of a cage holding his dejected mother and Mortimer – each covered in white flour – to the tune of Tchaikovsky's 'Dance of the Sugar Plum Fairy'.

Edward in the twenty-first century

From 2000 on *Edward II* begins to be staged with greater frequency in the UK and the US, with several productions clustering to the same time frame: 2007–9 and 2011–13, in major venues as well as smaller, lower-budget theatres. While still keeping a focus on same-sex attraction as a core motif of the tragedy, these productions often incorporate other topical contexts, including allusions to the war in Iraq during George W. Bush's last term of office; one should also mention a 1993 Washington Stage Guild production in DC that, as Lois Potter observes, was 'set against the background of President Clinton's attempts to liberalize the military attitude to homosexuality'.[51] Developing Robertson's conception of the assassin as sadistic lover, many directors have the actor who plays Gaveston also take the part of Lightborne (indeed, by 2015 the double-casting of the part is more or less conventional). Productions of *Edward II* since 2000 also include more instances of racial diversity and cross-gender casting than in the past, including René Thornton Jr. as the first African-American Edward in the 2014 American Shakespeare Center production at the Blackfriars Playhouse. So too was there a racially diverse, all-female production of the play directed by Rebecca Patterson at the Connolly Theatre in New York in 2004; here, English lords were costumed as Japanese samurai and a messenger was clothed as a modern postman, with one reviewer describing such embellishments as more 'self-indulgent' than ultimately clarifying.[52]

As part of the Stratford Festival of Canada's 2005 'Saints and Sinners' season, Richard Monette directed *Edward II* in the intimate Studio Theatre; this was the first time the Festival staged a Marlowe production. Monette used period costumes with the exception of Jamie Robinson as Gaveston, whom Justin Shaltz described as looking like he dropped into the production from a 'modern gay dance club ... clad in black leather' with a 'medallion' around his neck and 'sloppy afro'.[53] Shaltz interpreted the bond between King and favourite as entirely based upon 'physical lust' rather than anything more exalted – in this production Edward only briefly mourns Gaveston before turning his attention to Spencer. At Edward's death 'Lightborne and his accomplices tortured him with near drowning, three times splashing the stage with water from a large bucket. They then crashed a table down upon his back in scarlet lighting and skewered him from behind with a fireplace poker. Edward's screams of horror, pain, and disbelief were not only convincing, but unsettling' (Shaltz, 95).

In 2007 Gale Edwards directed *Edward II* at the Shakespeare Theatre Company's new venue Sidney Harman Hall as part of a season that also included *Tamburlaine*. In the words of the company artistic director Michael Kahn, Sidney Harman Hall was designed to allow artists 'to use their total imagination', the large space designed to sustain a wide range of stage and seating configurations. For Rachel Evans, Edwards's design concept evoked a 'Wildesque risqué 1920s aristocratic' atmosphere, with the King's court costumed as a 'hazy male phantasmagoria, not entirely unlike an R-rated, gender-bending burlesque a là *Cage aux Folles*'.[54] Returning from exile, Gaveston made a grand entrance by descending on a centre-stage lift wearing 'a gold lame tailcoat and angel wings'. Evans, however, found that the sheer size of the new venue 'privileged all things extroverted' and at times overwhelmed the action, although she praised Wallace Acton as Edward for his ability to convey moments of intimacy. In contrast, Tim Treanor thought that the director took 'full advantage of the new theatre's capacity, moving set pieces in from the most unexpected places while blanketing us with orchestral sound. Some of her effects are wonderfully subtle; her peers all seem to be at least eight inches taller than Edward and his Court, and it allows us to see where the power really is.'[55] At Edward's death a 'Ghost Gaveston' reappeared to shield or guard the 'violated body of his lover', a choice that innovatively revises the convention of double-casting Gaveston in the part of Lightborne and that mitigates the violence of the ending. As Lois Potter points out in a review of this same production, the spectacle of Gaveston in angel wings also evokes Tony Kushner's seminal play *Angels in America* (1993). Potter furthermore noted the play's emphasis upon 'the militarism of the barons, the corruption of the church, and the mainly silent child, the future Edward III, who observes it all' (66).

By comparison, in 2008 Sean Graney directed a streamlined and significantly more intimate promenade-style staging at the small 'Upstairs' theatre space in the Chicago Shakespeare Theater at Navy Pier. Graney articulated his vision of the play as follows: 'I thought that a play as unique as this, with its shifting points of view between protagonists, needed a unique staging ... breaking with traditional staging asks you to engage physically in the decision.'[56] The black-box space contained no discrete 'stage' area separate from the audience as such. Rather, the totality of the space was used, with actors performing in and among standing audience members who were in turn free to move where they pleased, including to take seats on low benches that the actors occasionally commandeered from them. At one corner of the room was a modern, tiled 'bathroom' containing a toilet full of stage blood. Separated off by a plastic curtain, this space was the location of the majority of the play's executions, all of which followed the same script: the victim was brought into the bathroom, shot with a gun produced from a plastic lunch box, and then blood was painted on the increasingly blood-spattered tiled wall. Once the execution had taken place the archetypal figure of 'Death', sporting a beaked Venetian mask, would – accompanied by tolling bells and fog effects – escort the body offstage. For the execution of Edward, Graney notably broke with this pattern, staging it instead with the house lights abruptly turned on and without any theatrical trappings of fog or dim lighting to distract from the sight of Edward's death. A bench that had moments before served as a seat for spectators was flipped over: Edward was placed on it, face-down, before he was smothered with a mattress and then graphically impaled on the poker (Graney did follow convention by doubling Gaveston and Lightborne). The effect was eviscerating: there was no ability for the audience to evade the violence before them (Stevens, 121).

Several more immersive and streamlined productions follow, including two at spaces that mimic the architectural configurations of Renaissance playhouses. In 2011 at the Rose Theatre in the 'Bankside' district of London – 'the theatre that helped make the playwright's name' – Peter Darney directed a 'fast-paced' and 'galloping' production in what Nicholas Hamilton described as a 'cramped' and 'atmospheric' venue. Hamilton praised Darney for:

> underlining the carnality and violence of Marlowe's play. When lovers are not kissing and groping one another, enemies are gouging eyes and pulling hair. Rather than reducing the production to a pantomime, the use of stage blood, filthy brown water and a severed head creates a grotesque atmosphere that would have engaged the Rose's original audience as much as it does today.[57]

The year 2011 also saw another production of the play at the Royal Exchange in Manchester. Director Toby Frow transformed the theatre's foyer into a 'fifties-style bar' in which members of the ensemble danced, creating an opening experience that Glenn Meads suggested contrasted provocatively against the 'gripping' action: 'Frow directs with a sense of urgency and creates a thriller of epic proportions.' Meads praised Emma Cunniffe as Isabella for her expertise in conveying the Queen's 'pain and rejection' and found Samuel Collings, double-cast in the role of Gaveston and Lightborne, as especially effective as the 'cold yet softly-spoken killer'.[58]

Finally, the most notable – or notorious – recent production of *Edward II* is surely Joe Hill-Gibbins's 2013 staging of the play at the National Theatre. Hill-Gibbins's 'hyper-stylised' design combined a range of theatrical devices including Brechtian scene captions projected onto screens; other video projections, including live-streaming footage from hand-held cameras; mixed-period costumes; and Jarman-esque anachronistic details such as characters smoking, drinking champagne and making 'telephone jokes'. In another 'Brechtian' touch the backstage area was visible to the audience, who for a portion of the production could see such behind-the-scenes gear as costume racks, props tables and lighting rigs. Played by Kirsty Bushell, Kent became Edward's sister, rather than his brother, and although the gender of the character remained the same, Edward III was played by Bettrys Jones, a petite adult woman 'dressed in a smart blazer and flannel shorts like a prep-school boy'.[59]

Played as an American (described in one review a 'bumptious, leather-jacketed clubber'), Kyle Soller as Gaveston made a spectacular entrance unexpectedly climbing down through the audience from the upper seats of the theatre, in Kirk Melnikoff's words seemingly 'conjured from without' the world of the play like a Vice or a Clown.[60] Soller also doubled the part of Lightborne, the scene of the murder-by-penetration working, for Melnikoff, 'as a discomforting fantasy conjured by those piqued and disturbed' by the men's physical affection for each other' (Melnikoff, 5). For the most part the reviews agree that the production seemed to take the side of Edward (John Heffernan), who struck viewers as both 'a moving, bewildered little boy lost' and a man 'more sinned against than sinning'.[61]

While all agreeing on the production's ambitiousness, the reviews of the play were nevertheless very mixed. Charles Spencer wrote that his 'heart sank' upon entering the Olivier theatre to encounter a set of 'unpainted plywood', the visible backstage revealing 'racks of costumes and stainless steel ladders', and found it impossible to take the adult woman playing Edward III seriously, especially given a wig and costume that made her resemble 'the female half of the Krankies', a Scottish comedy duo (5 September 2013). For Andrzej Lukowski, the production was 'aggressively modern and occasionally a bit of a mess'.[62] Michael Billington admired the play's 'visual bravura' but felt that the production's incorporation of live video footage, if 'innovative', had its drawbacks especially when it came to the delivery of verse:

> Characters are tracked by lightweight cameras and projected on to giant video screens. This pays off in the pained closeups of the captive Edward being mercilessly shunted around the kingdom; at other times, it gives the play a spurious documentary feel and muffles, rather than enhances, the language. (5 September 2013)

In contrast, Melnikoff felt that the 'multi-media moments heightened the emotional impact of Hills-Gibbins's scenes' even as they offered a 'not-so-subtle critique of the manipulative potential of modern media', although he, too, remarked that Marlowe's verse was often a 'casualty' of the director's 'spectacle-driven, conceptual approach' (4–5).

With a sharp uptick in productions of this play since 2000, we might well expect Marlowe's tragedy to continue to be staged with increasing frequency. For directors such as Murphy and Jarman, however, the importance of staging *Edward II* in the early 1990s had to do with visibility; that is, in the wake of the AIDs crisis, for example, merely representing same-sex attraction on stage – rather than suppressing it, as Poel did in 1903 – constituted a significant intervention. Thus for Murphy, Edward epitomized the 'modern gay lib man', but what might that phrase even mean for audiences in 2015, especially in light of pressing twenty-first century debates over such topics as same-sex marriage and, to be sure, related debates over the rights of trans people? Of course, this is not to suggest that every production of *Edward II* must constitute a political intervention in the area of identity politics, although – given the play's production history since the early 1990s – audiences may well come to the play expecting some kind of 'message' about homosexual desire rather than, say, the pressures of kingship.

3

The State of the Art: Desire, History and the Theatre

Judith Haber

Unlike most 'State of the Art' chapters on recent criticism in the Arden series, this one does not begin in the current century. I have chosen to start with the 1990s because it was then that the most groundbreaking examinations of Marlowe's *Edward II* were written, and those analyses – for both better and worse – continue to shape critical approaches to this day. In the following pages, I attempt to separate different perspectives on the play into reasonably coherent strands (although of course each of these intersects with the others, and some texts combine them all) and to locate areas of agreement and debate. I then examine how these various approaches have developed in the new century: some new ground has indeed been broken, but a number of pieces seem simply to rehearse, refine or sophisticate earlier ideas. Perhaps the least vital area of interest is that which was the most exciting in the 1990s – the construction of sexuality, which a number of critics have recently declared to be over-studied in the play, or to have been improperly emphasized in the first place. I end, however, by suggesting how some new perspectives could revivify work on *Edward II* and enable scholars in sexuality studies, as well in other areas of interest, to examine the play afresh and to deploy it as a central document in current critical and theoretical debates.

Edward II in the 1990s

The 1990s saw a tremendous upsurge of critical interest in *Edward II*. After listing no records for the 1970s and only twenty-eight for the 1980s, the MLA Bibliography lists sixty-one for the 1990s.[1] This interest (as well as that in the late 1980s) clearly reflected the growing influence of Michel Foucault, of Eve Kosofsky Sedgwick, and the coming to prominence of queer theory throughout the academy. The work of Alan Bray helped focus attention on the historical construction of homoeroticism in this period, and *Edward II* became the literary linchpin for academic discussion of the problems it posed; by the early 1990s, as Alan Stewart notes, it 'had become the English Renaissance play about male homosexuality'.[2] Major works by Gregory Bredbeck, Bruce Smith, Jonathan Goldberg and others used the play to help situate the paradoxes entailed by sodomy – that 'utterly confused category' that serves to disrupt all other categories – in the centre of the discussion.[3]

Bredbeck, at the beginning of the decade, focuses a fascinating chapter in his book *Sodomy and Interpretation* on the ways in which homoeroticism is 'written' – constructed and used – in the power politics of the play. He notes that Edward's death 'can be seen as an attempt to "write" onto him the homoeroticism constantly ascribed to him', and he concludes that 'the play demonstrates a crucial point in the epistemology of Renaissance sodomy: sodomy does not create disorder; rather, disorder demands sodomy'.[4] Goldberg, somewhat similarly, sees a 'sodometrie' as a kind of interpretation; he refuses, however, to limit 'sodomy' to a synonym for homoeroticism, broadening the category to include anyone or anything that transgresses normative boundaries and undermines orthodox hierarchy, including – to the consternation of some critics – Edward's queen, Isabella. He argues that 'the identity Marlowe gives to the sodomite is a fully negativized one. With no ground to stand upon, Marlowe envisions the possibility of sexuality and sexual difference as a separate category' (124). Bray himself, in an article reprinted in Goldberg's seminal anthology *Queering the Renaissance*, argues that many of characteristics of the relationship between Edward and Gaveston mark it ambiguously either as a socially acceptable friendship or as sodomitical: it only falls into the latter category, he maintains, because of Gaveston's class and mercenary intentions.[5] Moreover, he notes that similar ambiguities reappear in many male friendships of the time, making them always available targets for political enemies. Stephen Orgel, on the other hand, states that *Edward II* is 'to [his] knowledge the only dramatic instance of a homoerotic relationship being presented in the terms in which the culture formally conceived it – as antisocial, seditious, ultimately disastrous'.[6]

Bruce Smith, while agreeing with Bray in many respects, organizes his book *Homosexual Desire in Shakespeare's England* according to a number of recognized homoerotic 'types'. He discusses *Edward II* in his chapter on 'Master and Minion' and argues that it marks a crucial shift in perception: 'Marlowe introduces us to the possibility of a homosexual subjectivity' here.[7] Emily Bartels similarly finds that 'homosexuality' was, at this moment, starting 'to have a place, however nameless, formless, and faint, in Renaissance discourse'; she argues that it was therefore often occluded (along with the idea of the 'private') in that discourse, and that 'in countering its occlusion [Marlowe] begins to open a space that it will finally come to fill'.[8]

Mario DiGangi moves further away from Bray's position to assert that the equation of homoeroticism with sodomy in Renaissance studies 'depends upon certain problematic, and anachronistic, assumptions about homosexuality'.[9] He maintains that 'male homoerotic relations can be socially orderly as well as disorderly' and that '"sodomy" names not a homoerotic desire but a political transgression often associated with inappropriate forms of intimacy between men' (195, 204). Mortimer is therefore identified as the true sodomite here: 'Marlowe's Edward II and the historical James I' should be seen 'not as sodomitical monarchs, but as homoerotically inclined monarchs who had to define and defend themselves against sodomitical subjects' (209). Claude Summers also believes that Bray's 'construction of Renaissance homoeroticism as exclusively sodomitical is deeply problematic and dangerously constricting', maintaining that 'the literary discourse about homosexuality in Renaissance England is more various than his construction can accommodate'.[10] He further takes issue with Goldberg's 'elastic' version of that construction, since it erases sodomy's 'signal importance for discussions of same-sex desire in the period while expanding its application to social deviance generally' (29). In *Edward II*, he argues, the sodomitical construction is used only cynically (and finally murderously) by Edward's enemies, and it is contrasted with 'the world of erotic freedom represented by Edward's love for Gaveston' (42).

Other critics in the 1990s similarly contemplate Marlowe's representation of homoeroticism and its suppression. Jennifer Brady argues that 'the re-enactment of Edward's sin in his murder ... marks the crime as a phobic, sadistic denigration of homosexual love', but throughout the play, it is 'Edward's voice ... that Marlowe insists we hear'; she further identifies, in some earlier critical analyses, 'phobic responses to alternative sexualities'.[11] Stephen Guy-Bray makes this point even more forcefully: he surveys previous criticism and argues that 'the critical suppression of the possibility of a positive homosexual discourse imitates the action of Edward's murderer'; Marlowe dramatizes that murder 'in order to analyze the way society controls sexuality'.[12] In a psychoanalytic reading, Viviana Comensoli also explores the social 'regulation of desire' and contends that through deliberate departures from his sources, Marlowe demystifies Tudor historiography and illuminates the homophobia that helps to buttress the structures of a faltering patriarchal society.[13]

In contrast, Dympna Callaghan approaches *Edward II* from a feminist perspective and argues that the male homoerotic bonds in the play are themselves represented as supporting patriarchal structures – structures in which, she asserts (contra Goldberg), Marlowe's Isabella is helplessly caught. She compares the play to Elizabeth Cary's narrative, *The Reign and Death of Edward II,* in which the author 'uses sodomy to make femininity visible' and presents Isabella as 'a warrior queen'.[14] Kathleen Anderson also compares the two texts, but she finds that they both present Isabella as 'a powerful political figure' who uses every means at her disposal to obtain and maintain that power.[15] Sara Munson Deats reads Marlowe's work from a different feminist point of view in *Sex, Gender, and Desire in the Plays of Christopher Marlowe,* and sees both Edward and his queen as role-playing, 'androgynous characters who explode gender stereotypes'; the play itself, she believes, explores the performative nature of gender and identity.[16] Thomas Healy, who characterizes Isabella as a 'careful and diabolical' deceiver and positions Mortimer as the true sodomite, thinks that the play somewhat surprisingly combines homoeroticism with 'a perspective that is largely Protestant in its implications … mak[ing] a good case for viewing Marlowe as a Protestant dramatist'.[17]

Ian McAdam, in '*Edward II* and the Illusion of Integrity', reviews the work of many of the critics mentioned here and disagrees with most of them. 'The play is not primarily concerned with asserting homosexual subjectivity', he tells us; it is instead 'a tragedy about the failure of self-fashioning … . Edward opts for indulgence in fantasy rather than for skillful artistic control', and Marlowe's play is 'in a sense a self-consuming artefact, wherein imagination necessarily feeds on and destroys itself': it is shadowed by 'an Augustinian

Christianity that continued to haunt Marlowe, even as he fought to eradicate it'.[18]

A subset of the discussion explores Derek Jarman's revision of the play in his film and the accompanying book *Queer Edward II*.[19] I will generally leave these pieces to the chapter on performance, but it is worth mentioning here two essays that consider the play along with the film. Thomas Cartelli, in '*Queer Edward II*: Postmodern Sexualities and the Early Modern Subject', finds that 'by selectively foregrounding issues that the play's critics – as opposed to Marlowe himself – have chosen either to marginalize or to treat from a moralized perspective, Jarman has done more to hasten the demise of an already unraveling critical consensus on *Edward II* than he has to improve a play that, in many respects, invites the treatment Jarman has given it'.[20] Deborah Willis, in 'Marlowe Our Contemporary: *Edward II* on Stage and Screen', considers how Jarman's film and others that reference *Edward II* (Mel Gibson's *Braveheart*, Sidney Lumet's *The Deadly Affair*) have emphasized the homoerotic component in the play. She examines these alongside Bertolt Brecht's stage adaptation, which focuses on 'abuses of state power and class position', and she argues that '*Edward II* ... marks the spot where the two concerns intersect.' 'Thus', she maintains, 'Marlowe's play has provided an important testing ground for contemporary views of such matters as the relative importance of sexuality and class, the relation of "the personal" and "the political" and the tendency of liberation struggles to reinscribe pre-existing power relations'.[21]

Indeed, many critics in the 1990s do foreground the intersection of sexuality and politics within the play, especially as it bears upon the reigns of Elizabeth I and James VI. John Michael Archer, in a chapter of *Sovereignty and Intelligence* exploring Marlowe's putative careers as spy, sodomite and (failed) seeker of patronage, suggests that *Edward II* 'both underwrites the political erotics of Elizabeth's court ... and criticizes them by imagining a male monarch'; in so doing, the play 'both conceals and reveals the paradoxical link between patronage and homoeroticism as subversive practice and social bond'.[22] Lawrence Normand, in '"What Passions Call You These?": *Edward II* and James VI', places Edward's relationship with Gaveston alongside that of James and Esmé Stuart, not in order to argue for an exact correspondence, but to explore 'the available range of discourses in which same-sex eroticism might appear, ... thereby reaching a more complex and subtle sense of homoeroticism both in the historical episode and in Marlowe's play'.[23] Mark Thornton Burnett, while similarly eschewing 'mimetic analogy' in '*Edward II* and Elizabethan Politics', sees the play as responding to the complicated and contradictory positions of both Elizabeth and James, reading it 'in terms of a dialogue with civil unrest, an unruly noble faction, the security of the crown, and speculation about the direction that the monarchy might take: practices and processes that were, when the play was composed in 1591–2, specific products of its historical moment'.[24]

In an essay at the turn of the millennium, Curtis Perry investigates further the relationship between homoeroticism and royal patronage. He considers 'the image of the sodomite king', in Marlowe's *Edward II* and in popular representations of James I, 'as a figurative response to resentments stemming from the regulation of access to the monarch'.[25] Marlowe responds here to the scandal surrounding the French king Henri III, but 'the resemblance between Marlowe's Edward and the image of James that later arose in England' should be viewed as 'symptomatic, telling us more about the ongoing concern with the meaning and function of royal favour and the politics of access than about the sexual mores or personal character of James VI and I' (1056).

In contrast to these critics, others see precise parallels between the particulars of *Edward II* and contemporary events. Dennis Kay, in 'Marlowe, *Edward II* and the Cult of Elizabeth' argues that 'in Marlowe's play the image of the king may be construed as a negative exemplum, being defined negatively in terms of the well established cult of Queen Elizabeth'.[26] In addition, Curtis Breight, in *Surveillance,*

Militarism and Drama in the Elizabethan Era, sees the play as 'political allegory in which Gaveston and the Spencers stand for Burghley and, by analogy, King Edward for Queen Elizabeth'.[27]

William Zunder considers the politics of the play in much more general terms: 'Rejecting feudal particularism, and uncomfortable with capitalist self-interest, Marlowe chooses to occupy the only other terrain open to his generation: that of royal absolutism ... . The commitment to absolutism, itself a departure from traditional notions of limited monarchy, is complemented by a radical homosexuality'.[28] Articulating a more traditional view, Carla Prichard maintains that the resolution of the political conflicts viewed as 'unnatural' in the play is necessarily accomplished by the only person with whom Edward has a wholly 'natural' relationship – his son.[29]

Other readers approach the problems posed by the play from linguistic, psychoanalytic or theatrical perspectives. David Thurn, in 'Sovereignty, Disorder, and Fetishism in *Edward II*' brings these together to explore the 'dual function of specular structures as they work both to support and undermine the imaginary fictions of both self and state', resulting in an 'instability of affect'; 'Marlowe', he suggests, 'stages the events in the chronicles in anamophoric perspective, revealing "History" to be the sphere in which mutually exclusive possibilities are contested and sometimes held in exquisite tension'.[30] In a related exploration, I focus primarily on the linguistic paradoxes in the play, beginning with the '(un)pointed' letter, and demonstrate how these relate to the (non)concept of sodomy; I argue that *Edward II* ultimately closes those paradoxes down, enacting in both form and content a 'submission to history', while simultaneously gesturing toward the inadequacy of the closure it creates.[31] Fred Tromly, in a chapter in *Playing with Desire*, also considers the problems of writing a historically based drama and foregrounds, as he does throughout the book, Marlowe's tantalization of his characters and his audience.[32]

Catherine Belsey approaches the play from a more explicitly psychoanalytic point of view, and asserts: 'Marlowe's *Edward II* is a play about desire – and about desire's excess. ... Desire, which is an absence, takes possession of the subject, tantalizes with an imagined omnipotence, and ultimately delivers nothing more nor less than annihilation'.[33] Speaking in a different register, she also notes that the excesses presented within the play mirror those attributed to the Elizabethan theatre (89–92). Matthew Proser adopts a 'post-Freudian manner' in *The Gift of Fire* and identifies aggression as the motivating force behind both Marlowe's drama and his characters' actions.[34] Making an argument that, in an earlier form, was criticized by Guy-Bray and others, he maintains that 'Edward's aggressive self-indulgence actually provokes the sufferings that come upon him' and leads inevitably to his death (176). Katherine Sirluck sees Edward as defined, like all Marlowe's heroes, by the 'pleasure of outrage, ... the massing of self over and against all that seeks to control'.[35] William B. Kelly, in 'Mapping Subjects in Marlowe's *Edward II*', uses the work of Gilles Deleuze and Felix Guattari to consider the play 'as the site of contested ideas of subjectivity'.[36] While most of the other characters attempt to inscribe the king into a fixed, essentialist world view, Edward himself possesses a contingent, fluid subjectivity: he is a 'becoming-subject, in the several senses of that word' (4).

Marlowe's reimagining of historical material on the stage becomes the focus of several critical pieces. In *Christopher Marlowe,* Roger Sales looks generally at 'the difficulties that are created for spectators by the play's compressed, confusing version of history', and specifically at the ways in which the theatrical representation of the deposition and execution of an English king is made acceptable.[37] Douglas Cole, in *Christopher Marlowe and the Renaissance of Tragedy,* also examines Marlowe's transformation of Renaissance historiography, as well as of the *de casibus* tradition, into both of which the playwright 'worked ... ironic implications peculiarly his own', thus helping to create (with Shakespeare) 'a new form of historical tragedy',³⁸ Joan Parks considers carefully the chronicles by Fabyan, Stow and Holinshed that Marlowe used as sources, and concludes that 'Marlowe identifies artifice and fiction as fundamental principles governing not only the writing of history but also historical action itself. He thus establishes the historical significance of his own play even as he acknowledges its fictionality.'³⁹ Patrick Ryan, on the other hand, argues that continuity exists between *Edward II* and Medieval Passion plays: the depiction of the king's humiliation and torture 'rehearse ... symbolic degradations adapted from traditional lore of Christ's "secret passion"'. Ryan maintains that 'Marlowe, dramatizing the suffering of Edward, forges a powerful theatrical naturalism from interrelated conventions of Tudor piety and religious drama.'⁴⁰

Others approach Marlowe's relation to the theatre from different angles. Debra Belt, in 'Anti-Theatricalism and Rhetoric in Marlowe's *Edward II*', sees the play as an examination of 'the ways speakers, rhetoric, and plays act upon their hearers to shape judgments'.⁴¹ As such, it quite deliberately 'embod[ies] in dramatic form the ambiguities and contradictions of the anti-theatrical controversy' and 'allows Marlowe to conduct an extraordinarily wide-ranging anatomy of the criticisms levelled against the medium for which he is writing' (134, 149). Thomas Cartelli, in *Marlowe, Shakespeare, and the Economy of Theatrical Experience*, examines 'the ways in which Marlowe ... make[s] playgoers receptive to positions that effectively demystify established structures of meaning and belief', like Gaveston and Edward's homoeroticism and Lightborne's brutal murder of the king; while he notes that Marlowe's procedure here contrasts with that in some of Shakespeare's plays, he nevertheless argues that 'the work of the two playwrights' is drawn together by 'its common grounding in a poetics of demystification whose nominal theorist was Machiavelli'.⁴² In contrast, Patrick Cheney, in *Marlowe's Counterfeit Profession*, considers *Edward's* mixture of 'Machiavellian policy and Ovidian play' as part of its author's attempt to create a counter-national discourse: 'Marlowe's *professional* purpose in *Edward II* is to counter his rival colleagues' censoring of his works' and 'to simulate a triumph of Marlovian art over Spenserian and Shakespearean art'.[43]

A group of scholars focuses particularly on the relation between *Edward II* and Shakespeare's *Richard II*. Robert P. Merrix and Carole Levin examine the structure of the deposition scenes in both plays and find that they both follow a similar, three-part pattern, beginning with the king's questioning of his position, moving to 'introspection and delay' and then 'proceed[ing] with the physical divestiture and spiritual resignation, only to end by being diverted to anger and confusion at the loss of identity'.[44] In Marlowe's play, however, 'deposition is only a process, one from which the king slips from power into pathos', whereas for Shakespeare's king, it effectively becomes 'both process and role' (10). Maurice Charney examines a number of similar elements in the two plays and argues that '*Edward II* functioned as a model rather than a source for ... *Richard II*'; here, as elsewhere, 'Shakespeare is trying valiantly to outdo Marlowe and to go him one better.'[45] Charles R. Forker summarizes earlier scholarship on the connections between the two playwrights' works: he comments, 'That Marlowe in *Edward II* was indebted to Shakespeare's first histories is now taken as proved';[46] and Marlowe's play seems to have influenced *Richard II* and Shakespeare's later works in turn. Nevertheless, he concludes: 'Although the interests of Shakespeare and Marlowe patently converged in the pages of Holinshed, their attitudes and artistic sensibilities impelled them even from the beginning in different directions' (90). Meredith Skura argues, however, that 'Shakespeare was more influenced than we have realized by the erotic passion and erotic violence associated with male friendship and male rivalry in Marlowe': the love and violent death that 'have been ousted from Shakespeare's plot ... return in Shakespeare's language'.[47] She comments that 'the Marlovian echoes – and the fact that they are so muffled – tell us not so much about the play as about Shakespeare and the way he saw his rival, Marlowe' (90).

Criticism since the turn of the century

Interest in the play remains strong, despite having waned a bit (fifty-two MLA citations for the first decade of the new millennium and thirteen for the following three years), but while later examinations are often extremely sophisticated and interesting, they also frequently seem to refine earlier ideas and to explore pathways that have been trod before. Not surprisingly, more than a few provide (very useful) summaries of earlier criticism.

A number of critics make contributions to the ongoing debate about homoeroticism in early modern England and in the play. Thomas Cartelli reviews the terms of this debate in '*Edward II*', while also situating his argument 'in the context of ongoing efforts to analyse the early modern passions';[48] he sees the play as staging at least 'two competing forms of disorder … one focused on Edward's passionate obsession with Gaveston and the other on the arrogance, impatience, and downright fury of Edward's aristocratic opponents' (163). Jonathan Crewe revisits the scholarship on sodomy in more detail and argues that academics have reached a comfortable 'consensus' – 'the historicist dissolution of homosexual identity' – which has the drawbacks of allowing us to maintain a distance from the objects of our study and potentially leading to 'the supposition that sexual behaviours, even when officially disapproved or criminalized, coexisted relatively peacefully in early modernity'.[49] *Edward II* seems to reflect this consensus in many respects, but it also 'pushes back' against it, especially in its horrifying end, which calls our attention to a 'violent and deeply embedded "homophobia" against which enlightenment, modern or contemporary, makes headway with great difficulty' (389, 396). In 'Marlowe and Queer Theory', after an overview of the relevant criticism, David Clark concludes: 'If Marlowe had anything to say to queer theorists today, perhaps it would be a reminder to balance the pleasures of discourse and performativity with the need to critique a world in which people are murdered for failing to conform to a perceived norm.'[50] H. David Brumble believes that most recent interpretations 'obscure much that would seem important to Marlowe's audience' and offers a traditional 'corrective', maintaining that the play is particularly 'concerned with the necessity of control: personal, paternal, and kingly'.[51]

David Stymeist contends that 'the representation of sodomy in the play is strategically ambivalent .... *Edward II* constitutes a cleft text that simultaneously condemns and defends the practice of executing sodomites for sexual and social crimes.' Thus, the play 'figures as a culturally anomalous defense of gender transgression, which can be linked to wider theatrical concerns with the decriminalization of alternative sexualities', but it 'is also bound, in order to avoid detrimental financial and legal consequences ..., to defend the judicial and popular construction of the sodomite as an appropriate scapegoat'.[52] Alan Stewart, after examining the play's performance and critical history as well as its transformations of Holinshed, similarly concludes that its presentation of homoeroticism lends itself to conflicting interpretations: 'Marlowe simply cannot be pinned down to a single opinion of his subject matter.'[53] In an essay that focuses partially on Jarman's film, Lawrence Normand, after noting that 'in Marlowe's play sex is always political', argues that the contradictory interpretations of Edward's character and actions 'centre on the meaning of [his] ... death'.[54] He comments further: 'Jarman's rewriting of Marlowe's ending is anticipated in Marlowe's rewriting of Holinshed's account of Edward's death; and in both cases the changes work to diminish homophobia' (190).

Amanda Bailey, in a chapter of her book *Flaunting* entitled 'The Italian Vice and Bad Taste in *Edward II*', looks at this issue from a somewhat different perspective. Bailey foregrounds aesthetic expression within the play and explores how 'sexual and stylistic excess are linked ... and what is at stake in their overlay'.[55] The play presents a court that is infected (not unlike Elizabeth's) by a foreign style: 'The symptoms of the sickness contaminating Edward's realm are those "abhominable vices" that members of Marlowe's audience associated with the Italianified Englishman, namely "vaineglory, ſelfloue, [and] ſodomie"' (77).[56]

Critics continue to investigate questions of gender in the play, especially with regard to Isabella. Joanna Gibbs, in 'Marlowe's Politic Women', argues that Isabella is a complex, role-playing character, who operates in both the public and the private spheres: she has 'a pragmatic grasp of statecraft' and 'proves herself impressively capable of consolidating her position in a society hostile to female power'.[57] Jennifer L. Sheckter also views her as a powerful, self-conscious performer and creator of identities, contending that 'Isabella's self-assertions, particularly as a rejected, loyal wife and the mother to the future king of England, connect her with Marlowe's famous machiavels in their shared dedication to the pursuit of power.'[58] Kate Chedgzoy, in 'Marlowe's Men and Women: Gender and Sexuality', believes that the Queen's 'feminine grief at the destruction of her marriage motivates her to act in ways that challenge the gender stereotypes of the play's world' and that political ambition augments 'her increasing disorderly behaviour'.[59] Claire Hansen finds Isabella less flexible than many other critics. Using organizational management theory to examine the learning patterns and agency of the woman in three of Marlowe's plays, she notes that Isabella's strategies remain relatively consistent: she depends on powerful men to assure her position, and there is often a 'clear distinction between … [her] espoused theories' and the ideas that in reality govern her actions.[60]

Doris Feldman, in 'Construction and Deconstruction of Gendered Bodies in Selected Plays of Christopher Marlowe', argues that Marlowe always presents gender as unstable and socially constructed: '*Edward II* illustrates the extent to which masculinity and femininity are dependent on conscious attempts at formal bodily representation for and by others.'[61] In *Marlowe's Soldiers*, Alan Shepherd looks particularly at the construction of masculinity, especially as it enables a martial persona. He places *Edward II* in the context of post-Armada England, where a number of polemicists warned of the 'risks of self-indulgent prosperity', and he suggests that the peers' 'real problem with Edward's reign ... [is] that he favours peace over war as the preeminent episteme of English life';[62] Edward and Gaveston further trouble the nobles by repeatedly demonstrating that martial masculinity is performed, rather than possessed. In 'Masculinity, Performance, and Identity', Merry Perry examines father/son dyads in all of Marlowe's plays; she notes that Edward II 'defies the law of the name of the father'.[63] Taking a different perspective, Marie Rutkoski focuses on Prince Edward in 'Breeching the Boy in Marlowe's *Edward II*'; she argues that 'Marlowe deftly draws the prince, perhaps to our surprise, into the homoerotic and sodomitical dynamics of the play' and thus 'prevents us from viewing the boy ... as a solution to sexual and political subversion'.[64]

The play's reflection of contemporary politics (and their connection to sexual politics) remains a topic of discussion and disagreement. Marcie Bianco considers Anglo-Irish relations in 'To Sodomize a Nation: *Edward II*, Ireland, and the Threat of Penetration': she sees Gaveston as 'the metonymic embodiment of Ireland, which is very much related to his position of as a sodomite'; he is, in effect, 'the nodal point where Ireland and sodomy intersect in the play'.[65] Jeffrey Rufo looks at the figure of the minion in both *Edward II* and *The Massacre at Paris*, arguing that 'Marlowe's return to the minion and his immersion in contemporary French controversies in *Massacre* is an undervalued resource in analyzing the superior *Edward*.'[66]

Ronald Knowles sees the critical focus on sexuality as misdirected; he argues that 'to Marlowe's contemporaries', *Edward II* would have seemed 'a direct reflection on the most seditious political issues of the day – deposition and election of the monarch – which conflicted absolutely with Tudor orthodoxy'; Marlowe here skillfully incorporates the basic tenets of early modern 'resistance theory' into a more orthodox (and thus acceptable) form.[67] In *Marlowe's Literary*

Scepticism, Chloe Kathleen Preedy argues strongly for the pervasive presence of religious resistance theory in the play. She notes that 'the dual threat of Catholic and puritan rebellion was a terrifying prospect for loyal English subjects',[68] and that many of the elements in the play – equivocal language, the threat of being excommunicated (as Elizabeth was), and finally, regicide itself – were recommended by the polemical pamphlets of the time; in the character of Mortimer, Marlowe presents these ideas as 'framed by the language and imagery of religious faith, but in reality motivated by the self-interested ambitions of a hypocritical and skeptical rebel' (151).[69]

In *Literature and Favoritism in Early Modern England*, Curtis Perry develops and contextualizes more fully the ideas in his earlier article; he discusses several versions of the Edward II story, which is 'utterly ubiquitous in the period's controversial political writing, where it serves as a highly contested precedent for arguments about the nature and limitations of English monarchy'.[70] In Marlowe's version, 'both royal will and subjects' opposition tend ultimately toward the chaos of passion'; the play thus 'poses a query about ... England's supposedly balanced constitution' (201). Paulina Kewes, in 'Marlowe, History, and Politics', takes a somewhat similar view. She notes that Marlowe alters historical material in *Edward II* to make (often contradictory) topical allusions to contemporary England, Scotland and France; his purpose is not, however, to create a straightforward allegory, but to explore broader political issues. He wishes to 'call attention to the common condition of monarchy' in these countries: 'In all three, the burning question, which the prince's relation with his or her counsellors or favourites crystallizes, is the extent of the royal prerogative and the proprieties of resistance'; Marlowe further 'complicates the resonance of his story by inviting the audience to consider the contingent religious colouring of the conflict'.[71]

In *Sovereign Amity,* Laurie Shannon makes an important contribution to this conversation by considering *Edward II* in terms of a necessary contradiction between classical and

Renaissance discourses of ideal friendship and those of ethical monarchy. She explains: 'The precepts of ethical monarchy devise a sovereign self to fulfill a unique function: the personal representation of the body politic.' The king must 'sublimate ... private interests in the required interests of the realm'.[72] Friendship discourse, on the other hand, insists that friends are equals and more: they are 'one soul in two bodies'; a true friend is 'another self', who would give up the world for his peer (3–4).[73] Thus, the play presents 'an irresolvable dilemma of identity': the king describes his relationship with Gaveston in 'an exalted and classical friendship idiom; his nobles speak only of his improper *mignonnerie*' (13).[74] In 'Toward a Queer Address', Jeffrey Masten provides a delightful and thought-provoking meditation on the language of early modern male friendship in Marlowe's play and elsewhere: he considers the queerness of conventional modes of address (especially 'sweet') and letters between friends, illuminating the way they insist literally on the embodied nature of the friendship and the fungibility of the friends, on friendship 'as incorporation and simultaneity'.[75]

Several critics take up the relatively new topic of 'space' in the Renaissance and in the play. In '"Where is the court but here?": Undetermined Elite Space and Marlowe's *Edward II*', Peter Sillitoe focuses on the framing space of the 'court', which lent itself at the time to a number of contradictory definitions; the two models that dominate *Edward II* are one 'stressing the court as accompanying the king, wherever he may be' and another 'highlighting the fixed nature of the court, a political world that is merely in need of a figurehead'.[76] The various ideological conflicts (sexual as well as purely political) that these contested definitions suggest are played out in Marlowe's text. Emma Atwood takes issue with the critical focus on Edward's body and proposes instead to use the work of Henri Lefebvre to explore the 'mental place' of space in the play.[77] She builds on the work of Sillitoe and others, but 'instead of focusing on the court or elite space', she confronts the 'problem of warring imaginative spaces both in the world of the play and in the audience' (54). She finds that 'both Marlowe and Edward II favour the production of imaginative space that privileges the individual over the collective, thus challenging the nation-making projects of the 1590s' (67).

In *Marlowe's Republican Authorship,* Patrick Cheney interestingly combines a political perspective with his characteristic focus on Marlowe's classical sources. He suggests, with other critics, that we bracket the sexual politics that has made the play a 'gay classic' to focus on 'the government politics itself',[78] and he argues that Marlowe's allusions to Lucan (and implicitly, to Tacitus) connect the struggles in fourteenth-century England to the civil war in Rome, fought between supporters of the monarch and advocates of republicanism. Although Marlowe's sympathies are primarily republican, they are never simply so. The end of the play presents us, paradoxically, with 'a republican-minded king', and, in the heroic speeches as Edward approaches his death, 'Marlowe turns the freedom of sublimity not into a political state for the liberated citizen but rather into a tragic form of passionate language … . [He] boldly rehearses the Elizabethan age's most harrowing political language: a new sodomitical sublime' (160, 164). In an essay the following year, Cheney uses Longinus (as well as Ovid and Lucan) to develop this final suggestion; he focuses here on issues of genre and style and argues: 'The real legacy of *Edward II* is not the stoic humanism of suffering featured in earlier twentieth-century criticism, or the radical politics of anti-monarchism, passionate desire and gay rights celebrated in recent criticism, but rather the heightened poetics of a new English theatre: Marlowe's tragic theatre of the sublime.'[79]

A number of other critics are aware of the far-reaching importance of formal questions. Georgia Brown, investigating 'the disparities between Marlowe's text and the historical record', declares: 'Not only does *Edward II* unravel the historiographical practices behind *Holinshed's Chronicles*, it exposes how the representation of history has implications for issues of gender, sexuality, subjectivity, and dramatic form.'[80] She contends that the play challenges a masculinized, stoic, public version of English identity; Marlowe instead creates here 'a new form of lyrical narrative [that] gives voice to women and to passionate men, to the marginal elements that had been suppressed in *Holinshed*' (166).

In *Re-Citing Marlowe,* Clare Harraway also considers the project of writing a chronicle history play, emphasizing the text's concern with the nature of writing itself: she comments that 'by punctuating the action with an excess of official documents, political messages and letters, *Edward II* stages the textually-derived nature of its genre' and 'gives rise to textual debates about the nature of identity and the perpetuity of intent'.[81] Sara Deats, in 'Marlowe's Interrogative Drama', speculates that 'Marlowe may ... be the first English playwright to script dialogical dramas that inscribe the multiplicity and indecidibility of human experience'; *Edward II,* in her view, is an example of this achievement.[82] In '"Truest of the Twain": History and Poetry in *Edward II*', Lisa Hopkins traces the many ways – formally, thematically, characterologically and extradiegetically – in which Marlowe's play is 'haunted by doubleness'.[83] One of the most interesting dualities she explores involves the playwright's 'inherently dual and fissured' response to the work of Sir Philip Sidney: in *Edward II*, she asserts, Marlowe 'carves out for [him]self a liminal territory on the cusp of poetry' and demonstrates 'a newly discovered allegiance' to what Sidney 'might have given the name history'; he valorizes history for the same reason Sidney devalues it – because it is 'not susceptible to easy moralizing or pattern finding' (113, 112, 117).

Alan Dessen, on the other hand, suggests that we view the play in a manner that is not 'H.C. (i.e. Historically Correct)'.[84] He counters the generally accepted narrative of a move to realism in the drama of the 1590s by arguing that in these plays (and in *Edward II* in particular), a '"residual" allegory ... does persist,' even 'when they lack onstage abstract figures' (64). Marlowe often combines 'the verisimilar and the abstract' in ways that are more apparent (and permit of different interpretations) on the stage than on the page (70).

Ruth Lunney, in 'Marlowe's *Edward II* and the Early Playhouse Audience', also sees a connection between the play and earlier drama and stresses the importance of theatrical rather than textual experience, but she argues that Marlowe here significantly challenges and alters the expectations his audience brought to the playhouse. The most radical difference between *Edward II* and earlier plays was in 'its use of the exemplum', and, in particular, of the historical narrative as cautionary tale.[85] 'History', she explains, 'taught lessons; that was its point' (29). But in his staging of Edward's death and its consequences, Marlowe presents 'a new kind of theatrical experience that suggests that cautionary tales are irrelevant', and as result, he 'offer[s] his audiences empowerment, the possibility of making sense for themselves, of constructing new interpretative narratives' (36, 40).

Meg Pearson similarly emphasizes the audience's engaged participation as witnesses to both Edward's death and the resolution his son brings about at the end; in other histories, she avers, the state spectacle Edward III orchestrates might be accepted as a desirable restoration of order, but after the experience of his father's death, it seems 'politically expedient', but ultimately 'empty'.[86] Thomas Anderson focuses on Edward's murder as well, but he argues that 'Edward's body becomes both the site of commemoration and erasure, at once a monument of brutal murder and a reminder of the impossibility of bearing witness to the deed.'[87] In addition, the play as a whole, he demonstrates, 'exposes the contradiction at the source of royal power and its continuity', and thus 'lays open the limits of historical reflection' (93).

Roslyn L. Knutson and Evelyn Tribble consider the different ways in which the composition and performing styles of early modern acting companies both affected and are reflected in Marlowe's play. In 'Marlowe's Boy Actors', Tribble examines the playwright's practice of aiding inexperienced boy actors by building 'scaffolding' (i.e. cues, repetitions) and simple language into their scenes, and she demonstrates how this is done in the early interactions with the prince in *Edward*

II; she notes, however, that the boy's final three appearances 'contain increasing breaks with … scaffolding practices', and that in his coronation scene, he assumes 'independent command of the stage': the actor's trajectory during the play thus mirrors his character's and emphasizes the prince's transformation from a child into the powerful King Edward III.[88] Knutson argues more generally that Marlowe was familiar, since his boyhood, with various acting companies; he chose to place *Tamburlaine* with the Admiral's Men both because their approach was more 'modern' than that of the popular Queen's Men and because the commanding physical presence and acting style of their newly acquired actor, Edward Alleyn, were well suited to the title role.[89] She maintains that Marlowe also intended Alleyn to play the king in *Edward II* (as well as Barabas and Faustus), but that Pembroke's Men acquired the play and Richard Burbage assumed the part; it seems likely that Shakespeare saw this performance and that it had some influence on his subsequent work.

Other critics re-examine the specific connection to *Richard II*. George L. Geckle declares that Marlowe's alteration of Holinshed created the 'first great English history play' in *Edward II*, 'because of structural coherence, complexity of theme, development of character, and high degree of narrativity'; while *Richard II* may be stronger in some respects, it is not superior 'in terms of narrativity'.[90] In a chapter in *Shakespeare's Marlowe*, Robert Logan summarizes earlier assessments of the relation between the two plays and notes many disagreements, both in their interpretations and in their perceptions of Marlowe's influence on Shakespeare; rather than attempting to resolve the ambiguities in the plays in order to connect them, Logan argues that it is precisely 'in the development of an aesthetic of ambiguity that a similarity and, most likely, an influence of major importance lie'.[91] He also develops the idea that, despite characterological differences, the two title kings – and their creators – are tied together by participating in the 'will to play'.[92] David Bevington, in 'Christopher Marlowe: The Late Years', goes beyond the usual comparison and considers *Edward II* in relation to Shakespeare's *1 Henry IV* as well as his earlier plays; he argues that Marlowe and Shakespeare, 'acting separately more or less at the same time and perhaps in self-aware competition', effectively create the genre of the English history play, which is marked by 'sustained ideological duality and final resolution'.[93]

Jon Surgal, in 'The Rebel and the Red-Hot Spit', presents a psychoanalytic reading, asserting that Edward's 'psychological development is fixed ... at a stage corresponding so remarkably to Freud's description of the anal-sadistic phase of childhood that Marlowe's hero may be offered as a prototype of that phase'.[94] Christopher D. Foley reads 'The Woeful Lamentation of Jane Shore' (which offers 'a unique, albeit false, etymology of the northern suburb of Shoreditch that emphasizes the abject environmental conditions of the area's principal ditch') together with *Edward II* (which was 'likely first performed in Shoreditch at Burbage's Theatre') to make an ecocritical intervention: both texts, he argues, 'expose disorderly ... figures to the contemporary hazards of sewage in early modern London', thus 'reaffirming the ideological link between improperly disposed waste and social disorder', while 'explor[ing] the ... issue of waste exposure on a collective, rather than individual scale'.[95] The 'geographic marginality of the public theaters' made plays especially charged vehicles for this sort of exploration (30).

Siobhan Keenan describes a summary of *Edward II* written in May, 1601 by John Newdigate, apparently after reading an Elizabethan text of the play; Newdigate was also learning about Richard II at the time and seems to have had an 'interest in the lessons to be learned from historical rulers and statesmen'; his reading suggests that *Edward II*, like Shakespeare's play, 'became newly topical ... in 1601' after the Essex rebellion.[96]

Jeffrey Masten adds a particularly interesting twist to the discussion through his discovery and examination, in 'Bound for Germany', of a previously unremarked copy of the first edition of *Edward II* in a German library. Masten notes that the play is bound together with 'a long theological tract' that discusses whether 'it is permissible to execute heretics and a text on "the reign of the Turks" and other "oriental" religions'. He points out that early modern heresy was a category that was as 'confused' (to use Foucault's term) as sodomy and often conflated with it (in Marlowe's case and more generally), and he suggests: 'It seems possible that *Edward II* was thus bound … not as a play but as a theological-juridical text – a treatise (if you will) that explores the rightness of Edward's torture and horrific death.' This new contextualization of Marlowe's play 'underlines that, in Germany as well as in England, what we have come to call "homosexuality" exists in a complex network of legal, religious, ethnic, and national discourse'.[97]

Looking forward

Masten's recent discovery lends weight to my belief that, despite some appearances to the contrary, there remains much to be said about *Edward II* – even and perhaps especially as a document in the history of sexuality. Some (though not all) of the criticism since the millennium – especially criticism with this focus – does seem to rehearse and refine earlier positions, and a number of writers have suggested we should turn away from or at least downplay issues of sexuality here. Indeed, many of the most original recent contributions have been made in other areas, and critics interested in sexuality studies have often moved on, understandably and laudably, to consider less frequently analysed texts. However, Masten's discovery suggests that new ways of contextualizing – and therefore of interpreting – Marlowe's play can provide new perspectives and transform earlier critical views.

One important context is suggested by the ongoing debate about history and historicism among early modern queer theorists and critics. In recent years, a group of early modern scholars have adopted a position articulated by Jonathan Goldberg and Madhavi Menon in 'Queering History': decrying 'a historicism that privileges difference over similarity' and that is inevitably teleological, they suggest that '"queering" requires what [one] might term "unhistoricism"', and they recommend that scholars engage in creating a 'homohistory' that would 'be invested in suspending sexual and chronological differences while expanding the possibilities of the nonhetero, with all its connotations of sameness, similarity, proximity, and anachronism'.[98] In 'The New Unhistoricism in Queer Studies', Valerie Traub has criticized this stance, calling for instead a new 'queer historicism', which rather than simply challenging categories would be 'dedicated to showing how categories, however mythic, phantasmic, and incoherent, came to be'.[99] Of course, the construction of 'history' and the categories it creates, as well as its mode of presentation on the English stage, have been important strands running through the criticism of *Edward II,* as the above summaries make clear. In the 1990s, these concerns often intersected fruitfully with an interest in the construction of sexuality, but in recent years critics exploring ideas about history and the history play have turned, predictably, in other directions. While those directions have often proved productive, perhaps it is time for at least some of us to rejoin these interests (which may be nowhere better connected than in Marlowe's play) and to consider afresh how *Edward II* brings together 'sexuality' and 'history' (in the theatre), how it helped to create our current understanding of those concepts, and how it might, as a result, provide us with an invaluable perspective on – and enable us to make important interventions in – the current conversation.

4

Edoüard et Gaverston: New Ways of Looking at an English History Play

Alan Stewart

Critics and editors are unanimous in asserting that the materials of Christopher Marlowe's play *Edward II* (1592/3?; printed 1594) are drawn primarily from the 1587 edition of Raphael Holinshed's *Chronicles,* supplemented by the chronicles of Robert Fabyan and John Stow – indeed, the gruesome details of the play's climactic action, the murder of Edward by anal penetration with a red-hot spit, unclear from the playbook, are usually supplied by editors from these sources.[1] However, while it might seem commonsensical to read this literary work through its chronicle sources, this assumption keeps *Edward II*'s frame of reference firmly within the confines of English history. In this chapter, by contrast, I suggest that we should understand that English historical frame as co-existing with another: that of contemporary French politics.

It is nothing new to say that Marlowe was interested in recent French history. His *The Massacre at Paris* dramatizes events from the troubled French politics of the 1570s and

1580s. Long ago, Paul H. Kocher tracked Marlowe's use of English printed works about France, and Julia Briggs later showed that Marlowe's reading extended to French-language texts, a finding endorsed in Vivien Thomas and William Tydeman's 1994 survey of Marlowe's sources.[2] More recently, David Potter used *The Massacre at Paris* to explore the reputation of Henri III; Andrew M. Kirk devoted a chapter to the play in his book-length survey of the English drama's representation of French history; in his ongoing excavation of the French origins of English tragedy, Richard Hillman has demonstrated deeper connections between *The Massacre* and, in particular, Pierre Matthieu's *La Guisiade*; and Jeffrey Rufo has briefly explored Marlowe's 'immersion in contemporary French controversies'.[3]

While the argument is easy to make for *The Massacre at Paris*, however, the case for *Edward II* is not as clear-cut. It was the Cambridge poet J. A. Nicklin who in December 1895 first made an historicizing connection between Marlowe's play and the court of the French king Henri III, in an article on 'Marlowe's Gaveston' for the *Free Review*. The keyword for Nicklin is *minion*: '"Minion", a word used so often throughout the play to describe Gaveston, gives the key to his position. Marlowe is thinking of the *mignons* of the last of the Valois: Gaveston, as he lived for Marlowe, is the pet and darling of another Henri Trois.'[4] In 1942, John Bakeless, citing Nicklin and agreeing that the frequent usage of 'minion' 'suggests that the French court was more or less in [Marlowe's] mind', suggested a more concrete textual link between the courts of Edward II and Henri III: 'Marlowe may ... have read Jean Boucher's pamphlet on Gaveston, the favourite of Edward II, which was published in 1588 with satirical allusions to the Duc d'Espernon, the favourite of Henri III.'[5] Bakeless is here referring to an anonymous libel entitled *Histoire tragique et memorable de Pierre de Gauerston* (*The Tragic and Memorable History of Pierre de Gaverston*), an anonymously penned and published pamphlet that likened Gaveston to Henri III's favourite, Jean Louis de Nogaret, duc d'Épernon.

Nevertheless, Bakeless's tentative claim has not convinced most critics. Recent criticism of the play has fixated on Edward's relationship with Gaveston, exploring favouritism, friendship, sodomy and cross-dressing, but the possibility of a French analogue has been relatively unexplored.[6] No modern scholarly edition suggests the *Histoire tragique* as a direct source.[7] Richard Rowland's 1994 Clarendon Press edition mentions it in a footnote during a discussion that proposes instead James VI of Scotland as an important contemporary analogue for Edward II.[8] The 1997 New Mermaids edition by Martin Wiggins and Robert Lindsey allows only that the French situation might constitute one of '[t]he broader imaginative influences on Marlowe': 'At the time, the portrayal of a homosexual king, excessively devoted to "favourites" must have had resonances of Henry III of France' (xiv). The essays in a 1992 collection from the Université Stendhal at Grenoble fail to allude to any French context.[9] Almost alone, Hillman has insisted there must be a strong link, that 'the comparison between Edward II and Henri III, Épernon and Gaveston, was in the very discursive air breathed by Marlowe and his audiences'. But Hillman's analysis stops short at insisting on a specific relationship between the *Histoire tragique* and *Edward II*: Marlowe, he concludes, 'may or may not have known the *Histoire tragique*'.[10]

In what follows, I attempt to give a more substantial form to that 'discursive air'. In claiming the *Histoire tragique* as an important component in the making of *Edward II*, I am not however, suggesting that such an influence can be proven by the usual identification of 'source' material that provides precedents for plot, scenes, character or specific language. I shall instead suggest that in order to understand what Marlowe is doing in *Edward II*, we need to take our cue from the way that the *Histoire tragique* insistently posits an analogy between Pierre de Gaverston and the duc d'Épernon, and thus between Edward II and Henri III. Further, by triangulating *Edward II* and the *Histoire tragique* with Marlowe's play that explicitly deals with contemporary French politics, *The*

Massacre at Paris, we can begin to see the nature of the debt owed by Marlowe's English history play to the French politics of the dangerous summer of 1588.

§

On 6 June 1588, Elizabeth's ambassador to the French king, Sir Edward Stafford, included an enclosure in his regular packet to secretary of state Sir Francis Walsingham: 'I send your honor the vyldest book that euer I sawe.' The book was a libel, whose apparent target, he wrote, was the French king's favourite, the duc d'Épernon, a man 'whome thei [the book's authors] dare desire to offend', but its real aim lay higher: 'the drift of ytt in deede is against the kinge directly'.[11] From the 1570s onwards, France had been flooded by libels, both manuscript and printed, that commented, often scurrilously, on the contemporary Wars of Religion. By 1588, when this libel was printed, the king, Henri III, was under constant attack from the ultra-Catholic League, led by Henri, duc de Guise, who refused to countenance the prospect of the childless king's named successor, the Huguenot (Protestant) Henri de Navarre. As political and military tensions grew, libels printed on the League's behalf sky-rocketed, peaking at 362 in 1589 in Paris alone, almost one per day.[12] Many of these libels targeted the king's *mignons* (favourites), young men of the minor aristocracy whom he elevated to positions of wealth and power.[13] Since the end of 1587, the leading *archemignon* was Jean Louis de Nogaret, duc d'Épernon, promoted by Henri to admiral of France and governor of several provinces, who acted as a natural lightning rod for League attacks.[14]

For the English ambassador, monitoring this incendiary literature was a top priority, and his correspondence shows a predictable concern with works that dealt with Elizabeth (invariably renamed 'Jezebel' in League libels) and sensitive events such as the 1587 execution of Mary Queen of Scots. This libel against Épernon, however, also piqued him, perhaps because it dealt with a delicate moment in England's history. Its full title was *Histoire tragique et memorable, de Pierre de Gaverston, Gentil-homme Gascon, iadis le mignon d'Edoüard .2. Roy d'Angeleterre: tirée des Chroniques de Thomas Valsinghan, & tournée de Latin en François. Dediée à Monseigneur le Duc d'Espernon* (*The tragic and memorable history of Pierre de Gaverston, a Gascon gentleman, once the mignon of Edward II, King of England: pulled from the Chronicles of Thomas Walsingham, and turned from Latin into French. Dedicated to Monseigneur the duc d'Épernon*). As described in the manuscript journals of the Parlement de Paris clerk Pierre de l'Estoile, the libel represented the historical Gaverston, 'whose life and fortune provided a model for that of the duc d'Épernon, to conclude that, as this Gascon Gaverston – loved and uniquely favoured by King Edward II of England, preferred above all the king's other servants, enriched by the king's finances and the wealth of the people – was ultimately banished and exiled from the country at their demand and afterwards beheaded, the duc d'Épernon would reach the same tragic end [acheveroit ceste meme tragœdie] in France, under Henri III'.[15]

Ambassador Stafford was not the only one intrigued by this book. When news of 'a despiteful book written against M. D'Espernon' reached James VI of Scotland, he twice importuned his agent in Paris to acquire a copy.[16] And it struck a nerve in the Épernon camp, which responded with *Lettre d'vn gentil-homme*, a supposed 'letter from an Apostolic and Roman Catholic gentleman and true Frenchman, and faithful servant of the king to his friend', dated 1 July 1588, which became known as 'l'Anti-Gaverston'.[17] This prompted two further anti-Épernon attacks – *Responce a l'antigaverston de Nogaret; à M. l'Espernon* and *Replique à l'antigauerston* – the latter of which in turn produced a further pro-Épernon title, *Lettre missive en forme de reponse, à la replique de l'Antigaverston*, all dated 1588.[18] The Gaverston-Épernon libel was enough of a political event in its own right to be discussed at length in Pierre Matthieu's 1594 account of the

Wars of Religion, and Jacques-Auguste du Thou's standard *Histoire universelle*.[19] And it was clearly a best-seller: well over eighty copies of the libel are extant in European and North American libraries, an amazingly high number for an octavo pamphlet of its day.

It is almost impossible to identify who was behind this book, or any redaction of it. Like many French libels of the day, the *Histoire tragique* names no author – although its dedicatory epistle is signed 'P.H.D.T.' – no place of publication, no publisher, no printer, no bookseller and no place of sale (with one edition excepted, where that is given as 'Paris'). Its sole point of reference is its dedicatee and target, Épernon. Most reference volumes follow the identification made by l'Estoile: 'the [Catholic] League commissioned and had printed [fist courir et imprimer] in Paris the *Histoire ou fable de Pierre de Gaverston*' (VI, 64). Another early reader, the historian Pierre Victor Palma Cayet, recorded in 1608 that rumour had it that the *Histoire tragique* was penned by the radical Paris preacher Jean Boucher.[20] However, these Parisian co-ordinates are challenged by the response libel, *Lettre d'vn gentil-homme*, which claimed the *Histoire tragique* had been 'put into the light by the Archbishop of Lyon [Pierre l'Épinac] at the request of those of the League' (title page). Another possibility is suggested by the dedicatory epistle – dated 16 May 1588, from Havre de Grace (now Le Havre) – which might suggest that the libel, as Stuart Carroll argues, 'belongs to the local propaganda battle' in Normandy.[21] This hypothesis is strengthened if we accept Jacqueline Boucher's argument that the epistle's signatory, 'P.H.D.T.', was the poet Philippe Desportes, a follower of Épernon's late rival as favourite, the duc de Joyeuse, then resident in Normandy.[22] The book holds one further teasing possibility: 'P.H.D.T.' claims that he was given the chronicle history from which he translated the story by 'a Scottish gentleman' ('un gentilhomme Escossais'), which may imply a link between this libel and the prolific Scots-authored libels about the execution of Mary Queen of Scots that were rife in Paris in 1587 and 1588.[23] The situation is complicated by the fact that the *Histoire tragique* is not a single, stable entity. In the space of a few months the *Histoire tragique* went through some nineteen editions, but these were not merely reprintings: instead the text was added to, edited and rearranged in multifarious ways.[24] Perhaps the most likely scenario has the book originating in a shorter form in Normandy and later added to by someone associated with the bishop of Lyon, but, in short, the authorship and provenance of the *Histoire tragique* remain unknown and perhaps unknowable.

What is probably the earliest, 'original' version of the *Histoire tragique* is comprised of several components.[25] The title page claims that the book is '*Dedicated to Monseigneur the Duc d'Espernon*', but the reader need only turn the page to realize that the dedication is not sincere. There, an 'anagramme' turns 'Pierre de Gauerston' into 'Periure de Nogarets' ('Nogaret' being Épernon's family name), and a doggerel 'quatrain' proclaims that 'Gaverston caught England in his snares; you're doing the same to France, Perjure de Nogarets' (title page and sig. A1ᵛ). The ramifications of this identification are then spelled out in the book's lengthy (faux) dedicatory epistle to Épernon, dated 18 May 1588, and signed 'P.H.D.T.' from Havre de Grace:

> As you will see when you read this, the region, the relations, the character, the counsel, the ploys and tricks, the fortune and the sequence of actions of this PIERRE DE GAVERSTON agree entirely with yours [symbolisent entièrement auec les vostres]. All that's missing is your end, which we believe will be similar. For it's always the case that all those, like Gaverston and you, who abuse the favour of kings to the prejudice and detriment of the poor people, invariably receive a disastrous and shameful end as reward for their trespasses. (sig. A2ᵛ)

There then follows a 'Sonet av Roy' ('Sonnet to the King'), in which the epistle's second-person appeal to Épernon is replaced with another to the king himself. 'Sire', it opens, 'every man recognizes your necessity, but we don't have the power to help you – for if, for your part, you are in poverty, your people are reduced to utter destitution. The only thing we can do for your majesty is to give you counsel in our conscience: that you make your favourite king of France, and be the friend to him that he's been to you' – i.e. you'd be better off as favourite than as king. This suggested role reversal takes place as the sonnet moves from octave to sestet. 'You will change your luck, making a move similar to the hourglass: what was above comes below, filling what was above by putting it below. You'll take back the state, the goods and riches that you have lost through your generous gifts and you'll be without necessity – and so will we' (sig. B2ᵛ). And then, with its relevance to both Épernon and Henri fully established, the 'Histoire' of the rise and fall of Gaverston commences.

The translator claims he fell by chance on the Gaverston story in 'an English historian named Thomas Walsingham, who lived 150 years ago' (sig. A2ʳ); responding to a charge that this book never existed, the *Replique* clarifies that the Walsingham text was printed in London in 1574 by Henry Bynneman – the distinctive '-r-' spelling of Gave[r]ston derives from Walsingham.[26] The 'Histoire' is, indeed, generally quite faithful to Walsingham's Latin, but the anonymous translator reorders, contracts and expands Walsingham's references to Gaverston to produce the 'Histoire'. In so doing, he makes some subtle but notable changes. Walsingham calls the favourite by his Latin first name 'Petrus', but the 'Histoire' uses 'Gaverston' and refers to him repeatedly as a 'mignon', a 'Gascon' (native of Gascony) and therefore an 'estranger' (stranger, foreigner). While Gaverston was undoubtedly a Gascony native, that is of little consequence to Walsingham telling the story of Edward II; the mignon-Gascon-estranger epithets are aimed at the *Histoire tragique*'s 1588 French readers to substantiate the analogy between the Gascon mignon Épernon and the Gascon mignon Gaverston (whose name helpfully almost merges Gascon and Épernon). In keeping with the expectations of the *Histoire tragique* genre, the 'Histoire' introduces a trace of the supernatural, where none exists in its source. Walsingham describes the rise of Edward's initial infatuation with Gaverston with the phrase 'In tantumque lapsu temporis crevit amor' ('in time love grew'); the 'Histoire' embroiders this to become 'Et fut tellement ensorcelé de son amour' ('and [he] was so bewitched by his love'). Elsewhere, it elaborates that Gaverston came to 'occupy the good graces of his king, or, to put it better, infatuated and bewitched him (l'ayant infatué & ensorcelé)' (sig. B2^v). The 'Histoire' takes the story past the nobles' killing of Gaverston to detail how another quarrel between the king and his nobles is defused by the queen. The final step is the birth of a male heir, 'and from that day forth, by God's providence, the love of the father for his son began to grow, and his love for Gaverston vanished, and the king acquiesced to the wishes of his nobles. THE END' (sigs. G2^v–G3^r).

However, while the short early version boasts this wonderfully heteronormative happy ending, in most copies one turns the page to find another tract, addressed 'Au lecteur' ('To the reader') which commences 'If the condition of PIERRE DE GAVESTON [*sic*] was miserable, that of this King Edward was even worse.'[27] This second narrative sketches the disastrous post-Gaverston reign of Edward II, culminating with an account of his later favourites, the Despensers, father and son. In most copies, the break between the end of the Gaverston 'Histoire' and the beginning of the 'Au lecteur' section concerning the Despensers is bridged by a paragraph, set in italics, that makes crudely explicit what is implied by the juxtaposition:

However, as the character of this king was changeable and inconstant, he scarcely stayed in that [happy] state, through the advice of Hugh le Despenser, who succeeded GAVERSTON *to the same honors and malice, for he relit the fire that had never gone out, the fire of defiances, hates, and enmities between the king and queen, whom he chased from the kingdom; and the barons and nobles, whom he had beheaded, as will be deduced from this little warning, which I've added to this history, to conduct Edward to his grave, as we have done for his mignon.* (sig. G3ʳ)

'Au lecteur', then, explicitly replaces Gaverston with Despenser, and does for Edward what the 'Histoire' has done for Gaverston: traces his fatal downfall.

From the outset, the tone of 'Au lecteur' is different. Although we are still in the reign of Edward II, the narrative is larded with historical comparisons, classical and patristic references – Isidorus, Marc Antony, Aristotle, Livy – and even a glance toward Machiavelli. Thomas Walsingham is mentioned once, but the chronicle on which this section draws, it soon becomes clear, is not by Walsingham but by Jean Froissart:

Froissart, at the beginning of his history, tells of how there was ordinarily such a pattern in the succession of the kings of England, that between two good kings came a bad one: between two warlike and valiant kings, a lazy one; and between two wise and prudent kings, spendthrift and prodigal one. We see that in this Edward, his father, and his son … . (sig. G3ᵛ)

'Au lecteur' therefore opens, as does Froissart's account, with a highly moralized portrait of Edward II as a bad, lazy, spendthrift and prodigal king. It is Froissart who provides one of the most shocking moments in the libel: when Edward calls a parliament of his nobles in order to entrap and execute twenty-two of them. In addition, as Clare Sponsler argues, only Froissart includes the gruesome account of Hugh Despenser's execution.[28] The younger Despenser, we're told, 'was punished according to his faults', his bad counsel, perfidy and treason, 'for because of his detested sodomy [en detestation de sa sodomie], his shameful parts were cut off, his heart ripped out and thrown onto the fire' (sig H4ʳ). The introduction of this 'sodomy' is of crucial importance to the development of the Edward-Gaverston relationship in subsequent works: while Edward and Gaverston are not accused of sodomy in the 'Histoire', the effect of the 'Au lecteur' section is to fuse Gaverston to Despenser, and thus to imply that, if Despenser is guilty of sodomy, then Gaverston might also be guilty of sodomy. And the guilt of these favourites has a further impact. Some copies also add a single, crucial sentence to 'Au lecteur', immediately before the reference to Despenser's 'sodomy':

> I come now to the end, which was as shameful as his [Edward's] life. For after being degraded and deposed from his royal dignity, of which he had shown himself unworthy, the barons of the country put him to death using a red-hot poker, which they pushed into his fundament [les Seigneurs du pays le feirent mourir d'vne broche rouge de feu, laquelle il luys lancerent par le fondement]. (sigs. H3ᵛ–H4ʳ)

With this sentence, I would suggest, the stakes are raised significantly. The graphic and sexually suggestive account of the killing of Edward implicates him in the 'sodomy' of Despenser, and – perhaps more startlingly – in this telling, Edward's death is not only sanctioned but carried out by 'the barons of the country'. The implications for Henri are all too clear. Henri had for many years been the subject of innuendo concerning alleged sexual relations with his mignons, so the hint of sodomy here has particular resonance.[29] However, in a section which is directed 'To the reader', the analogy between Edward and Henri allows the public imagining that, just as the English barons did for Edward, it will be the nobles of France who will 'conduct [Henri] to his grave'. In its longer version, therefore, the libel moves from being an attack on Épernon and an implied critique of the king, to being a full-on assault on Henri himself, in which the central analogy is made between Edward II and Henri III, and Henri is effectively threatened with the deposition and murder that Edward suffered.

The impact of this pamphlet was quite remarkable. Its materials were redacted and rearranged in at least eighteen different versions, all within a single year.[30] Almost immediately, other libels, poems and plays started to employ the example of Edward and/or Gaverston, and as the tone of anti-royalist libels became much more strident after the summer of 1588, the *Histoire tragique*'s themes of sodomy and heresy, and its hint of associated sorcery, took off in spectacular fashion. André Rossant's 1589 *Les Mœurs, humeurs et comportemens* refers at some length to the English history 'which was last year represented in our vernacular' of the king who 'was too enamored of a Gascon, and had him so much *à mignon*, that, in short, he gave him everything he could, and shouldn't'.[31] In the preface to his 1588 tragedy *Aman*, Pierre Matthieu writes of the vicious conduct of other favourites, including 'the two Hugh Despensers towards King Edward II of England, Pierre de Gaverston towards Edward [being] another'.[32] A 1589 pamphlet lamenting Henri's assassination of the Guise brothers notes how the English had strongly hated the cruelty and perfidy used by their kings Richard II and Edward II against the nobles of their country, and for that cause principally had deposed them from their royal dignities.[33] The anti-Épernon *Replique à l'antigaverston* (1588) claims that the duc is a part of a cabal holding meetings with the devil, and that his original surname, Nogaret, identifies him with Guillaume de Nogaret, the 'greatest enemy and heretic of the Catholic church of his time' (sig. D2^r). *L'atheisme de Henry de Valoys* (1589) identified 'Espernon with his demons' as 'that pernicious man who is cause of the evils affecting France today', full of 'charms and sorceries', and then blithely refers to 'the little devils of his [Henri's] gaverston [les diablotins de son gauerston] ... this pernicious Gascon'.[34] While the *Histoire tragique* has Gaveston's sorcery seducing Edward (and therefore Épernon's sorcery seducing Henri), by the following year, Henri was himself the sorcerer.[35] In one particularly prurient piece, *Les Choses horribles* (1589), Henri is depicted instructing a cadre of would-be sorcerers at the

Louvre; giving life to the devil Épernon, with the help of Henri de Navarre and Pierre du Belloy; and then spending the night in bed with the devil Épernon, who sucks out all his body heat through his navel.[36]

And then, overnight, Épernon ceased to be Gaverston. On 1 August 1589, Henri III was fatally stabbed by a Dominican friar, and on his deathbed confirmed the Huguenot Henri de Navarre as his successor. Épernon opposed Navarre's accession with the same vigour as the League: fighting on the same side, he was no longer their favourite target, and the Gaverston libels disappeared from France.[37] There was a brief revival of interest in Gaverston among the network of exiled English Catholics, led by Robert Persons, who kept up a vigorous critique of Elizabethan religious policy.[38] Responding in 1592/3 to Elizabeth's 1591 proclamation against 'seminarie priests and jesuists', several polemicists accused the proclamation's supposed author, Lord Treasurer Burghley, of being a Gaverston.[39] One advised Burghley 'to thincke betimes upon the end of pierse of Gaverston, & the Spencers, & others that have abused their Princes favours in Ingland heretofore, to the debasing of true nobilitie, and pilling of the people'.[40] Richard Verstegan argued that Burghley was 'more noysome and pernitious to the realme, then euer were the *Spencers*, *Peeter* of *Gauerstone*, or any other that euer abused either Prince or people'.[41] Thomas Stapleton urged Burghley: 'Think of the Spencers, the Gaverstons, the Dudleys, the Cromwells, who in their day enjoyed the favour of their princes no less than you in yours; and since you know that virtually no trace, no memory remains of them except in disgrace and cursing, consider what will be the case with you, who surpass them all.'[42] (Note how the spelling of Gaverston mirrors that of the anti-Épernon libels.) Post-Épernon, then, polemicists' attempts to use Gaverston briefly functioned as an archetype of the evil favourite/counsellor, but I would argue the tactic failed. To some extent, this was because Gaverston was a bad fit with Burghley: no one believed that the elderly, respectable Lord Treasurer was a sorcerer-sodomite (Clancy, 25). But, more importantly, without the analogy with Épernon, Gaverston was simply not resonant enough an historical figure. It would take Christopher Marlowe to realize how the potent Gaverston of the *Histoire tragique* could be revived.

§

It is my contention that this attack on the duc d'Épernon shapes and informs Marlowe's play. This shaping works in ways that would elude the editor bent on retrieving the raw materials from which the playwright built his scenes – in this case, acknowledged to be the English chronicle histories of Holinshed, Fabyan and Stow. Instead, Marlowe takes from the *Histoire tragique* an understanding of the relationship between king and favourite that draws on the attack's analogizing between Gaverston and Épernon, and between Edward and Henri. Unlike the English Catholic campaign that sought to infuse Burghley with the evil reputation of Gaverston, Marlowe aims to infuse the Gaveston and Edward of his play with the potency of Épernon and Henri.

To get a sense of the strength of how this might work I turn to the final paragraph of the 'Au lecture' section of the *Histoire tragique*:

> We can judge by this short discourse, what state England was in during the reign of this foolish and effeminate Edward [ce fol & effeminé Edoüard]. It did not take more than a seed of heresy to take root to push it to complete ruin. Certainly that seed found easy access and much favour. The division between the king and the princes served it as a seed-bed. It found a king, who, in order not to lose the ease of his brutish life, suffered each and every sect rather than stamping them out. It met with a similar counsel, which, in order to fish better in troubled water, upheld it, and gave it liberty of conscience. It did not lack a Gaverston or a Hugues le Despensier who, to divert a war against the heretics, muddied the waters and fed the schism

between the Catholic princes; and forged alliance with all the devils of hell to prevent anyone probing too deeply into their lives. May God have pity on those republics which are under the yoke of such a leader, and governed by such dangerous counsel. (H4ʳ–H4ᵛ)

By this stage of the story, and despite the past historic tense and the references to Gaverston and Despenser, the author is clearly writing about contemporary France. For there was no 'seed of heresy' in the reign of Edward II, no schism between Catholic princes based on religion; when the author writes of 'such a leader', he means Henri, and the 'so dangerous counsel' is Épernon's. The analogy of one period for another has here become absolute – to the point of serious historical confusion. We are now reading Gaverston *through* Épernon, the reign of Edward II *through* the reign of Henri III, England through France.

Marlowe reverses the equation, without ever making explicit how his play is dealing with medieval England through the lens of near-contemporary France. Instead, he threads anachronisms – some subtle, some less subtle – through the play. Perhaps the most obvious, and certainly the most pervasive, is the one that J. A. Nicklin pointed out over a century ago: the fact that Marlowe's Gaveston is described repeatedly as a 'minion', an englishing of the term with which Gaverston is described on the title page of the *Histoire tragique*. In English, 'minion' had traditionally meant a male favourite or follower of a king or nobleman, and did not necessarily carry any sexual overtones. During the sixteenth century, it had also come to mean a pandered favourite child or a female paramour.[43] However, with *Edward II*, Marlowe makes quite clear that 'minion' denotes a man who is favoured both politically and sexually: Gaveston is not only an intimate favourite of Edward II, but a threat to Edward's wife. Isabella repeatedly bewails how Gaveston has stolen the attention and affections of her husband; Marlowe stages confrontations between wife and minion that grammatically insist on their analogous positions: '(ISABELLA) Villain, 'tis thou that robb'st me of my lord. / (GAVESTON) Madam, 'tis you that rob me of my lord' (4.160–1).

In most cases, the use of the epithet is derogatory. Lancaster calls him 'thy base minion' (1.132) and charges Edward that 'Your minion Gaveston hath taught you' how to raise taxes (6.146). The Queen says of her husband, 'let him frolic with his minion' (2.67), while Mortimer mocks, 'The King is love-sick for his minion' (3.87). Lancaster reassures the Queen, 'Fear ye not, madam; now his minion's gone, / His wanton humour will be quickly left' (4.198–9), but she continues to lament 'Hark how he harps upon his minion' (4.312), and complains to Lancaster that 'still his mind runs on his minion' (6.4); 'when I speak him fair, / He turns away and smiles upon his minion' (8.29–30). Nonetheless, the play also starts to recuperate the term. Mortimer Senior tells his nephew how 'The mightiest kings have had their minions' (4.392), and produces a list of worthy forebears: Alexander and Hephaestion, Hercules and Hylas, Patroclus and Achilles, Tully (Cicero) and Octavius, Socrates and Alcibiades. Most strikingly, Edward too uses the term, telling his barons: 'Were he a peasant, being my minion, / I'll make the proudest of you stoop to him' (4.30–1). 'Minion' is reserved for Gaveston: although we might see Spencer as taking Gaveston's place in the second half of the play, he is never a 'minion', always one of his (always plural) 'flatterers' (12.12, 12.17, 15.60, 17.25).

To explore further how the 'mignon' of the *Histoire tragique* intersects with the 'minion' of *Edward II*, we can triangulate it with *The Massacre at Paris*, in which Marlowe presents the other side of the analogy.[44] While the *Histoire tragique* deals with Edward and Gaverston as types for Henri and Épernon, and *Edward II* deals with Edward and Gaveston, *The Massacre at Paris* deals with Henri and Épernon – with Épernon identified quite clearly as a 'minion'. Indeed, Marlowe's first minions appear precisely at the moment of King Henri's first entrance – the stage direction specifies '*the kings Minions*' rather than naming them (14.0 SD). Henri has scarcely thanked his receiving party, before turning to his favourites:

> What saies our Minions, think they *Henries* heart
> Will not harbour love and Majestie?
> Put of that feare, they are already joynde,
> No person, place, or time, or circumstance,
> Shall slacke my loves affection from his bent:
> As now you are, so shall you still persist,
> Remooveles from the favours of your King. (14.16–22)

Here, with great economy, Marlowe introduces Henri's dependence on his minions, and his belief that his 'love' for them can co-exist with 'Majestie'. This assurance instantly gives licence to one minion, Mugeroun, to cut the ears off a cutpurse who has been stealing the gold buttons off his cloak; while Guise orders Mugeroun's arrest, Henri says he 'will be his baile' (14.35), showing immediately that his love for his minions compromises his majesty. The king and his retinue then depart 'to feast, / And spend some daies in barriers, tourney, tylte, and like disportes' (14.39–40), leaving the Queen Mother to lament to the Cardinal of Lorraine:

> How like your grace my sonnes pleasantness?
> His minde you see runnes on his minions,
> And all his heaven is to delight himselfe. (14.45–7)

The scene resonates closely with several elements in *Edward II*. Like Henri, Edward claims that nothing will divert his love from his minion; Gaveston gratuitously assaults the Bishop of Coventry, egged on by Edward (1.186–7); Edward, like Henri, enjoys the 'disportes', itemized by Gaveston ('Italian masques ..., / Sweet speeches, comedies, and pleasing shows' [1.54–5]); and Isabella's complaint about Edward closely echoes the Queen Mother's comment: 'still his mind runs on his minion' (6.4).

In other ways, however, *Edward II* is markedly different from *The Massacre at Paris* in its representation of minions.

Despite Henri's devotion to them, his minions are portrayed primarily as a group; only later in the play does Henri hand over power to Epernoun ('*Epernoune* I will be rulde by thee' [14.81]). Moreover, in *The Massacre at Paris*, there is no explicit suggestion that the relationship between king and minion is itself sexual. Instead, the minions' sexuality is used to cuckold the king's enemy, the duc de Guise. Henri taunts Guise that his wife had written a letter 'To my deare Minion, and her chosen freend' (17.14), saying 'So kindely Cosin of *Guise* you and your wife / Doe both salute our lovely Minions', while '*he makes hornes at the Guise*' (17.10–11 and SD). Guise's riposte to this recalls the remarks of Isabella – 'I love your Minions? dote on them your selfe' (17.21) – but the set-up is different. When the Guise has the upper hand, he boasts, 'Now sues the King for favour to the *Guise*, / And all his Minions stoup when I commaund' (21.48–9); given that he will be dead within the next forty lines, his language of enforced stooping reworks the vainglorious vaunts of both Gaveston ('Farewell, base stooping to the lordly peers' [1.18]) and Edward ('Were he a peasant, being my minion, / I'll make the proudest of you stoop to him' [3.30–1]).

Critics have objected to the lack of historical precedent when Marlowe's Edward launches an assault on the Catholic church:

> Why should a king be subject to a priest?
> Proud Rome, that hatchest such imperial grooms,
> With these thy superstitious taper-lights,
> Wherewith thy antichristian churches blaze,
> I'll fire thy crazèd buildings and enforce
> The papal towers to kiss the lowly ground. (4.96–101)

Here, again, anachronism is in place – and these words make more sense (though they are still historically unlikely) in the mouth of the dying Henri III in *The Massacre at Paris*: if he lives, he assures the English agent,

> the Papall Monarck goes
> To wrack, and antechristian kingdome falles.
> These bloudy hands shall teare his triple Crowne,
> And fire accursd *Rome* about his eares.
> Ile fire his crased buildings and incense
> The papall towers to kiss the holy earth. (24.59–64)

Here we can see the ways in which the *Histoire tragique*'s insistence on 'schism between the Catholic princes' might inform not only *The Massacre at Paris*, dealing with the same events, but also the historically removed *Edward II*.

The *Histoire tragique* focuses on the mignon's relationship with the king; *Edward II* does the same. In a play of twenty-five scenes, Gaveston is last seen in scene 10, and his death reported in scene 11. However, his memory lives on – as it does not in the *Chronicles* – shadowing Edward's later life: as he enters his final descent, the king memorably claims, 'O *Gaveston*, it is for thee that *I* am wronged' (22.41). Historically, Gaveston died in 1312, only five years into Edward's almost twenty-year reign. Marlowe condenses that reign in such a way that Gaveston seems to occupy half of it, and to be replaced by Spencer: in an audacious feat of historical compression, the play's eleventh scene covers events of more than ten years, which allows Edward to move from hearing of Gaveston's death to promoting Spencer in a matter of lines – the same telescoping of time achieved by the *Histoire tragique*'s two sections (the 'Histoire' and the 'Au lecteur'), the first dealing with Gaveston's fall and demise, the second with Edward's. Indeed, Marlowe's decision to open the story *in medias res*, with Gaveston '*reading on a letter*' that calls on him to 'come …, / And share the kingdom with thy dearest friend' (1.SD, 1–2) is notably close to a particular redaction of the *Histoire tragique* that opens with the line 'Edward II King of England repealed the ban [r'appella de ban] of Pierre de Gaverston' (*L'Estrange amitie*, sig. A1ᵛ).

Nevertheless, in the last lines of *The Massacre at Paris*, Marlowe allows the modern figures of Gaveston and Edward a final farewell, where lachrymose sentiment gives way to bloody revenge:

> Sweet *Epernoune*, thy King must dye ...
> Ah *Epernoune*, is this thy love to me?
> *Henry* thy King wipes of these childish tears,
> And bids thee whet thy sword on *Sextus* bones,
> That it may keenly slice the Catholicks.
> He loves me not that sheds most teares,
> But he that makes most lavish of his bloud.
> Fire *Paris* where these trecherous rebels lurke. (24.90, 96–103)

In historical reality, Épernon did not slice the Catholics or fire Paris: as mentioned above, he was staunchly opposed to Navarre's accession. But then, in historical reality, Épernon did not weep at Henri's deathbed: he had been effectively exiled from the king months earlier as Henri made one last attempt to appease his nobles.

At least one contemporary writer realized that Marlowe was doing something strange with the chronicle materials of the reign of Edward II. I would suggest that Michael Drayton's popular verse complaint *Piers Gaveston* (1594), in which the dead Gaveston recalls his time on earth in the tradition of the *Mirror for Magistrates*, can be read as an anti-Marlovian intervention. In an endnote, Drayton acknowledges that in recent discussions,

> Divers have been the opinions, of the byrth and first rysing of *Gaveston*, (amongst the Writers of these latter times:) some omitting things worthy of memory, some inferring things without probabilitie, disagreeing in many particulars, and cavelling in the circumstances of his sundry banishments; which hath bred some doubt amongst those who have but slightly run over the History of his fortune, seeing every man rove by his owne ayme in this confusion of opinion:[45]

Drayton claims that, in order to remedy this confusion, he 'relyed in the plot of my History' on 'some of those Writers who lyved in the tyme of *Edward II*, wherin he onely florisht, or immediatly after, in the golden raigne of *Edward* the third, when as yet his memory was fresh in every mans mouth'. In addition to these, he has had 'recourse to some especiall collections, gathered by the industrious labours of *John Stow*, a diligent Chronigrapher of our time' (sig. L1ᵛ). Drayton is, by his own account, being a good historicist – seeking to ground his poem in accounts deriving from the period of Gaveston's life, and not 'rov[ing] by his own ayme', as Marlowe does in injecting the politics of 1588 France into the early fourteenth century.[46]

The authors of the *Histoire tragique* produced a powerful analogy between the despised favourite of the current French king and a despised favourite of a medieval English king. Marlowe takes that analogy and produces a medieval English chronicle history that resonates with the libel-drenched culture of contemporary French politics. 'What call you this but private libelling / Against the Earle of Cornwall and my brother?' (6.34–5) asks the king, as he is warned that 'Libels are cast again thee in the street, / Ballads and rhymes made of thy overthrow' (6.174–5). While the *Histoire tragique* forces Épernon to follow the fate of Gaveston, and Henri III to follow the fate of Edward II, Marlowe's play gives us the reign of Edward II understood as the downfall of a king through his minion, a scenario made all the more powerful by its recent playing out for real just miles away from the English coast.

5

Edward II in Repertory

Roslyn L. Knutson

The facts about *Edward II* in repertory are few. They are derived from title-page advertisements on editions of the play in 1594 and 1622. The 1594 quarto, which was published by William Jones at the sign of the Gun near Holborn Conduit, declares on its title page that *Edward II* 'was sundrie times publiquely acted *in the honourable citie of London, by the* right honourable the Earle of Pem*brooke his seruants*'.[1] The 1622 quarto, which was published by Henry Bell at his shop at the Lame Hospital Gate in Smithfield, has variant title pages; one carries the old claim of Pembroke's Men, but another introduces an advertisement of performances 'by the late Queenes *Maiesties Seruants at the* Red Bull *in* S. Iohns *streete*'. These facts bookend the stage life of *Edward II*, enabling scholars to locate the play with Pembroke's Men early in its career and with Queen Anna's late. But what about in between? The title pages of quartos in 1598 and 1612 repeat the assignment to Pembroke's, but until recently scholars dismissed this information as out-of-date. For the most part, theatre historians have discussed *Edward II* in repertory in terms of Pembroke's Men, who first appear in records at court during the Christmas of 1592–3.[2] Here, I expand that discussion to address not only the theatrical marketplace in the early 1590s but also the status of Pembroke's Men in that marketplace. In addition, on the assumption that *Edward II* had a stage life after its registration at Stationers' Hall by William Jones on 6 July 1593, I explore narratives that track the migration of the play into other companies until it becomes the property of Queen Anna's Men. These narratives are necessarily conjectural, as are projections of the repertorial competition between *Edward II* and the offerings of its own and rival companies in the periods demarked by its second, third and fourth printings. Even so, the commercial environment envisioned here supports the argument that *Edward II* enjoyed a long career in the hands of skilled professionals; it was therefore a more significant contributor to the industry of early modern theatre than a brief tenure with Pembroke's Men in 1592–3 has implied.

Company ownership

For repertory studies, the place to begin is company ownership. The 1594 quarto confirms *Edward II* among the offerings of Pembroke's Men, but it does not reveal when or how that company acquired the play. Before it can be acquired, of course, *Edward II* must be written. Charles R. Forker, juggling the conflicting claims produced by a scholarly industry devoted to borrowed lines in suspect texts, chose the year 1591 'as the likeliest date' of composition but granted that 'early 1592' was 'theoretically' possible.[3] Either date gives *Edward II* a stage life prior to its tenure with the company of Pembroke's Men that was comparatively new in December 1592. But with whom? There are three plausible candidates: the Queen's Men, Lord Strange's Men and the Admiral's Men. When Marlowe put *Tamburlaine* on the market c. 1587, the Queen's Men had the players with the most theatrical prestige. But they did not acquire that play or any subsequent

Marlovian drama, in so far as is known.[4] According to Scott McMillin and Sally-Beth MacLean, the Queen's Men were waging an 'anti-Marlowe campaign' by the time *Edward II* appeared on stage, countering *Doctor Faustus* with *The Troublesome Reign of King John* and the *Tamburlaine* plays with *Selimus* (155–60, esp. 155). The company known as Lord Strange's Men was formed by late 1588, according to Lawrence Manley and Sally-Beth MacLean.[5] The company had leased the Rose by 19 February 1592, at which time Philip Henslowe began to keep performance records in his book of accounts (popularly known as Henslowe's diary). *Edward II* does not appear in Henslowe's entries for Strange's Men; and Manley and MacLean, who locate that company at the Rose in 1589, do not claim it for the 1589–92 repertory.

Therefore, if *Edward II* was composed before the fall of 1592, the Admiral's Men are most likely to have acquired it. Not only did they have a history with Marlowe's drama c. 1587, but they also acquired Edward Alleyn around that time. Scholars credit Alleyn with creating the character of Tamburlaine on early modern stages, as well as the roles of Barabas and Doctor Faustus, both of which he probably revived in 1594 and 1601–2. Yet scholars have not been as willing to see the role of Edward II as his. Constance B. Kuriyama, reflecting popular opinion, observes 'that the play has no part that seems to be meant for Edward Alleyn'.[6] Perhaps; but the role of Edward II is not significantly shorter in number of lines than that of Tamburlaine in part two of *Tamburlaine the Great*. Counting lines of lead players, Scott McMillin drew up a list of roles from adult company plays from 1580 to 1610 that had 800 or more lines. The roles of Tamburlaine in part one and Doctor Faustus did not make McMillin's list; Tamburlaine in part two (877 lines) and Barabas (1,138 lines) did.[7] By my count, the role of Edward II has 749 lines. That number makes it significantly longer than leading roles in two plays acquired by Pembroke's Men that shared the repertory with *Edward II*, namely *The First Part of the Contention Betwixt the Two Famous Houses of*

Yorke and Lancaster (*The Contention*, Q1594) and *The True Tragedy of Richard Duke of York* (*True Tragedy*, Q1595). According to T. J. King, the characters with the most lines in *The Contention* are King Henry (219 lines), Humphrey (205 lines), York (204 lines) and Suffolk (204 lines); those with the most lines in *True Tragedy* are Warwick (447 lines) and the York brothers, Edward (450 lines) and Richard (348 lines).[8] In the repertory of Pembroke's Men, therefore, *Edward II* would have been conspicuous for its dominant male role.

Whoever Marlowe had in mind for the part, by 1592 Alleyn was with Strange's Men at the Rose but *Edward II* was not (as indicated above). In addition, whatever its pre-1592 stage life might have been, scholars agree that the Earl of Pembroke's players acquired *Edward II*, a fact confirmed by its 1594 title-page advertisement. There is no similar agreement on the birth narrative of the 1592–3 configuration of the company. The venerable explanation of Pembroke's sudden appearance at court in December 1592 has been, in the words of E. K. Chambers, that the company was an offshoot 'for travelling purposes of the large London company formed by the amalgamation of Strange's and the Admiral's'.[9] A key feature of this explanation is the size of the company created by such a merger, and evidence for that size has long depended on the assignment of a lost play, '2 Seven Deadly Sins', to Strange's Men.[10] A Plot for '2 Seven Deadly Sins' survives, and it specifies parts for twenty named players plus two unnamed ones. Because Edward Alleyn was thought to have owned the Plot at one time (though he is not named in it), and because Richard Burbage is cast both as Gorboduc and Tereus (in the 'Envy' and 'Lechery' playlets, respectively), scholars have presumed that in the split Alleyn remained with Strange's Men at the Rose and Burbage moved to the newly formed Pembroke's Men.[11] In that separation of Alleyn and Burbage lie the seeds of a recently popular story of origin for Pembroke's. Andrew Gurr articulates the particulars: envisioning James Burbage with an empty playhouse in 1592 and his son Richard without a company affiliation, Gurr finds it 'conceivable that old

Burbage moved to set up a new company led by his son under a new patron'.[12] Manley and MacLean embrace and amplify this narrative. Connecting Henslowe's expansion of the Rose with subsequent renovations at the Theatre, they suggest that James Burbage had in mind as tenants 'Pembroke's Men, a company formed around some key members of Strange's Men, like Richard Burbage' (62).

Another venerable scholarly opinion seeks to explain Pembroke's acquisition of *Edward II*. It is based on an interpretation of a letter from Thomas Kyd, the playwright, to Sir John Puckering, Lord Keeper of the Great Seal of England. Kyd was arrested in May 1593, interrogated, perhaps tortured, and released. In June, shortly after Marlowe's death on 30 May, Kyd wrote a petitionary letter to Puckering, in which he asked Puckering's aid in re-establishing his good name with his patron. Kyd did not name that patron, but scholars incline to identify him as Ferdinando, Lord Strange (Kuriyama, 112). Marlowe figures in the letter because Kyd was trying to separate himself from some politically dangerous papers that were found in his lodgings. He asserted that the papers were Marlowe's and falsely mixed among his own when the men lodged together 'twoe yeares synce'; Kyd continued: 'My first acquaintance with this Marlowe, rose upon his bearing name to serve my Lo:[rd] although his L[ordshi]p never knewe his service, but in writing for his plaiers, for never cold my L.[ord] endure his name, or sight, when he had heard of his conditions ....'[13] Kyd's inference, clearly, is that his patron had tolerated the acquisition of Marlowe's plays by his players formerly but not recently. The fact that Lord Strange's Men acquired Marlowe's *Massacre at Paris* in January 1593 complicates a narrative of Marlovian rejection but facilitates one of Marlowe's commerce with Pembroke's Men late in 1592. Kuriyama, surrendering linguistically to the intractability of evidence, phrases Pembroke's ownership as follows: '*Somehow* [Pembroke's Men] were in possession of Marlowe's *Edward II*' (emphasis mine) (Kuriyama, 116). That 'somehow' is probably as accurate a way to describe

Pembroke's acquisition of *Edward II* as all the arguments made by Marlovian biographers and theatre historians.

Pembroke's Men, 1592–3: Venues

The history of Pembroke's Men begins officially on 26 December 1592, when the company performed at court; a second performance occurred ten days later on 6 January 1593. In its short year of existence, the company performed also in London and the provinces. One gauge of Pembroke's quality as a business – and thus the commercial value of its repertory – is the normalcy and aesthetics of its venues, both of which rank it on a par with its theatrical competitors.

According to the Chamber Accounts, the venue for royal performances in 1592–3 was Hampton Court.[14] Characterizing this space, John Astington contrasts the darkness of its medieval architecture against the light of its windowed interior; furthermore, 'chandeliers, each bearing multiple lights, … [lit] the faces of the actors' as well as that of the monarch.[15] The Chamber Accounts do not name the plays performed by Pembroke's Men, and scholarly opinion is divided on whether *Edward II* might have been one of them. Alfred Hart could not imagine Marlowe's play at court. He argued that the Queen would have taken 'mortal offence' at 'the scene in which the barons and archbishop combine to coerce King Edward'; further (Hart thought), she would have noted the relationship between Edward and Gaveston as parallel to hers with Essex, and 'almost choked with rage to hear such treason spoken by common players'.[16] Apparently though, Edmund Tilney, who authorized the play for performance generally, had had no such worries. A theatre historian today, inclined to privilege theatrical commerce over politics, might think that having the latest play by the notoriously popular Marlowe was sufficient reason for Pembroke's to choose *Edward II* as one of its court offerings.

Playing at court is not synonymous with playing in the city of London, the location advertised on the 1594 title page. A date for the public performances is cautiously advanced by H. B. Charlton and R. D. Waller, who suggested that 'December 1592 is the earliest time at which Pembroke's men could have played *Edward II* in London'.[17] Given that Strange's Men were at the Rose, the likeliest venue for Pembroke's was either the Theatre or Curtain. Marlowe was undoubtedly familiar with the Theatre because the Admiral's Men, who had acquired *Tamburlaine* and others of his plays, had leased that venue frequently through the late 1580s into 1591.[18] Also, Marlowe was a neighbour, having settled in 1587 in the liberty of Norton Folgate east of Shoreditch. If Pembroke's Men leased the Theatre at the end of 1592, Marlowe might have thought that *Edward II* was right at home.

Soon, however, the company took to the road. Plague, which had abbreviated playing in 1592, worsened in 1593. To date, scholars have identified ten provincial towns where Pembroke's Men played during the spring and summer. Because the records are rarely precise in terms of the dates on which companies performed, it is not possible to reconstruct Pembroke's itinerary; nonetheless, the company may be located along traditional circuits followed by troupes generally in the early modern period. Aligned according to routes identified by Sally-Beth MacLean, the travels of Pembroke's Men include East Anglia, where they played at Ipswich and King's Lynn; the Southeast, where they played at Rye; the Southwest, at Bath; the Midlands, at Coventry; the West Midlands, at Ludlow, Shrewbury and Bewdley; the East Midlands, at Leicester;[19] and the North, at York.[20] Between June and August 1593, Pembroke's Men performed at Caludon Castle, home of Henry, Lord Berkeley, where they earned 60s., as had the Queen's Men just weeks earlier.[21] Then, sometime in mid-August, Pembroke's Men returned to London. Edward Alleyn, on tour himself with Strange's Men, wrote to his father-in-law, Philip Henslowe, and asked about Pembroke's Men. In a letter dated 28 September 1593,

Henslowe replied that the players 'are all at home and hauffe ben t<his> v or sixe weackes for they cane not saue ther carges <w>th trauell as I heare & weare fayne to pane the<r> parell for ther carge'.²²

For more than a century, theatre historians have interpreted Henslowe's letter as evidence that Pembroke's Men were a failed commercial enterprise. Then, in the mid-1970s, research sponsored by the Toronto-based project, Records of Early English Drama (REED) began to be published. This cache of data prompted scholars to take a fresh look at received wisdom on provincial playing. In 1983, J. A. B. Somerset initiated the rehabilitation of Pembroke's Men by pointing out the frequency with which records of the players coincide with geographical locations over which their patron had influence.²³ Using REED data, I have argued elsewhere that nothing in the talent of Pembroke's players, the quality of their repertory or their choice of provincial stops accounts for the financial distress to which Henslowe referred.²⁴ On touring specifically: not only did Pembroke's receive sums comparable to those received by Lord Strange's Men in the summer of 1593, but also they visited many of the same towns. Therefore, they too probably performed in the guildhalls in these towns, offering shows attended by (and often sponsored by) the mayor and other civic dignitaries.

In a narrative about the repertorial commerce of *Edward II*, the venues of Pembroke's Men matter. Merely listing the sites rebuts an aspect of the old view of touring companies in which scholars imagined performances located on some common green along a country road leading into town.²⁵ To the contrary, as Peter Greenfield makes clear, theatrical companies on tour 'performed in many kinds of spaces, including the halls of noble households, churches, churchyards, streets, inns, private houses, and even a purpose-built theatre', but 'the most common location ... was the town hall'.²⁶ These halls stood at the centre of early modern urban life.²⁷ They were architecturally sophisticated, with decorated hammer beam roofs, bays of stained glass windows, candelabra and galleries. Some, as the guildhall at Coventry, were decorated with splendid tapestries and portraits. Any company performing in such a space would benefit both from the aesthetics of the building and its manifestation of civic authority. For Pembroke's Men to be one of those troupes gives it the status accorded to other London-based professional playing companies on tour in a summer during plague time.

But how likely is it that *Edward II* was taken on tour? Two conundrums are implicit in the question: the size and selection of the touring repertory. REED research has altered the paradigm on topics such as the economics of touring, the variety of theatrical venues and the ubiquity of provincial dramatic activity by companies with patrons along a spectrum from local dignitary to monarch. But it has been largely silent on the number and selection of plays that companies with a significant London presence such as the Queen's Men, the Admiral's Men or Lord Strange's Men might have chosen for a touring repertory. One piece of the scant documentary evidence is a letter from Edward Alleyn to his wife, written c. 1 August 1593, which gives the name of a play – 'harey of cornwell' – that Lord Strange's Men were preparing to perform in Bristol (Foakes, 276). Another is the trial concerning Lord Cholmeley's players at Gowthwaite Hall in Nidderdale in 1609; the Star Chamber proceedings name four of their plays: *The Travels of the Three English Brothers*, *Pericles*, a 'King Lere' and a Saint Christopher play.[28] Otherwise, theatre historians use logic and common sense to construct arguments about the drama taken on the road. Most agree that the major companies with London-sized caches of plays would travel with only a portion of their current repertory for two reasons: the troupes did not give many performances at any given stop, and the costumes and properties for a dozen or so plays would be too burdensome to cart from town to town. Still, as Greenfield acknowledges, 'the major London companies must have brought Shakespeare, Marlowe, and Jonson to the rest of the country, ... [as well as] a few of their surefire favourites' (264). Leslie Thomson, unimpressed by arguments that touring texts were habitually stripped of spectacular effects, posits that a company might have preferred 'to adapt the performance space' on the road than to leave its best plays in London.[29]

In a discussion of the 1592–3 tours of Strange's Men, Manley and MacLean provide the most informed and nuanced study currently in print on a company's choice of plays. They focus on *A Knack to Know a Knave* as exemplar of a text with a reduced cast (eleven men, two boys); they argue that abandoned characters and plot lines, plus absent clowning, suggest an abridged text (Manley and MacLean, 273, 274). Noting that Strange's Men offered the play soon after reopening at the Rose in December 1593, Manley and MacLean deduce its recent performance in the provinces. But not all of the evidence is compliant. The two shows that preceded *A Knack to Know a Knave* on stage at the Rose that December, as well as the one that followed, are large-cast plays: 'm*u*lomvr*co*' (if it is *The Battle of Alcazar*, as Manley and MacLean claim); 'Joronymo' (if it is *The Spanish Tragedy*, as is widely accepted); and 'the Jewe' (i.e. *The Jew of Malta*). According to Manley and MacLean's casting studies, these plays require thirteen men and five boys ('m*u*lomvr*co*'), fifteen men and five boys ('Joronymo') and fourteen men and three boys (*The Jew of Malta*). Moreover, Manley and MacLean argue that a play such as *John a Kent and John a Cumber* seems ideal for Strange's touring because it is 'so thoroughly a regional play', yet it too is large-cast (sixteen men and five boys) (276, 274). Additionally contradicting small-cast plays as the standard, 'harey of cornwell' – which Strange's Men undeniably took on tour in 1593 – was probably a large-cast play.[30]

Judged by Manley and MacLean's guidelines, *Edward II* compares favourably to the casting pattern of *A Knack to Know a Knave*. It requires eleven men and two to four boys, according to David Bevington.[31] However, unlike the plays in Strange's repertory that appear to have small casts because they have been abridged, the text of *Edward II* 'is almost universally regarded as good' (Charlton and Waller, 25).[32] Leslie Thomson, considering its demands upon a stage, characterizes *Edward II* as having 'minimal stage directions and staging requirements'; in her opinion, the play requires only 'a rear wall with at least two doors' plus a discovery space (perhaps curtained).[33] Thus there is no apparent technical impediment to an assignment of *Edward II* to the touring repertory of Pembroke's Men in 1593. Furthermore, Marlowe's play satisfies Greenfield's criterion of authorship by the top-tier dramatists of the day. Its longevity in print, if not also on stage, satisfies Greenfield's criterion of a sure-fire favourite.

Another consideration bolsters the odds that Pembroke's Men took *Edward II* on the road: the very fact that the company acquired the play. In December of 1592, Pembroke's Men knew that Strange's Men, who had a lease on a London playhouse (the Rose), had been on tour in the summer just past. If Pembroke's players had any professional savvy, they knew that the Queen's Men and Admiral's Men had also been in the provinces recently. Whether Pembroke's company secured the Theatre in the winter of 1592 or not, the players would have anticipated a tour in 1593. Touring was what companies did in the summer, plague or no. Why, then, would they acquire plays unsuited to provincial performance? Scholars know several other plays that shared the repertory of Pembroke's Men with Marlowe's play because, like *Edward II*, they were published with title-page advertisements advertising company ownership. These plays include *The Taming of a Shrew* (*A Shrew*, Q1594) and *The True Tragedy of Richard Duke of York* (*True Tragedy*, Q1595). Another play, *The First Part of the Contention Betwixt the Two Famous Houses of Yorke and Lancaster* (*The Contention*, Q1594), does not have a title-page advertisement of company ownership, but its serial relationship to *True Tragedy* has persuaded scholars to assign it also to Pembroke's Men. Despite their reputation as bad quartos, these plays, like Marlowe's, have ties to top-tier dramatists and qualify as sure-fire favourites. In terms of player requirements, only *A Shrew* has a small cast (ten men, five boys) (Bradley, 231). According to Manley and MacLean's charts, *The Contention* requires sixteen men and three boys, and *True Tragedy* requires sixteen men and four boys.[34] Received wisdom on plays chosen for touring would have Pembroke's Men exclude the members of their repertory that had first-class authorial credentials and strong appeal to publishers. But how plausible is that? Yet the alternative – that the company had additional repertory now invisible either because the texts are lost or the title pages of extant plays do not advertise a company owner – depends entirely on absent evidence. Maybe, then, Pembroke's Men did indeed take large-cast plays on the road.

Pembroke's Men, 1592–3: Repertory

The challenge of exploring the commercial value of *Edward II* is to identify its repertory mates as well as the plays with which it was in competition in the larger theatrical marketplace. Scholars agree that Pembroke's Men in 1592–3 acquired not only Marlowe's *Edward II* but the anonymous *A Shrew* and Shakespearean pair *The Contention* and *True Tragedy*. Other attributions – and they are numerous – are guesswork. Scott McMillin tentatively assigned the now-lost 'Dead Man's Fortune' to Pembroke's because the name of Richard Burbage appears in the extant Plot.[35] Believing that no company would perform in London or on the road without more offerings than *A Shrew* in the most populous early-modern genre, I have asked, 'Where are Pembroke's comedies?' ('Pembroke's Men', 135). Since the 1940s, the most influential argument for attributing plays to company holdings has been the textual phenomenon of borrowed lines. This methodology, in which similar phrases and lines are correlated across a body of texts, became in the hands of Alfred Hart a means of attributing plays to the repertory of Pembroke's Men. In

1942, he constructed a 'Pembroke Group' of plays linked by 'inter-play borrowings'.[36] As a result, he assigned *Arden of Faversham*, *Soliman and Perseda* and *The Massacre at Paris* to the repertory of Pembroke's Men (389–90). In Hart's wake, the list of plays assigned to Pembroke's repertory grew longer. In 1960, A. S. Cairncross assigned *Richard III*, *Romeo and Juliet*, *The Spanish Tragedy* and *1 Henry VI* to the company because, he said, 'all were reported by the same group' of actor-reporters.[37] In 1965, MacDonald Jackson added *Edward III*.[38] In the late 1970s, Karl P. Wentersdorf, who endorsed the assignments of *Arden of Faversham*, *The Massacre at Paris* and *Romeo and Juliet*, was sorely tempted to add W. W. Greg's suggestion of the A-Text *Faustus* also.[39] In 1985, Richard Proudfoot suggested that *The Famous Victories of Henry V*, *The Troublesome Reign of King John*, *The True Tragedy of Richard III* and *King Leir* might have joined Pembroke's repertory.[40]

Theatre historians have not conferred canonical status on these assignments. From a repertorial point of view, however, it matters little whether these plays – if current with *Edward II* in performance – belonged to Pembroke's Men or provided competition across company lines. In-house, the commercial context of *Edward II* is defined by its fellow chronicle histories, *The Contention* and *True Tragedy*.[41] Across company lines, Henslowe's *Diary* records the performances of Strange's Men at the Rose, 29 December 1592 through 1 February 1593. There, the chronicle history on offer was 'harey the 6' (usually identified as Shakespeare's *1 Henry VI* [*1H6*]), which received two performances with receipts averaging 34s. to Henslowe. Scholars now may be struck by the coincidence of two companies' sharing three plays that with *Richard III* would become a tetralogy on the Wars of the Roses; but in the winter of 1592–3, commercially speaking, the pair owned by Pembroke's had more in common with *Edward II* than with their competitor's *1H6*. Edward fights an insurrection against the forces led by Mortimer Junior and the barons, with superficial similarity to the Lancasters (who held the crown) and the Yorks (who wanted it) in *The Contention* and *True Tragedy*. In contrast, the war in *1H6* is fought in France by the English against the French to retain the lands won by Henry V. Strange's Men had another chronicle history, 'harey of cornwell', which had a faint chronological connection with the King Edward of *Edward II* through his father's youth as royal heir. The play, now lost, featured Henry of Almaine, who was raised at the court of Henry III where his companion was the young prince who would become Edward I.[42] Henry of Cornwall (Almaine) had a duplicitous political career that led to his death. In the Barons' War against King Henry III and Prince Edward, his loyalties fluctuated. Abandoning the barons a second time, he took the king's part against Simon de Montfort (his uncle and the barons' leader), who was killed in battle and his body dismembered (Manley and MacLean, 136).[43] Henry of Cornwall/Almaine was murdered by the sons of De Montfort in the Italian city of Viterbo in 1271. Not in Henslowe's lists for the Christmas period of 1592–3, 'harey of cornwell' was taken on tour by Strange's Men during the following summer.

In addition to 'harey of cornwell', there are two chronicle plays that were possibly contemporary with *Edward II* and thus participants in its repertorial value. The company affiliation of both is unknown. One is *Edward I*, by George Peele; the other is the anonymous *Edward III*. The date of composition and stage history of *Edward I* are also unknown, but its registration at Stationers' Hall on 8 October 1593 and publication later that year suggest a rough currency with *Edward II*. *Edward I* is rich with celebratory stage moments, one sequence of which foreshadows the reign of Edward II. The sequence begins with a discovery scene: the stage directions take Edward I and two counselors *'into the Queenes Chamber, the Queenes Tent opens, shee is discovered in her bed attended by Mary Dutches of Lancaster, Jone of Acon her daughter, and the Queen dandles his young sonne'* (10.1454).[44] Queen Elinor then presents the king with his son: 'Kisse him, and christen him after thine owne name' (10.1458–9). The presentation is followed by more festivity: musicians entertain the queen (10.1725); the infant prince, christened off stage, is publicly welcomed with a trumpet fanfare and parental kisses (12.1935–44); and Joan's groom leads the dancing during the ensuing marriage feast (12.1954–65). *Edward II* may recall the title character in 'harey of cornwell' only through the title the love-sick king bestows upon Gaveston; but, as Manley and MacLean point out, *Edward I* recalls the probable violent ending of that lost play. *Edward I* opens with a coronation procession in which Simon de Montfort's revenger-sons are paraded as prisoners; their explicit display as spoils of war invites consideration that 'harey of cornwell' was a repertorial prequel to *Edward I* (136–7).

Edward III transforms these three into a tetralogy of Plantagenet rule from 1272 to 1377. Like *Edward I*, the date of composition, company affiliation and stage history of *Edward III* are unknown. Printed in 1595 with a title-page advertisement of performances *'aboute the Citie of London'*, the play has been attributed to the repertory of Pembroke's Men (as noted above). Whether an in-house companion of *Edward II* or cross-company rival, *Edward III* locates Marlowe's play in an historical narrative, dramatizing not only the lapses in moral judgement of the boy crowned king in Marlowe's play but also his nation-building. As the fourth in the sequence, *Edward III* provides a comedic ending in that the king reassumes his monarchial duties and the Black Prince proves his mettle on the battlefield. In real life, that glory was temporary; but in drama *Edward III* ends the tetralogy on a triumphant note.

Edward II has both feet on English soil, even though the flight of Edward's French queen takes the action briefly abroad. In this it contrasts with the foreign histories that shared its marketplace in 1592–3. As noted above, Hart assigned *Soliman and Perseda* to Pembroke's Men, thus diversifying the categories of the company's history plays. The foreign history is amply represented in the repertory of Strange's Men at the Rose during the winter run of 1592–3 by continuations of the runs of *The Spanish Tragedy*, Part One of 'Tamar Cham' and 'mvlomvrco'.[45] However, the new foreign history in the offerings of Strange's Men at the end of January 1593 that had obvious repertorial resonance with *Edward II* is *The Massacre at Paris*. *Edward II*, being the only play by Marlowe known to belong to Pembroke's Men, is unique in competing across company offerings with its authorial siblings. In addition to being linked by lines in common and being taken from national chronicles, *Edward II* shares with *The Massacre at Paris* trademarks of Marlovian drama such as onstage violence, Machiavellian noblemen, scheming queens and stone cold killers. *The Jew of Malta*, also and always in cross-company competition with *Edward II*, shared at the least the horrific onstage death of the title character. London was one venue in which *The Massacre at Paris* could provide repertorial context for *Edward II* in the winter of 1592–3; the provinces were another. It therefore appears significant that *The Massacre at Paris*, which now survives only in a short form, was acquired by Strange's Men just as the company left the Rose for the provinces.[46] A projected tour of *Massacre at Paris* invites further conjecture that *Edward II* competed in the provinces against its sibling history play as well as a fellow member of the Plantagenet tetralogy, 'harey of cornwell'.

Whatever the commercial energy between 'harey of cornwell' and *Edward II* on the western touring circuits, Marlowe's play was in the hands of stationers when Edward Alleyn wrote to his wife from Bristol c. 1 August 1593 and mentioned the upcoming performance scheduled for that now-lost play. William Jones had entered *Edward II* in the Stationers' Register on 6 July, almost a month earlier. He published a copy in 1594. Scholars, looking ahead to Henslowe's 28 September letter about the return of Pembroke's Men to London some 'v or sixe weackes' previously, have viewed this sale to Jones as an early sign of the company's faltering commerce. More recent commentary has challenged that view. Peter W. M. Blayney determines that stationers could 'just about afford to spend two pounds on copy for [a] book' if that sum included 'the cost of having the manuscript properly allowed by the authorities'.[47] Blayney's research, by challenging the entire line of argument that stationers rated playbooks as commodities so highly that they would pirate copies, challenges also arguments that the sale of playbooks indicates a company's financial distress. Most theatre historians now grant that £2 would not have enabled Pembroke's Men to solve their cash flow problems. Attention has instead returned to a connection made in 1933 by Charlton and Waller, who noted that the play might have been marketed in July 1593 'to catch a public still excited by Marlowe's [recent] death' (4).[48]

1594–1622

When the finances of Pembroke's Men dominated the conversation on the sale of *Edward II*, the fact that the play itself might have continued to be some company's commercial property disappeared from scholars' radar. Pembroke's Men also disappeared from provincial records in 1594, and they had never been in London records except for the two court performances at Christmastide 1592–3. The appearance of *Edward II* in print in 1594 with an advertisement on its title page of ownership by the Earl of Pembroke's players seemed to close the stage history of the play. True, the play was published a second time in 1598, again with an advertisement of Pembroke's Men, but that claim looked old, as if copied from the earlier printing with insignificant variant phrasing. The third publication in 1612, with the same claim of company ownership, appeared to confirm the obsolescence of the advertisement on the second edition. But then there was a fourth edition; this one, which repeated Pembroke's Men on some copies but changed the advertisements on others to 'the late Queenes *Maiesties Seruants at the* Red Bull *in* S. Iohns streete*'*, implies that perhaps there had been a stage life in some co-ordination with the continued printing of the play.

Recently, in part because of new data about provincial circuits in the REED scholarship, theatre historians are asking where that life might have taken place and with what company. The result is alternative narratives of migration over the remaining 1590s, as well as attention to the repertory of the company confirmed as the owner of *Edward II* as it headed into print for the last time in the early modern period.

There are three likely contenders as owners of *Edward II* after 1593: Pembroke's Men, the Chamberlain's Men and the configuration of Worcester's Men that became Queen Anna's Men in 1604. Pembroke's Men have the best claim in that they had the play already.[49] Holger Syme makes a compelling case on available evidence for the resumption of Pembroke's company after their break with touring in August of 1593. Taking the letter of 28 September 1593 at face value, Syme makes several important points: (1) Henslowe does not specify 'a break-up'; (2) he calls the players (still) 'my lorde a penbrockes'; (3) he considers them 'at home' in London; and (4) he speaks of their pawning clothes, not liquidating their inventory.[50] In Syme's narrative, the players had regrouped for a touring stop at Ipswich by April 1595. They then continued to perform both in the provinces and in London until their fateful lease of the Swan playhouse in February 1597 that led to the uproar over the lost 'Isle of Dogs' and yet another reshuffling of players and scripts to the Admiral's Men and perhaps other organizations (280–3). According to this narrative, *Edward II* stayed with Pembroke's until the disruptions of 1597; the advertisement of ownership on its 1598 edition was therefore relatively current and accurate.[51]

The candidacy of the Chamberlain's Men rests initially on the fact that two plays published in 1594 with title-page advertisements of Pembroke's Men turn up in the playlist Henslowe recorded for the Admiral's Men and Chamberlain's Men, both newly formed, who shared a ten-day stretch of performances at the Newington playhouse, 3–13 June 1594. Those plays are *Titus Andronicus* and *The Taming of a Shrew*. Neither appears subsequently in playlists for the Admiral's

Men at the Rose; consequently, theatre historians assume that both migrated to the repertory of the Chamberlain's Men. If a larger batch of migrating texts included *Edward II*, the play was to enjoy its most extended London run yet. It might have been performed at three London playhouses: the Theatre, 1594–7; the Curtain, 1597–9; and the Globe, 1599 (depending on the timing of its eventual move to Worcester's Men). The Chamberlain's Men toured occasionally but not like Pembroke's Men did in 1592–3. By 1598, at which time (perhaps coincidentally) *Edward II* was published for a second time, there was a player with the Chamberlain's Men who could have carried the play to Worcester's Men sometime after 1599.[52] This player was Christopher Beeston. In his early tenure with Worcester's Men, Beeston was not yet the theatrical entrepreneur that he would become, but he might already have learned the value of acquiring plays.

The candidacy of Worcester's Men rests on the fact that, according to the title-page advertisement of its printing in 1622, *Edward II* migrated to the repertory of Queen Anna's Men, who had been the Earl of Worcester's players before 1604. Worcester's Men could have acquired the play as early as 1593. A company by that name performed in the provinces in 1593 (as did Pembroke's Men until mid-July), and their touring continued however sporadically into 1603. Worcester's Men had a London presence as well as an appearance at court during Christmastide of 1601–2 (3 January 1602). According to Herbert Berry, they leased the Boar's Head 'late in the summer or early in the autumn of 1601'.[53] Worcester's stayed at the Boar's Head into the summer of 1602, when they moved to the Rose for a year; they played at the Curtain and Boar's Head, c. 1603–6, until they settled at the Red Bull (now as Queen Anna's Men) (Berry, 72–3). Beeston is one constant in the flux of playing venues and patrons post-1602. By 1612 he was a sharer with Queen Anna's Men, and he continued in a management role when the company changed patrons to Queen Henrietta Maria in 1626 and revived other plays by Marlowe in 1633. This theatrical churning produced no records of *Edward II*. Therefore, its printing in 1622 probably signals the close of its stage life in the early modern period.[54]

The editions of *Edward II* mark three repertorial periods beyond its maiden run in 1592–3 with Pembroke's Men: 1594–8; 1598–1612; and 1612–22. Due to the nature of surviving records, the amount of information about repertorial competition for all of the companies diminishes from the first of these periods to the last. Furthermore, as has been demonstrated, both the stage life and company location of *Edward II* in these years is conjectural; consequently, much of the following is suggestive, not conclusive. Nevertheless, on the assumption that the play was performed by some company between 1594 and 1622, it does not strain credibility too much to envision a commercial environment that includes competition with other of Marlowe's plays, with plays that share its monarchial characters, with spin-offs of its narrative and with the family of plays about Richard II.

The repertorial environment of 1594–8 is rich for *Edward II*. As Henslowe's diary proves, five other Marlovian plays were on stage throughout the period: *The Massacre at Paris*, *The Jew of Malta*, *Doctor Faustus* and (by December 1594) both parts of *Tamburlaine the Great*. *Doctor Faustus* was still in performance, though barely, in the fall of 1597 when members of Pembroke's company came over from the Swan playhouse to join the Admiral's Men at the Rose. In 1598, the Admiral's Men acquired a play called 'dido & enevs', which they 'fyrst played ... at nyght' on 8 January (Foakes, 86).[55] Scholars such as F. G. Fleay and W. W. Greg, who often identified lost plays with similarly titled extant ones, were disinclined to identify this 'dido' as Marlowe's *Dido Queen of Carthage*, but the similar title nonetheless evokes subject matter already marked by Marlowe. Another cluster of plays on stage in this period shares the history of the Plantagenet line with *Edward II*. The Admiral's Men introduced 'longe shancke' on 29 August 1595, and Henslowe marked it with his enigmatic sign of 'ne' (Foakes, 30).[56] The play enjoyed fourteen performances into July 1596 and brought Henslowe average receipts of 31s. Scholars disagree about whether this entry identifies a new play on Edward I or a revival of Peele's play; either way, the currency of the story of Edward's father is evidence that Edward's own story had commercial value. The Admiral's Men did not have *Edward III*, but some company might have in 1594; in terms of dating its stage life, the registration of the play on 1 December 1595, followed by publication in 1596 pulls its currency from 1592–3 into 1594–5. Both it and Peele's *Edward I* were printed again in 1599. These publications, which follow chronologically if not also commercially upon the reprinting of *Edward II* in 1598, kept current the dynastic narrative that links the three plays. In this time period also, a now-lost play called 'Alls Perce' appears in payments by Henslowe for apparel including a bodice for a woman's gown in December 1597; the play is also listed in his inventory of playbooks on 3 March 1598/9. Martin Wiggins reflects current opinion among theatre historians that this 'Alls' was Alice Perrers, mistress of Edward III.[57] Such an identification connects the lost play to the family of drama about Plantagenet kings, specifically the tetralogy for which *Edward II* forms a titular third part.

The play to which *Edward II* has been most frequently compared is Shakespeare's *Richard II*. Scholarly commentary on this pairing is beyond the scope of this chapter; suffice it to say that similarities in structure and theme invite consideration of their repertorial relationship. Elsewhere, I have discussed *Edward II* as a context for *Richard II*; here, I make *Richard II* the context for Marlowe's play.[58] Lineally, Richard was Edward's great-grandson. Narratively, *Richard II* is the link between the Plantagenet plays to which *Edward II* belongs and Shakespeare's tetralogy on the Wars of the Roses, the middle two plays of which were in repertory with *Edward II* in 1592–3.[59] Being unquestionably successful in their families of related drama, *Richard II* and *Edward II* may well have triggered fresh commercial life for each other in the rhythm of their publication when, in 1597 and 1598 particularly, Shakespeare's play received three printings to

Marlowe's one.[60] *True Tragedy* (and, by association, *The Contention*) is linked by stationers' advertising to the stage life of *Edward II*. Scholars have believed that all of Shakespeare's pre-1594 plays migrated to the Chamberlain's Men early in the formation of that company, but Syme's narrative of a Pembroke's troupe that survived past 1594 with some of its previous offerings invites the conjecture that *Edward II* kept repertorial company with *The Contention* and *True Tragedy*, which together temporarily settled the issue of succession created when Edward III's first-born son died before he could become king. *The Contention*, with its serial mate *True Tragedy*, was published a second time in 1600, somewhat late for 'Edward' plays, but like that of *Edward II* in 1598 their title pages retained the advertisement of ownership by Pembroke's Men.[61] There is yet another play with Shakespearean associations as well as repertorial ties to *Edward II*. The reprinting of *A Shrew* in 1596 is a reminder of its 1594 quarto in its advertisement of Pembroke's Men on the title page, and it would advertise that company affiliation again in 1607.

The repertorial environment for *Edward II* between 1598 and 1603 resembles the patterns of 1594–8. The play again had siblings with which to share the London marketplace. In 1600, following the move to the Fortune, the Admiral's Men revived *The Jew of Malta*, c. May 1601; *The Massacre at Paris*, c. December 1601; and *Doctor Faustus*, c. November 1602 (Foakes, 170, 183–5, 206). Edward Alleyn, who had left playing in 1597, putatively revived the Marlovian roles to advertise the opening of the new Fortune playhouse. Even more suggestive of *Edward II*, the Admiral's Men made payments on two plays, now lost, that appear to be spin-offs. The first, 'The Spencers', was paid for and outfitted by mid-April 1599 (Foakes, 106–7, 118). The second, 'Mortimer', was bought in November 1601 for 40s.; on 10 September 1602 the company bought two suits alike ('a licke'), which cost £6 (Foakes, 184, 205).[62] Wiggins identifies the main characters of 'The Spencers' as the father and son with whom Edward associates after Gaveston's execution (IV, #1180). However, Wiggins is disinclined to identify the title character of 'Mortimer' as Edward's nemesis and Isabella's lover (IV, #1345).[63] From a repertorial viewpoint, though, the timing of 'Mortimer' fits neatly with the Marlovian revivals of 1601–2.

It is therefore tempting to imagine *Edward II* also in revival at another playhouse, competing with its siblings and spin-offs. Worcester's Men leased the Rose in 1602, available now that the Admiral's Men had moved to the Fortune. Henslowe recorded payments for Worcester's Men, but none of the plays is *Edward II* and few suggest an affinity with it except as they too have a claim on the genre of chronicle history: the two-part 'Lady Jane', 'Shore's Wife' and a revised 'Oldcastle'. Otherwise, the company's taste ran to the foreign history ('Albere Galles'), true-crime (the two-part 'Black Dog of Newgate', 'Cutting Dick'), comedies ('Medicine for a Curst Wife', 'Christmas Comes But Once a Year', 'The Blind Eats Many a Fly') and the domestic tragedy, *A Woman Killed with Kindness*. Berry provides an account of the theatrical enterprise at the Boar's Head, some of which plays belonged to Worcester's Men (124–7), but their chronicle histories such as the two-part *Edward IV*, the two-part *If You Know Not Me You Know Nobody* and *Sir Thomas Wyatt* do not suggest Marlovian influence. The Chamberlain's Men were at the Globe by 1599. The only hint of repertorial commerce with *Edward II* is the currency of their chronicle plays: *Henry V*, still in its debut run; and publications such as *2 Henry 4* (1600); *The Contention* and *True Tragedy* (1600, the latter still advertising Pembroke's Men); and *Richard III* (1602). *Richard II* was published again in 1608 with new additions, but this date seems too late to suggest co-ordination with a revival of Marlowe's play between 1598 and 1603.

Compared to the vibrant marketplace around the 1598 edition of *Edward II*, the printings of 1612 and 1622 look perfunctory. One reason is the absence of evidence. *Edward II*, though never in Henslowe's records, was in competition with plays that were; it was also in competition with

Shakespeare's plays, the stage history of which scholars have zealously researched. When Henslowe's records dry up in 1604, evidence of repertorial competition suffers 'archival attrition'; that is, many plays subsequently on stage are 'absent from the historical record' unless they appear in print.[64] Another reason is that the performances of Marlowe's plays had been on the wane for some time. Syme tracks their decline through Henslowe's records for the Admiral's Men, 1594–7; and he finds that, in the percentage of performances offered per play, 'Marlowe's share drops precipitously' from 19 per cent of performances offered in 1594–5, to 7.7 per cent in 1595–6, to 2.1 per cent in 1596–7 (500).[65] Also, the tide of printings of Marlowe's plays had ebbed. *Tamburlaine the Great* had not been published since 1605 (part 1) and 1606 (part 2). *Dido Queen of Carthage* had only the one edition in 1594; *The Massacre at Paris* had only the one in 1596.[66] Exceptions, in different ways, are *Doctor Faustus* and *The Jew of Malta*. The editions of *Doctor Faustus* escalated from the belated 1604 printing (S.R. 7 January 1601) until 1616 (the 4th edition, the so-called 'B' text) to five more printings – a total of nine – with those last five in tight succession: 1619, 1620, 1624, 1628 and 1631. Such a pattern suggests that perhaps as early as 1616 the stage runs of *Doctor Faustus* in England were no longer concurrent with its printings; from a repertorial perspective, it had made the transition from a play to a book.[67] In contrast, the eventual printing of *The Jew of Malta* was directly related to its revival for the stage. Registered at Stationers' Hall on 17 May 1594, *The Jew of Malta* was finally published in 1633 in conjunction with a revival of old stock by Queen Henrietta Maria's players. According to Jeremy Lopez, the revival was as much about Alleyn as Marlowe. Lopez argues that the Prologue by Thomas Heywood published with *The Jew of Malta* pays tribute to Alleyn by imagining the company's current star, Richard Perkins, 'haunted by the ghost of the old actor'.[68] The Alleyn remembered by Heywood was marked by a vigorous physical style of acting often evoked by the verb 'stalk' (169). This is the Alleyn of Tamburlaine; it is the image of Alleyn that has Kuriyama claim 'no part' for him in *Edward II* (*Christopher Marlowe*, 117). Despite the apparent similarity of company names, there was not a wholesale translation of players from Queen Anna's Men to Queen Henrietta's.[69] Except for Christopher Beeston. In full entrepreneurial mode, Beeston managed the company's venues and repertory until his death in 1638. A year later his son, William Beeston, submitted to the Lord Chamberlain a list of forty-five plays owned by Queen Henrietta Maria's Men; *Edward II* is not among them.[70] Neither is 'Mortimer His Fall', though its author, Ben Jonson, wrote at least one play for the company (*A Tale of a Tub*). Jonson's 'Mortimer' is a fragment; Karen Britland summarizes arguments for an early date c. 1600 but prefers the later date c. 1637.[71] Early or late, the play-scrap, with its shared characters and story, serves as the repertorial post-mortem of *Edward II*.

The fact that *Edward II* faded from the theatrical marketplace in the 1610s should not detract from the commercial power of its heyday. The play has suffered from not being with the Admiral's Men where its commercial history could be tracked through Henslowe's playlists and payments for diverse things and where its properties and apparel could have been in Henslowe's inventory along with the 'cauderm for the Jewe' and 'Tamberlanes breches of crymson vellvet' (Foakes, 321, 322). It therefore suffers from having been acquired by Pembroke's Men, who themselves have been treated with contempt by theatre historians. The fact that the players left touring and returned to London in mid-July 1593 has cast a pall over their achievements: the patronage of an earl among the Queen's favourites, performances at court on premier Christmastide dates when brand new as a company; perhaps instant access to the most venerable playhouse in London (the Theatre), with managerial assistance from the most experienced entrepreneur in the business (James Burbage); 'sundrie' public performances at this or another London venue; acquisition of scripts from the leading poets of the day (Marlowe, Shakespeare); and first-rate players (Richard Burbage), one of whom might have been a playwright (Shakespeare). Their provincial tour followed traditionally lucrative circuits, where its shows were authorized by the most powerful politicians in town and performed in its grandest civic spaces as well as its patron's residence. Unlike its repertorial companions in 1592–3, *Edward II* has not suffered from the label of 'bad quarto', but its company carries the stigma of having performed second-hand scripts hastily constructed by hack players with poor memories. Because the stage history of *Edward II* after its tenure with Pembroke's Men in 1592–3 is undocumented, it has remained isolated from the repertorial markets that are suggested by its subsequent printings. However, much of *that* market *can* be documented, and it suggests multiple contexts in which *Edward II* was a valuable property to acquire and to perform.

6

'Overpeered' and Understated: Conforming Transgressions and *Edward II*

James Siemon

Nothing classifies somebody more than the way he or she classifies.
PIERRE BOURDIEU, 'SOCIAL SPACE AND SYMBOLIC POWER'.[1]

For NOBLE MEN in generall itt is dangerouse to be familier with them, or to depend upon them, or to deale with or trust them too muche. For their thoughts are bestowed upon their owne waightie causes and their estates and actions are governed by pollicy. Againe albeitt they be most courtlie in wordes, yet they could be contented that riche gentlmen weare less able to liue without depending on them, even as the gentlman lookes with a discontented eye upon the stoute riche yeoman.

SIR WILLIAM WENTWORTH, 'ADVICE TO HIS SON'.[2]

Understatement is not the first quality that comes to mind when characterizing Marlowe's *Edward II*. The play's action takes the audience from initial angry confrontations between Edward and his nobles over his extravagant displays of favouritism toward an upwardly mobile male intimate, through repeated struggles that starkly pit political charges of 'traitor' against 'traitor' (4.20–1) or 'the barons' right' against 'King Edward's right' (12.35–6), to the rise of a would-be tyrant Machiavel and a concluding sequence juxtaposing the horrific onstage violation of the royal body with a final tableau that features the severed head of the regicide atop the hearse of his victim.[3] Yet, despite its spectacular theatricality and its insults directed at 'base born' characters, linguistically this play is no *Tamburlaine*.[4] Instead of declaiming at length, characters often stifle their own utterances, or are urged to do so.[5] Less obviously, despite its vividly evoked Marlovian themes, including individual aspiration, alienation, passionate desire, suffering and revulsion, *Edward II* is remarkable for its silences, re-iterations and ironical, sometimes just barely ironical, usage, especially in utterances that inflect familiar titles of rank and degree with estranging overtones.

It has often been noted that *Edward II* adapts the social status of the king's historical associates. As Claude J. Summers puts it, Marlowe altered Holinshed to make Gaveston 'a commoner and Spencer a servant'.[6] While this oversimplifies categories, Marlowe does emphasize an obvious social trajectory for Edward's companions as they rise rapidly and solely through royal favour, without the justifications provided by their historical alliances, inheritance or estates, military service, offices, or academic distinctions and do so amid insults from the play's hostile nobles, who label them 'basely born', 'upstarts' or 'night-grown mushroom[s]'.[7] It is less often remarked that *Edward II* is unusual among roughly contemporary history plays in the frequency with which it employs collective designations for those same nobles. This insistent nomenclatural presence in stage directions and dialogue referring to 'nobles', 'lords', 'barons', 'earls and barons' or 'peers' is accompanied by a complex treatment accorded the degrees and their holders.[8]

In rough outline, the play suggests obvious parallels with the *Tamburlaine* plays, in which an ambitious protagonist asserts and achieves ascendance amid detractors who presume superiority by rank, birth, religion, armed might or position. However, *Edward II* inflects its themes of aspiration, advancement, disparagement and competition for social distinction in rather different, complicated and period-specific ways. On the one hand, the nearly universal resistance to Edward's associates hyperbolically articulated by the play's aristocrats suggests a 'class for itself' defending the borders of that amalgam of ranks known as the *nobilitas maior* or 'gentlemen of the greater sort'.[9] On the other hand, the play insistently invokes recognized ranks and degrees and displays traditional forms of deference, but accompanies these instantiations of orthodox distinction with pervasive and often subtle ironies of tone and usage that register multi-level social competitions and antagonisms.

While the vocabulary of *class* should be employed tentatively in discussing the pre-industrial era, the argument which follows builds upon criticism concerned with 'class transgression' in *Edward II*.[10] Instead of focusing on 'class transgression' in the rise of the play's favourites, however, this chapter pursues an approach derived from Pierre Bourdieu's notion of 'conforming transgression'. Affirming that 'analysis of language is essential' to sociological inquiry 'inasmuch as language is the depository of a whole social philosophy', Bourdieu also recognizes the 'invisibility' within ordinary language of assumptions which constitute a society's 'taken-for-granted'. In confronting this dilemma, Bourdieu considers the poetry of non-literate cultures, which, though largely conforming to established expectations in values and terminology, yet manages to violate the well-worn, the well-known, the proverbial or familiar expression with miniscule alterations. Such formal deviations can be important because, while reiterating what is culturally 'sayable', conforming transgressions may nevertheless awaken active attention to shared presuppositions by injecting an element of surprise. Conforming transgressions appear throughout *Edward II* as countless 'little alterations' of utterance and implementation that re-render 'commonplace or routinized expression[s]' implicating rank and degree in surprisingly 'debanalized' and 'reactivated' forms even though their 'ordinary meaning remains present'.[11]

I

Recent scholarship has corrected and adjusted Lawrence Stone's classic account of early modern English nobility losing ground to a rising gentry. Many historians have stressed commonalities uniting the gentleman and the nobleman rather than their 'distinction' or 'tensions and conflicts of interest'.[12] Clive Heal and Felicity Holmes claim 'easy boundary fluidity and low inter-group aggression' between peers and gentlemen.[13] M. L. Bush argues that contemporaries thought nobles and gentry 'sufficiently alike to belong to the same social category'.[14] However, Marlowe's *Edward II* resonates with more conflictual accounts, such as that provided by Humfrey Braham:

> [I]n these oure dayes, more then euer hathe ben in times passed, an inordinate disdaigne emonge most sortes of parsons hathe rysen, in that one sort of men can not stand content with the state of an other. The high degree almost

contempneth the lower sorte, the low Degre loketh to
compare with his superior. The higher sort inflamed by the
opinio[n] of their ge[n]try, their noble aunce[s]tors, and
anceient houses, looke for that cause to be obeyed and
reuerenced of al men.[15]

Descriptions of social 'disdaigne' among the 'sortes' like that
of Braham or of tri-level suspicions among 'NOBLE MEN in
general', 'gentlmen' and 'yeomen' as evoked by Sir William
Wentworth moralize what Stone perceived as a demographic
issue.

'[W]ith large numbers of relatively new families pouring into
the gentry, the knightage, the baronetage, and the peerage, the
struggles of the status-seekers were particularly violent', Stone
writes, with 'competitive consumption' occurring at two social
divides: at the border between 'squirearchy and baronage' – in
effect, between the *armigeri*, the most socially elevated, arms-
bearing stratum of Wentworth's 'gentlmen', and the lowest
rank of Wentworth's 'NOBLE MEN', the barons – and at the
division between 'yeomen and lesser gentry' – that is, between
the 'mere' gentlemen, the *generosi*, and those who, though
perhaps wealthy and land-owning, were not considered gentle
(Wentworth's 'riche yeoman').[16] While *Edward II* betrays
traces of 'competitive consumption', it does not dominate the
play's action, despite passages evoking Gaveston's lavish provi-
sions for the King's delight or the fashionable extravagance of
the favourite's retainers.[17] Troops of Gaveston's followers never
appear on stage, and Marlowe ignores Holinshed's claim that
Mortimer and Isabella 'mainteined such ports, and kept among
them such a retinue of seruants, that their prouision was
woonderfull' (6:347). Marlowe's restraint may be contrasted
with contemporary works that treat Gaveston as embodying
competitive 'consumption' and associate him with stylistic
imitation or 'apishness' in order to criticize the Court, the
nobility in general or a broad swath of urban commonality.[18]

Drawing on the same sources that inspired Marlowe's
Gaveston to imagine delights to 'draw the pliant King which

way' he pleases (1.49–70) and Mortimer Junior to denounce Gaveston's extravagant attire and deportment (4.403–20), Samuel Daniel depicts Gaveston enlisting 'Buffons, Parasites, Minstrels, Players and all kinde of dissolute persons to entertaine and dissolue the King with delights and pleasures.'[19] However, Daniel claims that Gaveston's 'brauery, and daintines of attire … afterward … infected the Court of *England*' and eventually the whole social order with 'contagious … Consumption' as 'imitation thereof presently distend[ed] it selfe ouer all, and passe[d] beyond the example, and at length all meanes to maintaine it' (172–3).[20]

Gaveston similarly embodies contentious 'imitation' in Drayton's *Peirs Gaueston* (1594) and Dekker's *Seven Deadly Sins of London* (1606), though each work depicts a different social epidemiology.[21] While Gaveston's 'port and personage so magnificent' occasion noble criticism (sigs. F2r–F3v), Drayton's Gaveston describes the noblemen mimicking his attitude and behaviour:

> The Barrons now ambitious at my raigne,
> As one that stoode betwixt them and the Sunne.
> They vnderhand pursue me with disdaine,
> And play the game which I before had wonne. (sig. F3r)

Drayton's ambitious 'Nobilitie' attempt to play Gaveston's own 'game'. Collectively, 'they' spread 'disdaine' for him, just as he, as 'one' individual, had first done for them. To this end, 'the Barrons' mount lavish 'tryumphes', pooling resources to outdo him in 'entertain[ing] the King with wondrous cost' (sig. F3r). In this mimetic zero-sums struggle the baronial order collectively embraces Gaveston's own means to counter his attempts to 'counterpoyse the proude Nobilitie'.

By contrast, Dekker's Gaveston appears as an avatar of competitive consumption and 'imitation' within a contemporary urban setting where a downmarket youth subculture clashes with aged authority.[22] Without reference to 'barons', 'lords' or even to state politics, Dekker conjures up 'the

Gaueston of the Time' – a 'feirse, dapper fellow, more light headed then a Musitian: as phantastically attyred as a Court Ieaster: wanton in discourse: lasciuious in behauiour: iocond in good companie: nice in his trencher' (30) – as the catalyst for London fashion riots. Subsuming in himself the roles and qualities assigned to Marlowe's Gaveston and his hired 'Musicians', 'wanton poets' and retainers in 'proud fantastic liueries' (1.50–1; 4.411), including dapperness (4.413) and Italian and French associations (4.414–15, 2.7); Dekker's allegorical figure, having entered England 'when Monsieur came in', appears as 'Signior Ioculento', a 'prawncing' idol of 'apishness'. His forcible entry into contemporary London precipitates a civil mutiny pitting the desires of his riotous young adherents against the strictures of 'Reuerend Authoritie'. Galvanizing an identifiable faction out of a socio-economically disparate conglomerate consisting of 'richmens sonnes' with more money than 'wit how to bestow it', apprentices 'almost out of their yeers' and 'Tailors, Haberdashers, and Embroderers' who act as agents for 'yong and wanton dames of the Citie' who 'would not be seene to shewe their loue to him themselues', Dekker's Gaveston-of-the-Time represents the simultaneously attractive and divisive capacity of 'anie new-fangled upstart fashion' to redraw social divisions, including those of wealth and gender, and construct new subgroup identities, alliances and antagonisms.[23] By imitating the new, Dekker's followers of fashion proudly reject 'social aging' or resignation to gradually 'becom[ing] what they are' according to ascribed identities; instead they enlist under a new, dissimilative subgroup identity defined precisely by its *not* accepting prevailing norms in clothing, food and habitus.[24]

Surprisingly without any reference to Gaveston, a nearly contemporary text, William Camden's *Annales*, enlists virtually every aspect of Dekker's riotous urban nightmare to criticize the 'insolencie' of 'the Nobilitie' itself. Employing a chronology resembling Dekker's, Camden's history claims that at the time of Alençon's communications with Elizabeth, 'the Nobilitie' and those wishing 'they might seem noble' infected 'our apish nation' with a disease that has become chronic. The nobles first violated 'the habite of our Countrey', the '*patrius cultus*' – our national 'style of dress' or 'manner of life of our fathers' – by adopting 'outlandish Wares' and behaviour: 'jett[ing] vp and downe' wearing 'Silkes, glittering with gold and siluer'.[25] Here Camden's text might recall Mortimer Junior's Gaveston in his 'Italian hooded cloak/ Larded with pearl', 'riot[ing] it' and 'jet[ing] it in the court, / With base outlandish cullions' in 'proud fantastic liveries' (4.409–11); but Camden traces lasting, collective effects of the initial infection. In subsequent decades, this imitative syndrome has spread beyond dress and deportment to infect 'Hospitalitie' and great 'houses', the very practices and material embodiments of traditional aristocratic order, with riot and insubordination. 'Pride', he writes, 'grew more and more insolent: And withal crept in ryot in banqueting and brauerie in building' (Camden, 2: 69).[26] Thus, Camden, like Daniel and Drayton, locates imitative competition within the established order, as outrageous and threatening as the guerilla style wars of Dekker's youthful urban fashionistas. Camden's 'Nobilitie', like Daniel's 'Court' and Drayton's 'Barons', may enlist grander material means – tournaments, great houses, lavish banquets – but they manifest similar 'ambition', 'insolence', 'excess of pride' and 'disdaine'.

These works suggest that staging the conspicuous displays of clothing, behaviour and banquet evoked in Gaveston's speeches and Mortimer Junior's critiques could have readily elicited audience responses. Yet we never see that dramatic potential realized in *Edward II*.[27] Rather than staging a sartorial or gestural equivalent of Tamburlaine's spectacular self-indulgences, the play never shows us Gaveston styling with 'base outlandish cullions at his heels' (4.410). In fact, unless one counts Spencer Junior and Baldock, the others 'like to himself' never appear (Holinshed, 6:318).[28] This stage absence is not dictated by casting constraints, one presumes, given the play's many supernumeraries.[29] Instead of upstart minions in 'proud fantastic liveries' (4.411) or nobles 'ryoting' in 'outlandishe Wares', the play represents 'apish' competition of a different sort. For the 'love' of the king, we see disruptive competition between many 'nobles' and a very few 'upstarts'. Although Edward is wildly mistaken when he proclaims reconciliation with his barons, his equation – 'These silver hairs will more adorn my court / Than gaudy silks or rich embroidery' (4.347–8) – accurately suggests the predominance of attention devoted to staging established 'nobles' rather than 'gaudy' minions.

II

Attention does not equal respect. In fact, the 'lordly' ranks and degrees appear subjected to ironies of conforming transgression from the play's opening lines. Even before Gaveston bids 'Farewell' to 'base stooping to the lordly peers', and before he turns his mockery downward upon the ranks of 'POOR MEN' and all 'such as' they, who offer, in traditionally deferential terms, to serve 'your worship' before cursing him to 'perish by a soldier's hand' (1.18–48), Gaveston first reacts tellingly to a '*letter ... from the King*' (1.0). As he reads, Gaveston's lines pivot abruptly from passionate avowal of his 'Sweet prince' to an objectifying invocation of Edward's title: 'Ah, words that make me surfeit with delight! / What greater bliss can hap to Gaveston, / Than live and be the favourite of a king?' (1.3–5). Intensely individualized joy, aroused by Edward's declaration to be 'thy dearest friend' and by Gaveston's own self-recognition as uniquely 'the favourite', is abruptly contrasted by the impersonally indefinite article in speaking 'of a king' – any king. From this moment on, identities and relationships will be phrased and defined in relation to traditional rank and deference; but as here, terms and uses will be sometimes subtly, often brutally, and many times ironically invoked in ways that recognize but also compromise or complicate their nature and authority.

As these lines reveal, the play's treatment of noble ranks applies to the monarch. Stage directions include '*the King*' throughout *Edward II*, but in dialogue the plural 'kings' appears ten times while the non-restrictive 'a king' occurs a striking twenty-two times. Use of the indefinite article makes dramatic sense, since Edward struggles, like Shakespeare's Richard II and Henry VI, to embody a degree that he will forfeit, prompting such utterances as 'what are kings, when regiment is gone?' (5.1.26) or 'I was better when a king.'[30] Peele's *The Troublesome Reign of King John*, with its contending monarchs, employs 'kings' even more frequently in dialogue and uses 'a king' twenty-one times. Shakespeare's *3 Henry VI* provides comparable numbers for 'kings', but *Edward II* markedly exceeds each of Shakespeare's roughly contemporary histories, *2 Henry VI*, *3 Henry VI*, *Richard III* and *Richard II*, in its frequent use of 'a king'. The frequency of collective designations for the other degrees of the *nobilitas maior* – peers, earls, nobles or noblemen, lords and barons – appears particularly remarkable when *Edward II* is compared to roughly contemporary plays.[31]

However, it is not mere frequency but the ironies, and often extended ironies, of usage that matter in *Edward II*'s treatment of its nobles. Eight scenes after Gaveston's opening speech, for example, his exact self-denomination as 'the favourite of a king' returns at the fatal moment of his sentencing (9.27). In this wholly invented sequence, '*The nobles*' (9.7sd) first discuss the mode of death for their prisoner and insult him with typical epithets: 'proud disturber of thy country's peace, /Corrupter of thy King', 'Base flatterer', 'Monster of men', 'slave' and likeness of 'the Greekish strumpet' (9.9–19). Such terms may be predictable by this point in the play, but nomenclature and usage surrounding and implicating recognized degrees inflect the episode with odd conforming transgressions.

Just before 'soldiers' are ordered to kill Gaveston, recalling the poor 'soldier' who first bids him 'perish by a soldier's hand', Mortimer Junior surprisingly refuses to kill Gaveston precisely because doing so would bring 'shame– / Shame and dishonour to a soldier's name' (9.11–12). This sounds particularly odd coming from a character who twice contemplates and once co-operates in attacking Gaveston with his sword (2.8; 4.423; 6.83). It is even odder given that 'disdain' for Gaveston did not earlier prevent 'the mighty prince of Lancaster' (3.1) from enlisting his own sword in Mortimer Junior's assaults (6.78). Despite Lancaster's nobility, armed affront in the royal presence would have constituted a 'riotous deed', though such violent outbursts could invoke justifications in terms of martial honour, a confluence of group values claimed by the nobility and asserting a right to moral autonomy.[32] Yet, Mortimer Junior protests that the name of 'a soldier[]' prevents his killing Gaveston. This apparent inconsistency suggests still another available notion of nobility which could maintain – when convenient – that it might disparage a lord to employ arms against a commoner.[33] Such self-restriction appears objectively absurd in this instance, since '*the great Earle of* Cornewall' (Q2 1598 title page) would outrank Mortimer and his uncle, mere barons, in everything – except perhaps in recognition by the nobility.[34] In such twists and turns cultural terms and values that might otherwise be taken for granted solicit further scrutiny.

In light of other features of the play, this moment makes a – twisted but nevertheless recuperable – sense: here, as elsewhere, actions, words or gestures implicating degree may signify variably according to differing social contexts. Thus, Mortimer Junior is eager to use his sword against Gaveston except when *not* to do so would constitute a greater disparagement. Thomas Cartelli offers that Mortimer refuses to turn his sword on Gaveston because it is 'too suggestive of sodomitic contamination'; I am claiming instead that such an act is too suggestive of social assimilation.[35]

The bearing of rank on this sequence becomes further evident as the Earl of Warwick proceeds to issue blatantly self-contradictory orders regarding Gaveston's execution, while Gaveston himself displays surprisingly deferential punctiliousness:

156   EDWARD II

WARWICK	Lancaster, why talk'st thou to the slave?
	Go, soldiers, take him hence; for by my sword,
	His head shall off. Gaveston, short warning
	Shall serve thy turn; it is our country's cause
	That here severely we will execute
	Upon thy person: hang him at a bough!
GAVESTON	My lord –
WARWICK	Soldiers, have him away.
	But for thou wert the favourite of a king,
	Thou shalt have so much honour at our hands.
	[*He gestures to indicate beheading*]
GAVESTON	I thank you all, my lords; then I perceive
	That heading is one, and hanging is the other,
	And death is all. (9.21–31)

Swearing by his sword, and insultingly silencing Lancaster, Warwick commands beheading, reverses himself, orders hanging, and then relents to direct an unnamed mode of execution. Editors have speculated that Warwick's ultimate, re-revised death order may be conveyed by a gesture, but even without such prompting, 'Soldiers' might understand the mode of death betokening 'so much honour'. That is, the crux may depend on tacit recognition of noble status as entitling Gaveston to beheading rather than the hanging proper to the non-noble.[36] Mortimer Junior sarcastically invokes this same distinction when he taunts Spencer Senior with 'Your lordship cannot privilege your head' (18.79), a joke that could compound its ironies in light of Mortimer's own notorious death by hanging.[37] Yet in fact, Warwick articulates the 'honour' not on the basis of Gaveston's recognized degree, but solely upon his being one who 'wert the favourite of a king'. As his insulting familiar usage emphasizes, Warwick never here employs a single epithet, title, vocative or pronominal that would recognize the claims or even the existence of any rank whatsoever pertaining to Gaveston. It is as if to use them would burn his tongue.

Warwick's surprising leniency, moreover, is articulated in a highly suspect way. He adopts regal usage, employing self-referential plurals ('we will execute', 'at our hands') and kingly command ('Thou shalt'). Elsewhere such locutions signal the ambitions of Mortimer Junior (18.44; 23.101). Thus, while denying Gaveston any recognized degree, Warwick edges himself up the ladder. To echo Mortimer Junior's attack on Gaveston, it is Warwick (as later Mortimer Junior himself) who begins to *over-peer* (4.19) his fellow nobles.[38] In fact, even his rapid changes of mind and arbitrary award of 'honour' to Gaveston mime royal prerogatives exercised by King Edward, not only in handing out 'honours' but in violating chrono-normative standards of nobly deliberate consistency.[39]

Gaveston's own utterances, by contrast, consistently observe the expected timing, forms and titles appropriate to the nobility of his interlocutors. Awaiting Warwick's sentence before responding, Gaveston addresses 'my lord' and thanks 'my lords' collectively. Yet to read this respectful invocation of respected titles as going back on his resolution never to stoop to 'lordly peers' would be to miss the way the play inflects terms of respect and entitlement to function contextually as insults: Gaveston thanks his 'lords', in essence, *for nothing*, since, as he points out, what he thanks them for amounts to a distinction without difference.

If the ironies implicating rank were not already complex enough within this sequence, ultimately, Gaveston's beheading registers contempt rather than 'honour' since he dies 'in a trench' by Warwick's 'ambush', a 'bloody' act that Spencer Junior and King Edward judge 'flatly against law of arms' (11.118–21; 13.18). Thus, when the anonymous soldier's play-opening curse finally comes home to rest, it does so, thanks to Marlowe's re-imagination of Gaveston's assassination, with a nobleman's self-violation of foundational values of nobility.[40] In murdering Gaveston, 'Guy of Warwick, that redoubted knight' (3.4), noted for 'silver hairs' of reverend wisdom (4.347), betrays his oaths and bonds to fellow peers. The treachery he himself calls 'wit and policy' (9.96) others deem 'dishonour to [him]self' (10.8).[41] Warwick's betrayal of his own rank is further compounded by the flippant mock he dictates to his 'honourable friend', the Earl of Pembroke: 'Commend me to your master, / My friend, and tell him that I watched it well' (10.9, 12–13).[42]

Thus, Warwick becomes the 'Treacherous Earl' that Marlowe's Gaveston calls him, but history's Gaveston called Warwick names far worse than 'Earl'; or rather, names that would have been worse outside the context provided by the play's insinuations concerning established titles. Although Marlowe clearly alters his sources to lend point to the baronial attacks on Gaveston's status, he simultaneously de-fangs Gaveston's notorious insults directed toward the nobles, rendering titles of respect as functional insults. Holinshed's Gaveston 'called the earle of Glocester bastard, the earle of Lincolne latelie deceased bursten bellie, the earle of Warwike the blacke hound of Arderne, and the earle of Lancaster churle' (6:321). These terms attack key points of noble self-definition: lineage, warlike physical prowess, bodily elegance and gentility. Other slurs (drawn upon by Drayton) call Lancaster and Pembroke 'the stage player' and 'Ioseph the Iew', adding hypocrisy and alien cultural identity to the attacks and thus resonating with insults that Marlowe's barons direct at the 'sly inveigling Frenchman' (2.57) and at Edward and his troops who march 'like players' (6.180). By contrast, Marlowe's Gaveston often grants the nobles respectable terms, letting strategic modifiers, or even silence, perform the work of insult.

In the first scene, despite having informed the audience that he 'abhor[s]' the Earl of Lancaster and 'that villain' Mortimer Senior (1.75, 80), Gaveston speaks rather differently about them to Kent:

Edmund, the mighty prince of Lancaster,
That hath more earldoms than an ass can bear,
And both the Mortimers, two goodly men,
With Guy of Warwick, that redoubted knight,
Are gone towards Lambeth; there let them remain. (3.1–5)

Opening with a triple compliment – acknowledging Lancaster's *might*, the multiple *earldoms* of which he himself boasts (1.101) and the 'princely born' status he proudly shares with the king (4.81) – Gaveston then allows the lords Mortimer to be 'goodly', and lauds Warwick, the 'redoubted knight', as the nobles elsewhere title themselves ('valiant knights' [9.16]). So what exactly conveys what some consider Gaveston's 'gay contemptuousness' and 'superb insouciance'?[43]

The context of hostility and the comparison to the slavish ass are relevant, but there is more than the obvious here.[44] One of the play's repeated motifs is the act of recognizing that denies the claims of what is recognized by virtue of the form in which the recognition is given utterance. Thus, the ostensibly positive 'goodly' may express condescension or a title may insult. For instance, the single time that Baldock is exactly entitled 'chancellor', Isabella, having first insultingly omitted his title – 'Baldock is with the king' – immediately adds, as if on second thought, 'A goodly chancellor, is he not, my lord?' (18.52–3). Speedy correction emphasizes the initial omission, and respectable entitlement is qualified by interrogative form and by the slippery adjective 'goodly'.[45]

This still frames analysis too simply, since any move to type, to class, may be demeaning even in exactly invoked titles. Here Baldock is 'a' chancellor, as Edward is initially 'a' king, neither determined by a definite article. So, too, in Gaveston's utterance, the 'Lord Mortimer of Chirke' (4.358) and the lord Mortimer of Wigmore (6.193) are compactly grouped as 'Mortimers' rather than individuated.[46] Similar grouping may be obviously demeaning when coupled with use of titles. When Mortimer Junior refers to 'a night-grown mushroom – / Such a one as my lord of Cornwall is', he doubles down on his insult by coupling the formally correct version of Gaveston's title by categorizing him among others who are 'such a one as' he (4.284–5). For his part, Gaveston addresses the needy soldier as 'sir' while dismissing 'such as you' (1.34–5). Furthermore, Gaveston's mock praises for 'the Mortimers' and the earls employs a hyperbolic Spenserism

– 'that redoubted knight' – to exaggerate an epithet the nobles use for themselves.[47] Strikingly, silver-haired Warwick, the character who joins other Marlovian Machiavels in admiring his own 'wit and policy' (9.96), is awarded Spenser's epithet for young Red Cross. Finally, Gaveston's utterance concludes by dismissing his opponents from Court in a regal phrase that lumps together earls, barons and clerical peers as 'them': 'there let them remain'.

The features of utterance which here serve to both recognize established social identities of rank, degree and office while also de-legitimizing them work in both directions: from the nobles toward the upstarts, as from the upstarts toward the nobles, offering in linguistic form an understated version of Daniel's, Drayton's and Camden's infectious imitation. The most striking instance of such conforming transgression occurs when the nobles simultaneously recognize and de-recognize Gaveston's titles. Introducing the sequence by announcing Gaveston's arrival with punctiliously correct form, 'look where his lordship comes' (6.49), the Earl of Lancaster then joins the other peers in a corporate silence, followed by a bizarre acclamation:

EDWARD	Will none of you salute my Gaveston?
LANCASTER	Salute him? Yes! Welcome, Lord Chamberlain.
MORTIMER JUNIOR	Welcome is the good Earl of Cornwall.
WARWICK	Welcome, Lord Governor of the Isle of Man.
PEMBROKE	Welcome, Master Secretary. (6.64–8)

These nominally positive salutes prompt angry reaction:

KENT	Brother, do you hear them?
EDWARD	Still will these earls and barons use me thus!
GAVESTON	My lord, I cannot brook these injuries. (6.69–71)

And backed with Edward's 'warrant', Gaveston responds with insults that provoke riotous violence:

GAVESTON	Base leaden earls that glory in your birth,
	Go sit at home and eat your tenants' beef,
	And come not here to scoff at Gaveston,
	Whose mounting thoughts did never creep so low
	As to bestow a look on such as you.
LANCASTER	Yet I disdain not to do this for you.
	[*Draws his sword.*] (6.74–9)

Like the lords themselves, Gaveston invokes the degree of his adversaries, his obvious contempt registered only in the modifiers 'Base leaden' and 'low'. There is more to say, however. The noble seats from which good lordship and hospitality should be actively dispensed become the sites of non-courtly exile to which Gaveston commands them 'Go' and 'sit', exploiting their tenants.[48] Their diet itself conveys old-fashioned Englishness.[49] Furthermore, Gaveston responds only to the 'earls' who share his own degree, ignoring the merely baronial Mortimer Junior, and he deploys the dismissive collective, 'such as you'. This replays Gaveston's opening dismissal of the poor soldier with the uselessness of 'such as you' (1.34). It also replicates noble contempt for 'any such upstart' as Gaveston (4.424) and 'such friends' as he might buy for himself (4.259), or 'such pernicious upstarts' as the Spencers and Baldock and 'such as you are' (11.165; 19.113).

But what exactly makes the nobles' uninflected salutes to Gaveston register as 'injuries', ill 'use' and 'scoff'? After all, Pembroke's 'punctilious' greeting has been cited for its lack of 'class-hostility'.[50] As in Isabella's mock entitlement of Baldock, delay plays a part; but choric and exhaustive declamation may also convey contempt. These formal elements assert the lords' group prerogative to withhold or grant recognition, but they further corporately and collectively mimic the royal prerogative of abrupt, arbitrary and excessive bestowal that Edward himself exercises so egregiously. The nobles verbally ape the power of 'kingly regiment' to bestow multiple titles upon whomever it may 'please' (1.164), 'merely of our love', and to do so specifically to show 'despite of' others (11.145–7).[51] Their rapid-fire iteration exactly mimes Edward's sudden grants of title upon title to Gaveston, 'I here create thee Lord High Chamberlain, / Chief Secretary to the state and me, / Earl of Cornwall, King and Lord of Man', and its addition to boot of gold, guards, the royal seal and 'What so thy mind affects or fancy likes' (1.153–69). The lords also anticipate Edward's grants to Spencer Junior, first creating him 'Earl of Wiltshire', with 'crowns of us, t'outbid the barons' (11.49–55) in estate acquisition, before ecstatically elevating him even further: 'Spencer, sweet Spencer, I adopt thee here; / And merely of our love we do create thee / Earl of Gloucester and Lord Chamberlain, / Despite of times, despite of enemies' (11.144–7).

In sum, the lords mock kingly practice by imitating it, expressing 'despite' in acclamation. Yet when the king directs 'love' their way, 'these nobles' (4.338) greet with utmost respect the royal behaviour here mocked. Precisely repeating the sequences in which he receives and elevates 'sweet' Gaveston or later 'sweet Spencer' (1.139–55; 11.144–7), Edward raises the kneeling lords, commands 'embrace' and grants offices. First, 'Courageous Lancaster' is commanded, 'embrace thy King … . Live thou with me as my companion' (4.341–4); then 'Sweet' Warwick is named 'chiefest counsellor' (4.346); Pembroke is ordered to 'bear the sword' immediately 'before the King' (4.352). Finally, the pouting Mortimer Junior is granted that very freedom of choice which Edward first bestows on Gaveston, who is offered 'What so thy mind affects or fancy likes' (1.169); Edward creates, then recreates, Mortimer till Mortimer finds an office he might 'like':

> But wherefore walks young Mortimer aside?
> Be thou commander of our royal fleet,
> Or if that lofty office like thee not,
> I make thee here Lord Marshal of the realm. (4.3547)

The off-handed reshuffle of 'lofty' offices is breathtaking, but one has seen it before. Furthermore, this episode ends with serial ironies that reveal 'love', lavish entertainments, self-indulgence and casual bestowal of honors to be ingrained in the culture of the court rather than specific to Edward's relations with 'sweet Gaveston' (4.48) or with 'Sweet Spencer, gentle Baldock' (19.95).

Who apes whom? Does Edward mock the nobles as the nobles mocked Gaveston, by giving them exactly what they feel entitled to get, but in a way that cheapens the giving? The nobles do not detect any ironies the way Gaveston registers their mockery of him. Instead, Isabella affirms Edward's lavish bestowal of offices to be requited by a 'love of his renownèd peers' that makes 'the King of England rich and strong' (4.367–8). The sequence then rapidly replays corporately and collectively Edward's intimate relationships with his favourites: Edward invites his 'sweet' noble companions 'Now let us in and feast it royally'; orders 'tilt and tournament' with 'Spare no cost; we will requite your love'; and commands 'gentle Warwick' to 'come, let's in and revel' (4.375–86). This joyful celebration of a 'love' relationship with banquets, revels, largesse and lavish display that is said to make Edward 'rich and strong', exactly mirrors and inverts Mortimer Junior's attack on Edward for 'idle triumphs' and 'prodigal gifts bestowed on Gaveston' that have 'drawn thy treasure dry and made thee weak' (6.154–6).[52] While one might categorize the former as 'public' and the latter as 'private' matters, the relationship between the monarch and his nobles is clearly portrayed as self-interested – and disorderly.[53] The sequences illuminate one another, but importantly this competitive consumption crosses a divide between noble and non-noble, where words and things may change their meanings.

III

The lords call Gaveston many insulting names, but when Mortimer Junior calls him 'thief', Gaveston's objection elicits an explanation, or rather, a translation:

GAVESTON	How meanst thou, Mortimer? That is over-base!
MORTIMER JUNIOR	Away, base groom, robber of kings' renown. Question with thy companions and thy mates. (9.71–3)

As 'base groom' rather than 'true man', Gaveston has stolen the credit that belongs collectively to the royal estate of 'kings'. Here, Marlowe understates and Mortimer overstates.[54] On the one hand, Gaveston's worst enemy tacitly omits actual theft from Gaveston's offences. On the other, Mortimer denies what he elsewhere grudgingly acknowledges – Gaveston's gentle birth. Though Mortimer's acknowledgement renders the term 'gentleman' insulting, he does, amid his usual vilifications ('base peasant' and 'base villain'), grant Gaveston to be 'hardly' – that is barely or merely – 'a gentleman by birth' (4.7–29).[55] In other words, Mortimer, who occupies the lowest recognized *noble* degree, as a mere baron and thus 'hardly' noble, perhaps indeed 'the meanest nobleman' among earls and 'princely' earls, dares to delimit the *royal* rank of 'kings' above him and to disdain the highest *non-noble* degree, that of born gentlemen, below him, and to speak thus to one who has been elevated above him as Earl of Cornwall.

When Edward first creates Gaveston a 'new earl', placing him in the place appropriate to the Queen with 'we will have it so', the Earl of Lancaster protests that Edward 'may not thus disparage us', and the baron Mortimer Senior demands, 'What man of noble birth can brook this sight?' (4.9–12, 32). Thus, from highest to lowest degree, the nobles define 'us' by 'noble birth', excluding one born merely 'a gentleman'. To 'disparage' meant to undervalue but also to dishonour by marrying unequally. In advancing a bare gentleman, Edward enforces upon 'us that be his peers' (2.42) an unequal, degrading union, effectively dis-peering the nobles by over-peering Gaveston. Related contentions involve the other 'upstarts'.

As the nobles attempt to seize Edward, the Spencers face off against Lancaster and Pembroke over just who are the real 'traitors'. Lancaster's admonishment bidding Edward to forsake them 'For they'll betray thee, traitors as they are', prompts a combative exchange:

SPENCER JUNIOR	Traitor on thy face, rebellious Lancaster.
PEMBROKE	Away, base upstart; brav'st thou nobles thus?
SPENCER SENIOR	A noble attempt and honourable deed Is it not, trow ye, to assemble aid And levy arms against your lawful King? (12.18–24)

Pembroke never answers the charge of treason, but reflexively speaks for 'nobles', deploying the same classifying terms previously directed at 'base' Gaveston.[56] The factitiousness of this disparagement of Spencer is emphasized by the onstage presence of *'noblemen of the King's side'* (12.0sd) and Spencer's *'old'* father bearing the *'truncheon'* of command over his attending *'soldiers'* (11.31sd). Obviously 'well allied' (6.246), Spencer Junior and his father pointedly translate Pembroke's terms back across the divide between the self-recognizing nobility and everyone else by questioning master terms of 'noble' hegemony. Their 'deed', treasonously levying arms against their 'lawful king', contradicts their birth claim to be 'noble' and 'honourable'.[57]

Finally, to turn away from 'great' earls and peers, there remain the last moments of the play's lowliest-born main character. The historical Baldock, like Marlowe himself, could claim 'gentry' by academic pedigree, but the play's Baldock, who affirms 'my gentry / I fetched from Oxford, not from heraldry' (6.240–1), is left undistinguished by the degree of Bachelor of Civil Law that would render him, by most early modern definitions, 'gentle' and entitled at least to address as an esquire.[58] Instead, Marlowe's Baldock initially appears reduced to household tutoring (5.29–30), to exaggerated verbal and bodily deference, a straitened wardrobe (5.46–9) and menial functions such as saying grace at the lower end of the table or running trivial errands (5.37, 71–3). Although later called a 'smooth-tongued scholar' (18.66), Marlowe's needy tutor initially requires tutoring in conducting himself 'like a gentleman' rather than like 'common pedants' (5.32, 52).[59]

Despite having attained the exalted office of Lord Chancellor, Baldock is arrested by Leicester without title: 'Spencer and Baldock, by no other names, / I arrest you of high treason here. / Stand not on titles, but obey th'arrest' (19.56–8).[60] But even when he is addressed in terms befitting his learning and office, Baldock is mocked. No sooner does Baldock conclude his final valedictories of Edward and Spencer (19.104–11) by urging 'new life' in heaven, proverbial 'lessons' concerning 'nature's debt' and a resigned *de casibus* couplet about rising to fall, than Rhys Ap Howell caps his attempted eloquence with a withering, literally prosaic response: 'Come, come, keep these preachments till you come to the place appointed. You, and such as you are, have made wise work in England. Will your lordships away?' (19.112–14).[61]

Rhys's 'Come, come' not only violates the chrono-normativity of deference demanded by exalted office, but he proceeds to unleash the powers of understatement in mock-recognition and classification one last time. Dismissing Baldock's rhetorical flights as 'preachments' indecorous outside 'the place appointed', Rhys reduces clerical calling to cliché-mongering while turning the cleric's 'appointed place' into a joke as the pulpit morphs into the scaffold appointed for the condemned.[62] Academic distinction appears in Rhys's ironic praise for Baldock's 'wise work'. Finally, Baldock's 'lordship' is scorned in its very naming, as Rhys employs a formula of address mandated by the favourites' high offices, deferentially bidding them to their doom with grimly solicitous courtesy – 'Will your lordships away?' (19.114).⁶³ Ultimately, Baldock and Spencer leave the play reduced to a nameless category: 'You, and such as you are'.⁶⁴

IV

'Such as you are' – that insulting refusal to grant a name resonates with the play's intense interest in recognized, un-recognized and mis-recognized classifications and their uses. This interest is perhaps relatable to social categories, both recognized and elusive, that appear in traces surrounding the playwright in the years of the writing, performing and publication of *Edward II*. The initial printed text of *Edward II*, after all, is the first – and until 1619 the only – English history play proclaiming authorship by a 'gentleman' ('Chri. Marlowe, Gent').⁶⁵ Objectively, this claim rests on the same grounds as Baldock's initial claim to 'gentry ... fetch[ed] from Oxford, not from heraldry'.⁶⁶ However, Baldock rises beyond 'apocrasate' (apocryphal) gentleman to Lord Chancellor; properly addressed as his 'lordship', Baldock could claim arms and precedence over non-royal earls and barons.⁶⁷ This dizzying social trajectory could have inspired fantasies of upward mobility, status recognition and tragic martyrdom for a playwriting university-man-on-the-make. But instead of ending with Faustus's tragic grandeur, the Lord Chancellor of England leaves the stage an object of condescending jokes that offer cool, precisely-tailored conforming transgressions, sarcastically recognizing his 'lordship's' calling, precedence and 'wise' learning.

Marlowe's own 'gentry' is subject to some uncertainties in the years immediately surrounding the writing of *Edward II*. Although he had acquired the title 'Dominus' or 'sir' in college documents of 1584, Marlowe's arrest record from 18

September 1589 labels him 'yoman', differentiating him from Thomas Watson 'generosus' (gentleman).[68] This sub-gentle classification might have been accurate enough – as it would be for Ben Jonson 'yeoman' in 1598 – absent Marlowe's advanced degrees; however, his release on 1 October 1589 denotes him 'generoso'[69] Just why Marlowe was initially classed as Watson's social inferior presents a puzzle, since Marlowe and Watson, though residents of the same down-at-the-heels neighbourhood, could both assert scholarly credentials. Was Marlowe less elegant, less articulate, less convincingly 'gentle' than Watson?[70] Nor is it clear what other than his academic attainment could have effected the correction of Marlowe's rank to 'generoso', although David Riggs suggests the substantial bail posted by two rate-payers, one gentle, could have credentialed his gentility by demonstrating connections with the better sort.[71]

Marlowe certainly invokes his educational status when arrested in Flushing in 1592. Sir Robert Sidney records that Marlowe professed himself 'a scholer', adding that Marlowe claimed to be 'very wel known both to the Earle of Northumberland and my lord Strang'.[72] This evidence, along with that provided by Marlowe's Latin dedication to Mary Sidney Herbert, Countess of Pembroke, of Watson's *Amintae Gaudia* (S.R. 10 November 1592), suggests attempting to profit from noble associations. Marlowe's fulsome dedication urges the Countess to 'receive and watch over' one who is 'Most desirous to do [her] honour'.[73] The poem further praises her for a 'sincerity of mind which Jove the father of men and of gods hath linked as hereditary to thy noble family'. Is *Edward II*'s ironic treatment of hereditary nobility simply at odds with such nearly concurrent attempts to assert noble association and enlist noble patronage?

It has been claimed that *Edward II* singles out the Earl of Pembroke as 'the only English aristocrat [it] portrays in a favourable light' (Riggs, 282). Although such selective portrayal could have served Marlowe's evident needs by flattering one who may have been the patron of the play's actors, 'the right honourable the Earle of Pembrooke his seruants' (Q1), and by anticipating his bid for patronage from the Countess, I do not find this claim convincing. Pembroke fits right in with the play's other aristocrats: wishing Gaveston dead (4.253), plotting his murder (4.293), insulting him (6.68) and berating Spencer in their collective behalf, with 'Away, base upstart; brav'st thou nobles thus?' (12.21). His single act of ostensible 'honour' – the attempt to spare Gaveston – ends in disgraceful failure for trivial, and wholly invented, reasons when Pembroke cavalierly abandons his post with 'We that have pretty wenches to our wives, / Sir, must not come so near and balk their lips' (9.102–3). If Pembroke were exceptional, then the play could easily be assimilated to a familiar rhetorical strategy – distinguishing 'true' nobility from false – and to an equally familiar historical narrative about Marlowe's generation of economically superfluous, university-educated writers pursuing noble patronage rather than barely viable clerical positions or turning, like Watson, to tutoring.[74] So why might Marlowe forego the opportunity to praise the Pembroke name, and why cheapen the very idea of hereditary nobility that he extols to the Countess of Pembroke?[75]

Leaving aside the usual narratives about the social resentments of Marlowe's literary generation or about Marlowe's own social, political or psycho-sexual alienation, I offer one more notional socio-genesis for the play's stylistic sensitivity to conforming transgressions implicating degree. Whatever the scholarship boy might have experienced among wealthy and entitled students at Cambridge, Marlowe's experience of family and neighbourhood could also have contributed to forming a *habitus* keenly attuned to conforming transgression. Accounts have often emphasized economic and social negatives when discussing the playwright's father.[76] Yet despite humble origins and recurring financial insecurities, John Marlowe was a literate and by many measures substantial Canterbury figure, distinguished by professional and community offices: Searcher (inspector) for the Company of Shoemakers (1581–2); Warden Treasurer of the Company (1589); Sidesman for St George the Martyr (1573) and St Andrew (1578); Churchwarden for St Mary Bredin (or Breadman) (1591–4); and Constable of Westgate (1591–2). He frequently appears as a juryman, bondsman or witness for weddings, christenings and burials. On at least one occasion in August 1585, Christopher accompanied him in an official function (Urry, 28–9); there must have been other such occasions during John Marlowe's long career. Though lacking the birth, wealth, land and leisure sufficient to climb much higher in the social ladder, John Marlowe, as William Urry puts it, 'hover[ed] about the edge of greater men's affairs', often in positions of considerable trust (Urry, 26). His roles as Sidesman and Churchwarden suggest particular relevance to the combination of recognition and ironic distance regarding rank that this chapter has traced.

The substantial responsibilities of Sidesmen (assistant Churchwardens) and Churchwardens included the Wardens' duties to look after the church's material condition, to provide parish soldiers with arms, and to offer – unlike the play's Gaveston – relief to maimed veterans, roles that demanded considerable out of pocket expenses.[77] But of most relevance to our argument, both positions entailed the obligation and the power to correct and to seat parishioners in church 'according to their own conceptions of status and reputation'. These offices required a capacity to make difficult multi-factorial social evaluations; understandably, they entailed routine exposure to verbal and even physical abuse.[78] Attacks by irate parishioners upon Churchwardens and upon one another over seating arrangements are extensively documented.[79] These fights are all about degree and status, often invoking birth, family position and disparagement.

For all its inconveniences and risks, the Warden's office signalled its holder as 'somebody' in the parish. While Sir Thomas Smith condescended to Wardens as 'lowe and base persons' with 'no voice nor authoritie', in fact, the Wardens' office was part of the accepted London '*cursus honorum* of local office and could be a prerequisite for serving in higher offices'; in the village, Godfrey Goodman claims, 'a sufficient man; one that is able to do the King and country good seruice, wee make him a Constable, a Sides-man, a Head-borough, and at length a Church-warden: thus wee raise him by degrees'.[80]

This elevation 'by degrees' did not entail gentle standing, which makes it interesting that most litigation over seating involved 'middle and upper ranks of the local community', and disproportionately those of gentle status.[81] Thus, John Marlowe had to be prepared to intervene in disputes involving his 'betters' in an urban parish, where mobility could make determining the relative status of disputants particularly challenging. Furthermore, among the behaviours that had to be adjudicated were verbal and physical strategies of utterance such as this chapter has traced. Besides blows and rude gestures, antagonistic competitions for standing were sometimes registered by keeping a hat on or by omitting proper titles of address. Perhaps most relevantly, parish antagonisms could appear as mock deference. For example, Abraham Comyns is reported for having over-acted subservience by means of gestures that might otherwise have expressed respect, treating George Badcock 'gent' as follows: 'as he came into the church neere to Mr Badcocke's stoole or pue, Comyn made a low obeisance with his head bowed towards the ground before Mr Badcock's pue (he being then in it) and afterwards once or twice more did the like obeysance in way of derision to Mr Badcock, laughing in his face which moved a great part of the congregation to laughter'.[82] Or for a conforming transgression of title, Thomas Clement 'laughing said to [the minister] if it like your worship or your lordship if you will, mockingly after such time as he called him lord'.[83] John Marlowe may never have had to intervene in cases precisely like these, but perhaps young Christopher, on his way to becoming a 'gent', could extrapolate from such behavioural raw materials to a drama that would pit established nobles and upstart gentry against one another, each mocking the other as 'your lordships' or 'redoubted knight[s]', while 'a king' proves incapable of restraining them or the conforming transgressions through which they express their reciprocal resentments.

Table 1 Word Frequencies: Edward II and Selected Contemporary Plays[1]

	E2	1C	TR	1H6	2H6	3H6	R2	R3	TR3	E1	R3F	E3	TRJ	KJ	J4	ST	JS	T1	T2	DF	MP
Kings	10	3	6	4	5	9	7	5	2	10	5	8	20	15	7	10	7	26	20	5	1
vocative	0	0	0	0	1	1	0	0	0	0	0	0	6	5	1	0	0	6	7	0	0
SDD	0	0	0	0	0	0	0	0	0	0	0	0	2	1	2	1	0	2	3	0	0
A king	22	2	15	13	6	15	9	6	9	4	7	9	21	5	9	1	10	10	11	0	6
A king's	2	0	0	0	0	0	0	0	1	1	0	0	1	1	0	0	0	0	0	1	0
Gentlemen[2]	0	1	1	3	3	1	1	2	1	3	2	1	0	1	5	1	0	3	0	0	1
Vocative	0	0	1	4	0	1	4	8	4	1	9	1	2	0	3	3	0	0	0	8	0
SDD	0	0	0	0	0	0	0	0	0	0	0	0	0	0	0	0	1	0	0	0	0
Gentle[3]	23	6	17	8	10	20	13	21	1	20	27	5	2	15	16	8	2	4	3	1	3
Gentleman	5	1	1	4	3	2	8	6	4	4	6	0	1	4	16	1	6[4]	0	1	3	0
Earls	7	3	1	0	2	1	0	0	0	0	0	0	1	0	0	0	0	0	0	0	0
vocative	2	0	0	0	0	0	0	1	0	0	1	0	0	0	0	0	0	0	0	0	0
SDD	0	4	1	0	1	0	0	0	0	0	0	0	3	0	0	0	0	0	0	0	0
Barons	14	1	0	0	1	0	0	0	0	5[5]	0	1	9	0	0	0	0	0	0	0	0
vocative	1	0	0	0	0	0	0	0	0	4	0	0	4	0	0	0	0	0	0	0	0
SDD	3	0	0	0	0	0	0	0	0	3	0	0	1	0	0	0	0	0	0	0	0

	E2	1C	TR	1H6	2H6	3H6	R2	R3	TR3	E1	R3F	E3	TRJ	KJ	J4	ST	JS	T1	T2	DF	MP
Peers	13	5	1	4	7	2	1	3	13	4	3	5	5	3	1	0	0	0	2	0	0
vocative	1	2	0	1	2	0	1	3	2	3	4	2	3	0	4	0	0	0	2	0	0
SDD	0	0	0	0	0	0	0	0	0	0	0	0	0	0	0	0	0	0	0	0	0
Nobles[6]	11	0	0	3	2	0	2	1	5	2	1	0	8	2	5	0	3	3	0	1	2
vocative	0	0	0	0	1	0	0	0	2	4	0	0	0	2	1	0	0	0	0	0	0
SDD	8	0	0	0	0	0	2	1	0	0	1	0	3	0	1	1	1	0	0	0	0
Lords	11	2	4	7	5	5	4	2	1	7	2	5	6	8	5	0	5	6	2	1	1
vocative	31	21	29	33	31	39	13	12	11	23	14	13	42	5	6	9	11	10	10	0	18
SDD	1	0	0	0	0	0	1	4	0	5	2	0	6	2	2	0	0	3	1	0	1

Abbreviations:

E2 = *Edward II* (1594)
1C = *The First Part of the Contention* (1594)
TR = *True Tragedy of Richard, Duke of York* (1595)
1H6 = *Henry VI, Part One* (1623)
2H6 = *Henry VI, Part Two* (1623)
3H6 = *Henry VI, Part Three* (1623)
R2 = *Richard II*, Q1 (1597)
R3 = *Richard III*, Q1 (1597)
TR3 = *True Tragedy of Richard III* (1594)
E1 = *Edward I* (1593)
R3F = *Richard III* (1623)
E3 = *Edward III* (1596)
TRJ = *The Troublesome Reign of King John* (1592)
KJ = *King John* (1623)
J4 = *Scottish History of James IV* (1598)
ST = *Spanish Tragedy* (1592)
JS = *Jack Straw* (1593)
T1 = *Tamburlaine, Part 1* (1590)
T2 = *Tamburlaine, Part 2* (1590)
DF = *Doctor Faustus* (1604)
MP = *Massacre at Paris* (1596?)

Notes

1. Speech Prefixes (e.g., 'Lords' in R3F), singular 'gentlewoman' and 'Lordship' and 'lordships' are not included in totals. *First Part of the Contention* from Oxford Text Archive (OTA), checked against Early English Books Online (EEBO); all other texts from EEBO TCP1 and TCP2. Table includes variant forms throughout: 'kings'/'kinges'; 'nobles'/'nobiles'; 'lords'/'lordes'; 'peeres'/'peares'; etc.
2. 'Gentlemen' includes plural forms: 'gentle men', 'gentlefolks', 'gentlewomen', 'gentles'.
3. 'Gentle' includes 'Ungentle,' and also includes adjectival modifiers that are non-human in reference.
4. 'Gentleman' (*Jack Straw*) includes 2 titles as 'gentleman usher' in SD.
5. 'Barons' (*Edward I*) includes 2 references to 'the barons warres'.
6. 'Nobles' includes 'noble men' but does not include the currency ('nobles').

7

'My Life, My Company': Amity, Enmity and Vitality in *Edward II*

Garrett A. Sullivan, Jr.

In recent years, vitality has emerged as a major critical concern within early modern studies. Some scholars, inspired by the work of Michel Foucault and Giorgio Agamben, have taken up life from the perspective of biopolitics and political theology;[1] others have argued for literary character as a form of artificial life;[2] while still others interested in the history of embodiment have attended both to relations among plant, animal and human life and to the slippery distinction between the living and non-living.[3] Christopher Marlowe has had a role to play in these critical conversations.[4] And yet, scholars have only started to grapple with Marlowe's profound engagement with the category of vitality.[5] *Edward II* in particular explores numerous different ways in which life might be conceptualized.

That the category of life might *need* conceptualizing will likely appear strange to some. After all, the difference between the animate and inanimate would seem to be obvious. And yet, as philosophers and cultural critics have pointed out, almost all definitions of life prove profoundly inadequate. Ferris Jabr notes this in a 2014 editorial in the *New York Times*:

> Some things we regard as inanimate are capable of some of the processes we want to make exclusive of life. And some things we say are alive get along just fine without some of these processes. Yet we have insisted that all matter naturally segregates into two categories—life and nonlife—and have searched in vain for the dividing line … . We must accept that the concept of life sometimes has its pragmatic value for our particular human purposes, but it does not reflect the reality of the universe outside the mind.[6]

Jabr invites us to recognize the ontological fallacy of the life-concept: there is no vital principle – whether it is soul, spark or breath – that is shared by every animate thing. Despite this, different life-concepts obviously have cultural currency in different sociohistorical contexts. Indeed, the category of life has throughout history migrated beyond the boundaries of biological existence and across various discourses, including religious, political and poetic ones. This is how, to offer one familiar example, John Milton can claim that 'books contain a potencie of life in them'.[7] If life is ontologically void or variable, it is also culturally powerful. Moreover, vitality is a value-laden concept, something to be arrogated to some beings, objects (such as Milton's books), institutions and practices while being denied to or pitted against others. Perhaps no early modern English playwright sees this more clearly than Christopher Marlowe.

In *Edward II*, Gaveston and Edward seek to construct a life that, insofar as it is constituted out of a refusal of paternal authority and an indifference to dynastic legacy, also goes by the name of death.[8] At issue here is not merely a *way of* life, however (meaning, habitual patterns of behaviour performed by these two individuals), but also a *concept* of life that is untethered from the demands of past and future. To demonstrate this, I will consider different ways in which 'life' means in *Edward II* by first turning to scene 19, a watershed moment in the play's treatment of vitality. From there, I will show how Gaveston's opening monologue establishes the terms for a corporate model of vitality that for both Edward and Gaveston is indistinguishable from sharing the kingdom. This model emerges out of opposition to the imperatives of dynastic kingship, which sutures the perpetuation of the polity to the temporal extension of life. However, when Edward finally gives up the throne, he accedes to the dynastic imperatives he had earlier spurned. Moreover, his post-deposition existence is marked by the tragic reworking of the model of corporate vitality – of amity and enmity – first established in Edward's relationship with Gaveston. I will conclude by suggesting that *Edward II* develops a non-teleological vision of vitality whose future lies in the theatrical present.

§

At the end of scene 19 of *Edward II*, Edward is forcibly separated from his favourites Spencer Jr. and Baldock before being taken to Killingworth Castle, where he will eventually renounce his kingship. As the king parts from 'Sweet Spencer [and] gentle Baldock', he bids adieu both to them and, seemingly, to his own animate existence: 'Life, farewell with my friends'.[9] Edward's declaration echoes an earlier question he posed to Leicester: 'Com[e you], then, in Isabella's name / To take *my life, my company*, from me?' (64–5, emphasis mine). In both instances, Edward locates his vitality in his relationship with his favourites.

Like Edward, Baldock describes the separation of the king from his favourites in terms of a vital loss: 'Spencer, I see our souls are fleeted hence; / We are deprived the sunshine of our life' (104–5). In this formulation, Spencer and Baldock have individual souls, but, puzzlingly, they also share a life that is forfeited at the very moment Baldock attests to it. The fleeting of their souls follows from the loss of royal 'sunshine' that,

Baldock suggests, animated both their individual and corporate lives. Some thirty-five lines later, near the beginning of scene 20, Edward ponders, 'But what are kings, when regiment is gone, / But perfect shadows in a sunshine day?' (26–7). Without 'regiment', the king is leached of his own vitality; once 'the sunshine of [Baldock and Spencer's corporate] life', the imprisoned Edward is now a talking shadow.[10]

If Edward's departure strips Spencer and Baldock of life, the effect is momentary, as Baldock quickly recasts the terms of their vitality:

> Make for a new life, man; throw up thy eyes,
> And heart and hand to heaven's immortal throne,
> Pay nature's debt with cheerful countenance.
> Reduce we all our lessons unto this:
> To die, sweet Spencer, therefore live we all;
> Spencer, all live to die, and rise to fall. (19.106–11)

The 'new life' to which Baldock exhorts his companion centres upon the prospect of Christian immortality. Insofar as the word 'life' appears in the singular, it is once again corporate. Indeed, the entire passage focuses on 'we', not 'I'. And yet, the 'we' on display here is less a collective being than a generic one that Baldock is exhorting to reform: we are all sinners, we all die, etc. Consequently, Baldock suggests, each of these two men will need to reform his *own* life, attend to his *own* spiritual needs. Of course, this will affect how these characters both live the rest of their lives and conclude them. '[A]ll live to die, and rise to fall'; each should aspire to '[p]ay nature's debt with cheerful countenance'.

It is worth lingering over the different views of life and death assumed in these last two statements. Confidence in his salvation enables the Christian to face death cheerfully. This salvific world view understands death to inaugurate a new, better life, and thus we all fall to rise. However, Baldock's final couplet – the last lines he utters in the play – asserts the opposite. As Martin Wiggins and Robert Lindsey observe,

Baldock here 'invokes the medieval "de casibus" notion of tragedy in which an individual's rise to success is always followed by their fall' (19. n.110–11). In the space of six lines, Baldock juxtaposes a pair of different templates for construing the nature and shape of human existence: a *salvific* template in which death inaugurates a new, better life; and a *tragic* one in which decline and death mark a humbling end. Crucially, both of these have a compensatory dimension ('Make for a *new* life, man'); they are what Baldock and Spencer turn to when deprived of the royal sunshine of both their corporate *life* and their individual *lives*.

At the end of scene 19, then, Edward's favourites seek to reframe their lives in the wake of their separation from him; at the beginning of that scene, before Edward is severed from his 'company', he fantasizes about how they might all together conduct their lives:

> Come Spencer, come Baldock, come sit down by me;
> Make trial now of that philosophy
> That in our famous nurseries of arts
> Thou sucked'st from Plato and from Aristotle.
> Father, this life contemplative is heaven –
> Oh that I might this life in quiet lead! (16–21)

Edward figures the contemplative life in terms both collective ('Come Spencer, come Baldock') and individual ('Oh that *I* might this life in quiet lead'). He also recognizes the impossibility of sustaining it: 'But we, alas, are chased; and you, my friends, / Your lives and my dishonour they pursue' (22–3). 'This life contemplative' is a present-tense vitality, predicated upon 'making trial' of the philosophical tradition, that is evoked only to be quashed. Moreover, the intimate connection between 'your lives' – the lives of Spencer and Baldock – and Edward's dishonour is articulated later in the scene, when the king's impending imprisonment and deposition deprive his favourites of the force that animates them.

In sum, both Edward and his favourites understand the king's separation from his 'company' as having ontological effects; it changes not only their lives but also how they conceptualize their own vitality. For Edward, kingly 'regiment' encompasses company and life, and forfeiting it transforms him into a shadow. For Baldock (who seemingly also speaks for Spencer), separation from Edward forces him to 'make for a new life'; his body bereft of the royal sunshine that had heretofore animated it, Baldock turns his attention to the state of his own soul. Additionally, life is now figured in terms that are more diachronic ('all live to die, and rise to fall') than synchronic ('my life, my company').[11]

Edward's separation from Spencer and Baldock is only the most prominent example of the play's sustained engagement with the issue of life. Indeed, the opening lines of *Edward II* introduce a conception of vitality predicated upon amity and enmity – a conception that both encapsulates and serves as the ontological basis for Edward's view of kingly regiment. The first scene of *Edward II* finds Gaveston rhapsodizing about his new life as royal favourite: 'What greater bliss can hap to Gaveston, / Than live and be the favourite of a king?' (1.4–5). His question is blasphemous; in suggesting there is no 'greater bliss', Gaveston prefers the mortal life of the royal favourite to the eternal life of his soul. This question also rhetorically ushers a new life into existence: the blissful life of the favourite begins *now*, in the immediate wake of Edward's ascension to the throne. In other words, the lives of the new monarch and his new favourite are functionally co-emergent.[12]

While Edward II's ascension to the throne in the wake of his royal father's death suggests dynastic continuity, the new king's letter to Gaveston signifies otherwise. '"My father is deceased; come, Gaveston, / And share the kingdom with thy dearest friend"' (1.1–2). In ushering us briskly from one reign to the next, these lines would seem to serve a rhetorical purpose similar to that of the familiar declaration, 'The king is dead; long live the king.' However, in place of a reference to his new regal authority, Edward alludes to sharing the kingdom with Gaveston. Jonathan Goldberg notes that these lines 'instigat[e] a sodomitical order, one that alienates his peers and his wife, driving Queen Isabella and the younger Mortimer into an adulterous and rebellious embrace'.[13] The invocation of Edward I is, paradoxically, crucial to the instigation of this sodomitical order. Thus, while Edward's kingship *depends upon* (the death of) his father for its legitimacy, the nature of his reign is constituted out of the *repudiation of* his father's wishes. Within the play, Edward's first monarchical action is to defy his father's edict that Gaveston be banished. The play's opening lines have a quasi-emblematic function, as they establish Edward II's reign as simultaneously *continuous with* the past – the son succeeds his father – and *discontinuous* with it – the son establishes a 'sodomitical order' in defiance of both his father and the barons. (Mortimer Junior's very first lines underscore this second point: 'Mine uncle here [Mortimer Senior], this earl [Lancaster], and I myself / Were *sworn to your father at his death, / That [Gaveston] should ne'er return* into the realm' [1.81–3, emphasis mine].) In its discontinuity, the sodomitical order is framed in spatial more than temporal terms, as a form of sharing.

What does it mean for Edward to 'share the kingdom with [his] dearest friend', though? Critics have suggested this statement portends co-rule between the monarch and his favourite, even though neither man proves terribly interested in the business of governing. More pertinent to our understanding of Edward's sodomitical regime is the association of the verb 'share' with not only mutuality but also dismemberment: 'To cut into parts; to cut off' (*OED*, v. 1 *Obs*. a. *trans.*) or 'To divide and apportion in shares between two or more recipients' (v. 2. 1.a. *trans.*). In light of these definitions, 'sharing' connotes the dissevering and reallocation of portions of the kingdom in the name of friendship. Moreover, it offers one possible definition of what Gaveston – and, I would argue, Edward – understands 'liv[ing] and be[ing] the favourite of a king' to entail; as the king says to his favourite, 'If for these dignities thou be envied, / I'll give thee more, *for but to honour thee / Is Edward pleased with kingly regiment*' (1.162–4, emphasis mine). Instead of following past monarchical practice or respecting the obligations attendant upon rank, Edward and Gaveston perform a type of kingdom sharing in which lands and titles are repeatedly reallocated among Edward's allies and enemies. The most notable early example is Edward's stripping the Bishop of Coventry of property and position, to his favourite's benefit: '[Gaveston, b]e thou lord bishop, and receive his rents. / And make him serve thee as thy chaplain'; 'And take possession of his house and goods' (1.193–4, 202). This particular act of kingdom sharing has a strong symbolic significance, as the divestiture of the Bishop of Coventry's titles and possessions interrupts the Bishop's plans to 'celebrate [Edward I's] exequies' (175). The Bishop, whom Gaveston identifies as having been responsible for his exile (191), seeks to perform his mourning for Edward I's death in a way that the new king never does. More importantly, his arrest highlights the extent to which Edward II's reign constitutes a rupture with the past, a new sodomitical order predicated upon 'sharing' the kingdom between friends.[14]

While in *Edward II* sharing connotes division at the level of the kingdom, it implies mutuality at the level of Edward and Gaveston's relationship. Indeed, as numerous critics have pointed out, that relationship is discursively grounded in classical and early modern friendship theory.[15] The central trope of friendship discourse posits that true friends have, in the words of Florio's Montaigne, 'one soule in two bodies'.[16] This figure describes radical likeness: if two bodies share one soul, then those bodies are taken to be equivalent; as Laurie Shannon describes it, '[T]wo equal corporeal bodies bound in friendship constitute a single corporate or juridical body, a legal fiction creating an operative unity' (4). In Marlowe's reworking of friendship discourse, he positions *amity* – the mutuality of male friendship, figured as a single corporate body – within a broader context of political *enmity*. That is, the sodomitical order initiated by Edward and Gaveston necessitates not only that their friendship take precedence over matters of state, but also that the king and his favourite maintain an oppositional relationship with England's political order. Gaveston suggests as much in his opening speech through his striking articulation of the fusion of amity and enmity: 'The King, upon whose bosom let me die, / And with the world be still at enmity' (14–15). Certainly 'die' has its conventional sexual resonance here, suggesting orgasm. It also describes a way of living, in both amity with the king and enmity with the world. Here and throughout the play, amity seems to need enmity for its existence, or at least one is closely bound up in the other; to be Edward II's favourite is also to be at odds with, if not the whole world, then nearly the entirety of the political class. Moreover, this fusion of amity and enmity has an ontological dimension; the vision of Gaveston upon the king's bosom emblematizes what he means when he alludes ten lines earlier to '*liv[ing] and be[ing]* the favourite of a king'.

If death connotes life (as well as sex) here, it also necessarily elicits thoughts of mortality. Indeed, Gaveston's first speech is peppered with references to life, death and/or afterlife. Gaveston compares the 'sight of London to [his] exiled eyes' to that of 'Elysium to a new-come soul'; he envisions himself as 'Leander, gasp[ing] upon the sand' after swimming to meet his lover, which image evokes both Leander's nightly journeys across the Hellespont and his eventual drowning; and, as we have seen, Gaveston fantasizes about simultaneously dying, living and ejaculating on the king's breast. If Gaveston's vision of living and being the favourite of a king encompasses both amity and enmity, it also rhetorically smudges the difference between conventional understandings of life and death.

We have seen that Edward and Gaveston's kingdom sharing is predicated upon the new monarch's repudiation of his father's (royal) authority. As such, it is also at odds with the dynastic logic at the heart of hereditary monarchy. The medieval doctrine of the King's Two Bodies offers a famous articulation of this dynastic logic. This doctrine depicts the monarch as one who combines in his royal being a mortal 'body natural' – the imperfect physical body of the king – and the immortal 'body politic', which both pre-exists each individual king and survives him. The difference between these two bodies has implications for thinking about the monarch as a being living in time:

> [I]n some respects the king ... was a 'temporal being,' strictly 'within Time,' and subjected, like any ordinary human being, to the effects of Time. In other respects, however, that is, with regard to things *quasi sacrae* or public, he was unaffected by Time and its prescriptive power; like the 'holy sprites and angels,' he was beyond Time and therewith perpetual and sempiternal. The king, at least with regard to Time, had obviously 'two natures'—one which was temporal and by which he conformed with the conditions of other men, and another which was perpetual and by which he outlasted and defeated all other beings.[17]

The nature and significance of the immortal 'body politic' has been the subject of much debate. Some scholars working in the wake of Ernst Kantorowicz have approached it as a metaphysical principle undergirding sovereignty;[18] others have stressed the space the 'body politic' creates for thinking popular authority and commonweal;[19] still others have questioned the cultural reach of this doctrine.[20] For our purposes, it is enough to note that the King's Two Bodies captures monarchy's 'temporal' (or synchronic) and 'perpetual' (or diachronic) dimensions. With these dimensions in mind, we learn something important about Edward's sodomitical regime: it is constituted out of the attempted refusal of a sempiternal conception of kingship.

Now, this might seem farfetched, insofar as differences between Edward I and Edward II can be easily explained in terms of the vicissitudes of their respective 'bodies natural'. From this perspective, Edward II's overturning of a paternal edict speaks only to the temperamental distance between father and son. As we have seen, though, Edward does much more than disobey his father when he urges Gaveston to share the kingdom; with Gaveston, he embarks on the reimagining of sovereignty in terms of both amity and enmity (the king and his favourite against the world). To do this, Edward requires the legitimation provided by being his father's son; at the same time, though, his reign is inaugurated by and out of an action that signifies radical rupture rather than continuity. To put this differently, Edward and Gaveston's kingdom sharing, in its combination of mutuality and dismemberment, stands as their ultimately (and inevitably) unsuccessful attempt to figure sovereignty solely in synchronic terms, outside of any debt owed to either the past or the future. With this in mind, it is worth returning to Gaveston's initial statement of alliance to the king: 'upon [his] bosom let me die, / And with the world be still at enmity'. Dying here *precedes* enmity and *inaugurates* a way of 'living and being' that encompasses Edward, Gaveston and the political class to which they oppose themselves. Moreover, this is living and being in the present tense; the life of king and favourite as imagined here is untethered from the claims of the past or the imperatives of the future.[21]

'Dying' not only inaugurates 'living and being', as if in a parodic reworking of Christian salvation, it also enables them. As a euphemism for orgasm, dying upon the king's bosom connotes sexuality untethered from an economy of sexual (and dynastic) reproduction. Put differently, it signifies a conception of life that is not dependent upon its perpetuation for legitimacy. The significance of such a conception becomes plain when we consider the extent to which biological life was understood to require reproduction for its cultural legibility. The physician Helkiah Crooke begins Book 4 of *Mikrokosmographia*, which focuses upon 'the Naturall Parts belonging to generation', thusly:

> The greatest argument of diuinity, or of a nature relishing thereof is perpetuitie and immutability, the perfection whereof as it is incompetent to any compound creature (for the soule is therefore immortall because it hath no parts) so

> it is most resembled in that we cal *Life*; wherein there is a perpetuity though not of all the parts of time *Past*, *Present*, and *to Come*; (for *Time* is the measure thereof) yet of that which in time is subsistent, that is the *Present*. For as the production of points perpetuateth a line, so the coherence of *present* times make a kinde of eternity. Life therefore so long as it is prolonged hath no end, and may be compared to a clew of yarne, such as the Poets faigned the Destinies to spin, which so long as there is flaxe to supply, may be drawne into an endlesse length.[22]

For Crooke, 'perpetuitie and immutability' present the 'greatest argument [for] diuinity', and, in the material world, life comes closest to attaining such perfection. Life represents a 'kinde of eternity', Crooke argues, that is best defined as a close sequence of present moments that, when connected, 'perpetuateth a line'. And, of course, perpetuation is all: 'Life *therefore so long as it is prolonged* hath no end.' One can go farther, however, as Crooke's own discussion indirectly suggests: it is not merely that life will *end* if not prolonged, it is that it will no longer be, and will not have been, life. As life by definition describes 'a perpetuity' or 'a kinde of eternity', so is its prolongation a precondition for its existence in the first place.

Now, Crooke is focused on the perpetuation of matter in the above passage, not the subsistence or generation of specific living creatures.[23] Nevertheless, the assumption undergirding his analysis – that life must perpetuate itself in order to be life – is, in early modern literature and culture, operative at the level of the individual being. Unsurprisingly, it usually takes a distinctly patriarchal form and pertains to notions of dynastic extension. We can go to Crooke one last time for a positive articulation of this cultural logic: 'The father liueth in the sonne, and dyeth not as long as his expresse and liuing Image stands vpon the earth' (sig. S4ᵛ). Crooke's statement is more ideological than scientific; it reflects the cultural imperative succinctly articulated by Fred Tromly: 'In early modern England the mutually reinforcing voices of religious, political, and pedagogical authority insisted that it was the duty of sons to emulate and indeed replicate their fathers.'[24] Put differently, the vitality of both patriarch and dynastic house requires reproduction for its very existence. 'The father liueth in the sonne.' In cultural terms, this statement means not only that the father *continues to live on* in the son, but also that *the vitality and identity of the father depend upon his replication in order to exist in the first place*. It is this view that is famously explored in Shakespeare's procreation sonnets, in which the Poet offers the Young Man both the carrot – if you reproduce, you shall be 'Yourself again after yourself's decease' (13.7) – and the stick – if you remain single and don't reproduce, you will '"prove none"' (8.14).[25] The paradoxes of vitality and identity are wonderfully captured in the opening lines of sonnet 13: 'O that you were yourself! But, love, you are / No longer yours, than you yourself here live' (13.1–2). On the one hand, because the Young Man does not reproduce, he is himself only for as long as he 'here live[s]'; on the other hand, he is not himself even now – O that he were! – because he doesn't perpetuate his life. The stakes are not merely personal, as the Young Man 'lets so fair a [dynastic] house fall to decay' (13.9) by not procreating. According to the Poet, the lives of both the Young Man and his family depend for their very existence upon the Young Man reproducing himself.[26]

In this formulation, then, vitality depends upon its perpetuation in order to be itself; and fathers both live on in their sons and require sons in order to live and be themselves in the first place. With this cultural logic in mind, the stakes of Gaveston's association of *dying* with *living and being* become clearer. 'Dying' is a figure for Gaveston and Edward's efforts to uncouple vitality and sexuality from the dictates of generation, replication and dynasticism, from both the past and the future; insofar as it is associated with kingdom sharing, *dying* also has a political dimension, drawing into itself both the amity of king and favourite and their enmity with the barons.

§

In opposition to the dynastic logic that structures his play – it begins and ends with the deaths of kings and the installation of their successors – Marlowe presents us with forms of vitality that are located in male homosocial relations that seemingly have no future. In addition to Gaveston and Edward's vital 'dying', we have the life that, after his favourite's death, Edward locates in his 'company', not to mention the 'royal sunshine' animating Spencer and Baldock. These two men invoke the 'new life' of Christian immortality after they separate from Edward and in anticipation of their own deaths. But how do we make sense of the king's *own* vitality once regiment and company are gone?

In scene 20, shortly after Baldock has uttered his last words, Edward vacillates between affirming his kingliness and lamenting its passing. At one moment, Edward differentiates his suffering from that of his fellow man through reference to 'the imperial lion's flesh' (11); at the next, he bemoans the loss of kingly regiment (26–7). While he describes that loss as having already occurred, the 'imperial lion' metaphor attests to his continued sovereignty. At the same time, these lines are uttered on the eve of his deposition, the moment at which he will no longer be king. In other words, Edward here experiences his life in terms of a temporal confounding, with past, present and future converging on him all at once. He construes himself as both king and no king; even though his deposition is yet to occur, he experiences it as having already happened. And yet, despite this, he is still the 'imperial lion'.[27]

This temporal confounding is materialized for Edward through references to his crown. Immediately after figuring kings without regiment as 'perfect shadows', Edward observes, 'My nobles rule; I bear the name of King. / I wear the crown, but am controlled by them – / By Mortimer and my unconstant Queen' (20.28–30). The crown and the 'name of King' attest mostly to what he once was. Shortly thereafter, though, Edward clings to the crown as a marker of what he still is:

'See, monsters, see, I'll wear my crown again. / What, fear you not the fury of your King?' (74–5). And in between these two moments, he has described the crown as a locus of kingly vitality: 'Here, take my crown – the life of Edward too' (57). Once again, all of this occurs before his deposition, at a time at which he understands himself to be and not to be the king.

Scene 20 demands that we differentiate between kingly consciousness and kingly ontology, both of which stand in complex relationship to the vitality of the monarch. For the first two thirds of this scene, before he has given up the crown, Edward is still the king; the body politic resides in him. In subjective terms, however, Edward is already torn between past, present and future. If his royal vitality is relinquished along with kingly regiment, it will be lost again with the crown. And yet, he obviously survives these losses. Indeed, there are traces of a distinctly kingly vitality in Edward's hardihood while he is being subjected to torture:

> Gourney, I wonder the King dies not.
> Being in a vault up to the knees in water,
> To which the channels of the castle run,
> From whence a damp continually ariseth
> That were enough to poison any man,
> Much more a king, brought up so tenderly. (24.1–6)

Having been deposed, Edward II's kingliness *is* dead, or, better yet, transferred to his son. And yet, Maltravers observes, 'the *King* dies not'. He refers here not to the sempiternal idea of kingship enshrined in the body politic – 'the king is dead, long live the king' – but instead to the monarch's body natural. Even when Edward's being is divorced from that of the body politic, a residue of kingly vitality remains for Maltravers and Gourney to wonder at. Stripped of the crown, Edward is not just 'any man'; otherwise he would have succumbed to the poisonous atmosphere of the vault. As Maltravers notes twice in six lines, Edward *is* still (at least some part) a king, even when he is king no longer.

The hardiness that Maltravers wonders at is a funhouse mirror version of the sunshine that we have seen Baldock locate in Edward II; both are figures of a sovereign vitality that is bound up in relations of amity and enmity. Indeed, Maltravers, Gourney and even Lightborne appear in Marlowe as a dark reworking of the kingly company that for Edward once defined both life and regiment. 'My lord, be not pensive; we are your friends', insists Maltravers (22.1), while, a few lines later, Gourney reassures Edward 'the Queen hath given this charge / To keep your grace in safety' (13–14). Even the murderous Lightborne feigns companionable sympathy when Edward reports his mistreatment at the hands of his keepers: 'Oh speak no more, my lord; this breaks my heart. / Lie on this bed and rest yourself awhile' (24.70–1). Of course, the relationship between amity and enmity is configured very differently here than it was with Edward and Gaveston. In the prison scenes, gestures of amity on the part of Edward's 'friendly' captors, who intermittently refer to him as king, are stalking horses for torture, abuse and, finally, murder. Consider Lightborne's instructions to his accomplices: 'lay the table down and stamp on it; / But not too hard, lest that you bruise his body' (111–12). While Lightborne's concern for the state of Edward's body is born of the need to mask evidence of foul play, his lines combine a will to violence – 'lay the table down and stamp on it' – with a strange murderous solicitude – 'not too hard, lest that you bruise his body'. The murder itself conjoins duplicitious care and physical intimacy with horrific violence. It is a brutal distortion of Gaveston's description of living and being with '[t]he King, upon whose bosom let me die, / And with the world be still at enmity'.

The prison scenes, then, both echo and unravel Edward's conception of kingly regiment, a conception he inaugurated with Gaveston and maintained with Spencer and Baldock only to see it brutally parodied by Maltravers, Gourney and Lightborne. It is also while he is in prison that Edward acknowledges the force of the dynastic logic he at first resisted. Edward agrees to his own deposition so that 'the Prince shall

[not] lose his right [to the crown]' (20.92).[28] Most critics have read Edward III's ascension to the throne as 'a solution to the problems the play poses'.[29] In this view, Edward III represents the restoration of the dynastic order that is violated by Edward II's sodomitical one. As we have seen, Edward II's break from the past is emblematized by his non-performance of funeral rites for his father. In contrast, Edward III establishes the legitimacy of his reign not only by imprisoning his mother and having Mortimer killed, but also by adhering to the ritual practices his father eschewed: 'Go fetch my father's hearse, where it shall lie, / And bring my funeral robes... . / ... / Here comes the hearse; help me to mourn, my lords' (25.94–8). Note also that Edward III calls upon his lords to grieve alongside him ('help me to mourn'), signalling the end of enmity between the monarch and the political class.

If one way that Edward III establishes his *bona fides* as a ruler is by imprisoning his mother – that is, by not succumbing to family feeling when faced with her murderous actions – Isabella is of course necessary to his claim to the throne in the first place. So far in this analysis, dynasticism has appeared as a homosocial, quasi-parthenogenetic affair, one conducted by the Poet and Young Man in the procreation sonnets (with fleeting acknowledgement of the latter's would-be wife), or by father and son in Crooke (with no such acknowledgement). Isabella has more of a role in the drama of dynastic perpetuation, but it is of an oblique nature.[30] Isabella's status as, in Edward's phrase, an 'unconstant queen' is a mark of her perfidy, one that might be expected to jeopardize her son's legitimacy. However, her love for Mortimer does not cast a shadow over Edward III's claim to the throne; their relationship comes late, and in the wake of her husband's cruelty toward her. In this regard, the question that often puzzles readers – when exactly does Isabella redirect her affections toward Mortimer? – is important not for any answer it yields, but because it assumes no shadow of wifely infidelity is cast over Edward III's birth.[31] At play's end, the 'unconstant' Isabella represents a threat to the emotional constancy of the new king, one that he successfully quells: 'Away with her. Her words enforce these tears, / And I shall pity her if she speak again' (25.85–6). Or, to put it differently, Isabella is the site onto which Edward III's own inconstancy – his capacity for tears and pity – is projected in order to be symbolically mastered. In this regard, the son mimics the father. Edward II's disparagement of the queen's 'unconstant' nature elides his own mutability, as in the early scene in which he spurns his wife at one moment only to pledge 'A second marriage 'twixt thyself and me' (4.336) at the next. Why the change of heart? Because Isabella speaks in favour of Gaveston's return from exile. Edward's loyalty to his friend engenders inconstancy in many other arenas of his life.

This discussion of Edward III's ascent has associated him with the restoration of dynastic order, but critics have offered trenchant alternatives to such a view. Marie Rutkoski has argued that 'Marlowe deftly draws the prince, perhaps to our surprise, into the homoerotic and sodomitical dynamics of the play', while Jeffrey Masten has noted that in his final lines 'the Child king Edward III tak[es] up or resum[es] Edward and Gaveston's syrupy language of male affection and pleasure'.[32] In concluding, I want to suggest that, for this analysis, the final status of the dynastic order is not terribly important, for the simple reason that the conceptual legitimacy of 'living and being' can survive its apparent supercession. To see this, we must first consider what Judith Haber has famously identified as Marlowe's penchant for 'pointless play'. Haber's term describes 'the non-reproductive [or] unconsummated sexuality towards which [Marlowe's] texts repeatedly gesture'.[33] This chapter extends Haber's line of reasoning to encompass what we might call a 'pointless vitality', a non-telological conception of life. This is the kind of life that Gaveston aspires to in 'liv[ing] and be[ing] the favourite of a king', or that Edward associates with 'company', or that is manifest in the hardihood of a king who is not a king. The play's final bend toward the dynastic, then, might seem to mark the 'end' of pointless vitality, as might Baldock and Spencer's turn to their own last 'ends' once the sunshine of their collective life has gone out. Certainly Crooke and Shakespeare's Poet would seem to lend credence to this view, as they each suggest life is not life if it is not perpetuated. By this measure, 'pointless vitality' is no vitality at all.

To think this way, however, is to usher *telos* into a little room where it does not belong. To argue for pointless vitality's conquest or erasure – to see dynastic life as somehow supplanting or superceding 'living and being' – is to misrecognize the intellectual daring of Marlowe's sustained investigation of the meanings of life. This investigation is particularly well suited to the theatre in its performative and textual dimensions. From a teleological perspective, we might conclude that *Edward II* demonstrates 'living and being' have no future, but we would be wrong; that future is realized every time the play is staged or read, every time Edward and Gaveston re-inaugurate their model of corporate vitality. Pointless vitality exists in a theatrical present whose future lies in that present's next iteration. It is a future that, to repurpose Crooke, is a 'coherence of present times' in which, every time we engage the play, we witness anew each of its characters make a new life, either individually or collectively. Pointless vitality may have no end, but it does have a home. It's called the theatre.

8

A Survey of Resources: Teaching *Edward II*

Edward Gieskes

Despite what Jeremy Lopez calls the 'modern editorial consensus' that *Edward II* is 'Marlowe's greatest play' and the fact that it is 'the only play to appear in every anthology of early modern drama published since 1911', it is not taught as often as *Doctor Faustus*.[1] Indeed, Marlowe's other plays and poems are more mentioned than taught in the high school and undergraduate classroom. Given the usual organization of undergraduate courses in the drama of the English Renaissance, Marlowe's work tends only to appear in the sophomore survey, in courses on non-Shakespearean drama, and in classes focused on nondramatic verse. In the sophomore survey, students typically might read *Doctor Faustus* or some of the poetry. Courses on lyric or nondramatic poetry may include his translations from Ovid, *Hero and Leander*, along with the 'The Passionate Shepherd to His Love'. His translation of the *Pharsalia* almost never appears on an undergraduate syllabus.

In my own non-Shakespearean drama course, *Edward II* competes for space with other Marlowe plays and the obligation to cover drama from the 1580s to the 1630s. Given these constraints, *Tamburlaine, Part 1, Doctor Faustus* or *The Jew of Malta* often represent Marlowe. Based on my own experience, examinations of sample syllabi and discussions with colleagues, it appears that only rarely does an undergraduate course focus on Marlowe's work and only occasionally does his drama figure in courses on Shakespeare. Despite having taken more than one undergraduate course in early modern literature, my own first encounter with *Edward II* was in graduate school as part of a seminar on Marlowe. What all of this suggests is that *Edward II* is routinely overlooked as a classroom text for undergraduate students, which is a shame not just because the play can provide a powerful experience as book or production but also because its particular workings as a history play can complicate student understanding of the period's drama. The graduate classroom is a different story, naturally, but even there *Edward II* can take a secondary position to *Tamburlaine, Part 1, Doctor Faustus* or *The Jew of Malta* or, more commonly, to Shakespeare's historical drama.

As Martin Wiggins writes in his excellent introduction to his New Mermaids edition of the play, *Edward II* is 'uncomfortable and challenging' because it is so hard to 'reduce it to rule' (xxxvii). I have taught the play at both the undergraduate and graduate levels, in courses on the history play as well as in general surveys of non-Shakespearean drama, and in my experience, the difficulty of reducing it to 'rule' is precisely what makes it a great play for the classroom. For me, *Edward II* has much to offer undergraduate and graduate students. It can be taught as a history play and as a play engaged in political questions about tyranny. At the same time, students can be introduced to the context of both Marlowe's career and the more general field of the drama of the 1580s and 1590s. It also offers opportunities to bring up questions of gender and sexuality because of its representation of homoerotic relationships. My central claim is that the play's complexity and its links to the broader literary field are what make it a productive and exciting play in the classroom. In what follows, I will present some ideas about opportunities in teaching the play before proceeding to an annotated bibliography.

While I do not want to dwell on personal classroom anecdotes, a few remarks on my particular experience teaching the play will help explain my approach below. In my undergraduate courses on non-Shakespearean drama, the play has figured as the only history play on the syllabus.[2] This has inevitably given rise to opportunities to present the play as history, requiring some attention to other examples from other playwrights. I also have had much success treating the play as a tragedy that can be compared to the roughly contemporary *Spanish Tragedy* or *Arden of Feversham* or later plays like *The Duchess of Malfi*. Once students have been introduced to the products of Marlowe's career, efforts to locate *Edward II* among his other plays and the poetry have been rewarding as well. The play's particularly tricky relation to generic categories has made it an especially useful play for raising questions about form, questions that complement and complicate the historical, political and gender issues that we discuss. Over the years, my students have also taken an interest in: (1) how the political and emotional stakes of the play centre on Gaveston, conflating politics and the personal in ways that resonate with Shakespeare's *Richard II*; (2) how the play's poetics – its investment in spectacle in terms familiar from Marlowe's lyric poetry – and display relates to its politics; (3) how the play's characters talk about tyranny; and (4) how relatively little interest the barons take in questions about gender and sexuality.

Genre and Marlowe's history play

As *Edward II* fits into the Elizabethan genre of the history play, an attention to genre can bear much fruit in the classroom. One could begin by highlighting the full first title of the play: *The Troublesome Reign and Lamentable Death of Edward II, with the Tragic Fall of Proud Mortimer*. This title differentiates the fates of Edward II ('*Lamentable*') and Mortimer ('*Tragic*'). Pointing out to students that tragedy gets attached to Mortimer, not Edward, immediately raises questions about genre and purpose. Students will want to discuss what is tragic about Mortimer's fall and why Gaveston is not mentioned at all. They will be interested as well in thinking of the play as a hybrid of a more abstract *de casibus* and romantic tragedy.

As its beginning and end can well demonstrate to students, *Edward II* is also deeply engaged in the dramatic and poetic conversations of its late-Elizabethan moment. Gaveston's reference to the Hero and Leander story in his first speech (which may or not be a reference to Marlowe's own poem) and Edward's citation of lines from Lodge's *Wounds of Civil War* at the close of the play together can be used to demonstrate Marlowe's investments in the literary and dramatic culture of the 1590s. *Edward II*'s connections to plays in a range of genres from history to revenge tragedy encourage discussions about how Marlowe's play (and others) fit into the broader contemporary dramatic field. In my graduate survey of non-Shakespearean drama, reading *Edward II* shortly after reading Kyd's *Spanish Tragedy* has allowed students to see generic and poetic links between works that, on the surface, can appear quite different.

An attention to genre in the classroom invariably sparks interest in the broader field of early-modern literature, and in some cases it will allow short forays into the period's non-dramatic literary offerings. In discussing *Edward II* as tragedy, for example, one could fruitfully turn to Michael Drayton's twin historical poems *Piers Gaveston* and *Mortimeriados*. These treat the events that Marlowe dramatizes and were written shortly after the play. They both insistently ally themselves with the dramatic genre of tragedy.[3] In the eponymous poem, Gaveston invokes the 'mournful Maidens of the sacred nine', the Destinies, who dwell in 'the shades beneath', desiring them 'with sable pens of direfull Ebonie, / To pen the processe of [his] tragedie'.[4] After this plea, Gaveston's ghost makes explicit allusion to Marlowe's contemporary Thomas Kyd's work in a stanza structured like Hieronimo's lament in *The Spanish Tragedy*, but in a joyful vein:

> O daies, no daies, but little worlds of mirth,
> O yeeres, no yeeres, time sliding with a trice;
> O world, no world, a very heauen on earth,
> O earth, no earth, a verie Paradice:
> A King, a man, nay more then this was hee,
> If earthly man, more then a man might be. (sig. K5r)

This is, of course, not an uncommon rhetorical pattern, but the lines echo and play on specific parts of Hieronimo's speech ('O world' and 'O earth').[5] His imitation (or emulation) of Kyd's combination of anaphora and correctio signals the connections between this poem and drama.[6] Weirdly, this stanza praises Edward I, the father whose death is the cause of Gaveston's rejoicing in Marlowe's play. Drayton's complete poems are too long to be more than touched on in a drama course, but focused references to specific moments where Drayton invokes the theatre can help place Marlowe's work into a broader picture of the literary field.[7]

Questions about genre can drive other types of discussion about the play as well. If the play is presented as a history play, matters related to the dangers of favourites or to rebellion, for example, can come to the fore. If instead, the play is presented as a love story, the thematics of desire, jealousy and gender move into clearer view. If the play appears to students as tragedy, links to tragic historical plays like *Richard II* come to the foreground. Historical poetry helps to show how difficult it is to approach the narrative in any straightforward way. More importantly, thinking about the play's own shifting emphases encourages students to raise questions about how genre works in shaping response.

Politics

Since the play can be usefully thought of as a play about English history, its politics necessarily become an important part of classroom discussion. Students are generally alive to questions about how the play represents the monarchy, especially if they have some previous exposure to Shakespeare's histories. Unlike the plays of Shakespeare's tetralogies, *Edward II* does not engage directly in dynastic questions because linear succession is never really in doubt in the play. Nor is the play deeply invested in representations of political transitions between models of kingship or in chronicling the emergence of a Machiavellian mode of politics.[8] The play's depiction of a failed monarch and the negative effects of his indulgence of favourites has obvious links to traditional *de casibus* portraits of bad monarchs as well as to other historical drama and these connections can be stressed in the classroom through focused examples from texts like *The Mirror for Magistrates* or Shakespeare's plays. At the same time, those comparisons can show students that Marlowe's representation of Edward's tyranny in terms of his discarding of the traditional aristocracy and their values in favour of the affection of first Gaveston and then the Spencers separates his play from those of his contemporaries. Marlowe's emphasis on Edward's love for his favourites places the play's engagement with politics in an affective context – Edward's failures as a monarch stem from his valuing the personal over the political. Edward's most vociferous critics focus less on the love affair between the king and Gaveston than on Gaveston's baseness and the excesses of Edward's court. In a speech that has been consistently rewarding to discuss in the classroom, Mortimer Junior says in response to his uncle's suggestion that the King will grow out of his doting on Gaveston, the King's

> wanton humour grieves not me,
> But this I scorn, that one so basely born

Should by his sovereign's favour grow so pert,
And riot it with the treasure of the realm
While soldiers mutiny for want of pay.
He wears a lord's revenue on his back,
And Midas-like he jets it in the court. (4.403–9)

Instead of being concerned about the King's desire for his favourite, Mortimer Junior focuses on the spendthrift ways of his favourite and their consequence for the kingdom.[9] Whether or not Mortimer Junior's animus is driven by homophobia, envy or, as he claims, the best interest of the kingdom is hard to discern, but his *expressed* reasons derive from concern about the state of the kingdom.

Emphasizing the title's focus on Edward's '*Troublesome Reign*' also enables classroom comparisons to the kinds of political (and religious) questions raised by the anonymous *The Troublesome Reign of King John*, the only other extant play with '*Troublesome Reign*' in the title. Both plays are about kings who share difficult relationships with their subjects. Both plays' monarchs have problems with Catholic clergy, and the distinction between Edward's murder and what amounts to John's martyrdom open up varying perspectives on what the project of Marlowe's play might be.

Comparing the approaches to dynastic politics in *Edward II* and Shakespeare's *Richard II* can also be very productive in the classroom. *Richard II*, often said to be similar to Marlowe's play, focuses on broad questions of state and legitimacy that rarely figure in complaints about Edward's reign. Even in Edward's resignation scene, the historical threat of a disrupted succession is only hinted at, and that briefly. In the sources, however, the barons threaten to turn the succession over to a Parliament hostile to Edward, effectively threatening to disinherit Edward III. Characters like the Bishop of Winchester dismiss Edward's complaint that he is giving the crown to Mortimer, not his son. Paulina Kewes has recently argued that Marlowe's *Edward II* is less interested in being specifically topical than it is in offering more general reflections on the religion and the monarchy in a 'confessionally polarized world' (152). Comparing this to Shakespeare's approach in his plays about the Wars of the Roses is an opportunity to show students some of the complexities of political thought in the period, a complexity sometimes obscured by an otherwise-understandable focus on Shakespeare (or other plays by Marlowe).[10]

Marlowe's career

As one of the so-called first generation of Elizabethan playwrights, Marlowe and his body of work for page and stage can provide a productive example in classroom considerations of the Marlowe corpus, of the idea of a writing career, and of the history of printed drama. His sensational biography may be a draw for students, and the fact that his career was cut short by Ingram Frizer's dagger encourages speculation on what might have been. At the same time, the details of Marlowe's life can also obscure the work by overshadowing it with biographical speculation and sensationalism. Teachers of Marlowe well know the difficulties in balancing discussion of his life and his work. *Edward II* figures centrally in these questions about Marlowe's writing because of the way it refers to other parts of his body of work, because it is one of the first of his plays to appear in print under his name, and because it is his only specifically English history play (indeed his only play set in England at all).

Edward II invites students to pay attention to other parts of Marlowe's corpus from its very beginning when Gaveston invokes the Hero and Leander story. This invitation is issued by specific allusions as much as by what have come to be recognized as Marlovian motifs and habits of representation. Gaveston enters reading a letter from Edward whose 'amorous lines / Might have enforced me to have swum from France, / And, like Leander, gasped upon the sand, / So thou wouldst smile and take me in thy arms' (1.6–9). Whether or not these lines predated Marlowe's unfinished epyllion, they mark his interest in the story and can be used as a bridge to his popular narrative poem. They also align Gaveston with the Leander of the poem who is the object of Neptune's sexual attention. Edward, in a characteristically Marlovian mythological reference, occupies the position of Hero in the narrative. This is, of course, a passing reference but the play goes on to describe other displacements of gender norms – the 'lovely boy in Dian's shape' of Gaveston's imagined entertainments, for example – that draw the hearer's attention and can be used to underscore Marlowe's constant working at troubling norms. Emphasizing the ways that Marlowe's allusions to the classics often carry unexpected meaning has generally been productive in the classroom, not least because it encourages close attention to the language of the play.

Later in the play, Edward swears an epic revenge on the killers of Gaveston in an oath whose language echoes *Tamburlaine*:

> By earth, the common mother of us all,
> By heaven and all the moving orbs thereof,
> By this right hand and by my father's sword,
> And all the honours 'longing to my crown,
> I will have heads and lives for him as many
> Treacherous Warwick! Traitorous Mortimer!
> As I have manors, castles, towns, and towers.
> If I be England's king, in lakes of gore
> Your headless trunks, your bodies will I trail,
> That you make drink your fill and quaff in blood,
> And stain my royal standard with the same,
> That so my bloody colours may suggest
> Remembrance of revenge immortally
> On your accursed traitorous progeny –
> You villains that have slain my Gaveston. (11.128–47)

The speech has clear echoes of Tamburlaine's speech on the satisfactions of an earthly crown, and the piling up of guarantors of Edward's oath and the extremity of the promised violence seem calculated references to Marlowe's earlier plays. At the same time the fact that no lakes of gore await vast numbers of headless trunks in the play points toward Faustus' equally grand and unfulfilled oaths about walling Germany with brass or ruling the world. Intertextual references like these allow students to make connections between this and others of Marlowe's plays and poems in productive ways.

Just as *Edward II* can be a gateway to Marlowe's other work, the print history of *Edward II* can introduce compelling discussions about Marlowe's own sense of career and about the reception of his work. *Edward II,* whose first quarto appeared in 1594, was one of the first of Marlowe's plays to appear under his name – the other was *Dido Queen of Carthage,* printed as a collaboration with Thomas Nashe in 1594 – and there were four editions of *Edward II* before 1642. The more famous *Tamburlaine* never appeared under his name in the period.[11] *Edward II* was published a full decade before the first edition of *Doctor Faustus* and almost forty years before *The Jew of Malta* first saw print. Offering these facts in the classroom can generate questions about what 'Marlowe's career' might actually mean. For starters, as there were few printed texts ascribed to Marlowe in the early 1590s, how would an early modern reader or theatre-goer have thought about Marlowe's career? The related question of how Marlowe might have seen his 'career' has been taken up by Patrick Cheney and Richard Helgerson, among others, and the work of those scholars can open up further questions about how early modern writers saw their work. Marlowe's non-dramatic work adds even more questions. How might Marlowe's translations of Ovid and Lucan and his epyllion on Hero and Leander fit into what his career was or how it might have been perceived?[12]

Marlowe's other plays are set in locations remote in space and time – *Tamburlaine* in the Near East, *Dido* in pre-Roman North Africa, *Doctor Faustus* in Europe, *The Massacre at Paris* in France and *Jew of Malta* in the Mediterranean world – and while several of these plays can be thought of as historical, only *Edward II* is about English history. Students can productively compare Marlowe's apparent interest in history to that of other playwrights. While it is impossible to know if he would have written more plays about England, it is still striking that he seems not to have when other playwrights were producing many plays on English history. His treatment of history is broad in that he treats historical subjects from many parts of the world and calling attention to this breadth offers an opportunity for students to consider what the scope of Marlowe's project may have been in both *Edward II* and the rest of his dramatic work – how, for instance, does his interest in history outside of England shape his career?

Gender and sexuality

Martin Wiggins' introduction to the second New Mermaids edition of the play reminds readers that seeing the play as a 'gay classic' makes good sense, but at the same time he reminds us that the play does not emphasize Edward's homosexuality. If Edward is often an unsympathetic figure 'it is not his homosexuality in itself which makes him so. His devotion to his lover is single-minded and obsessive, and this makes his behaviour to everyone else abominably insensitive' (xix).[13] One of the more remarkable things about the play is how little characters seem concerned with the sex of Edward's favourite. Instead, problems come from the intensity of the affection and the consequences of how much Edward favours Gaveston.[14] Students do not always notice this on a first reading – partly due to an understandable focus on the fact that the play centres on a same-sex relationship and the reputation of the play as a 'gay classic' – but pointing this out in the classroom is a reliable way to begin a discussion of the complicated way Marlowe's play engages in questions about gender and sexuality.

Characters within the play have a curiously blasé attitude toward the homoerotic relationship between the King and Gaveston. Neither man is criticized for it as such, and even Edward's murder, while it has been discussed in reference to his sexual preferences, is not presented in the play in those terms and is instead described as a way to kill him without external signs of murder. It also comes from the historical record, not purely from Marlowe's imagination.[15] Rather than condemning either Edward or Gaveston in directly homophobic terms, characters criticize them for their wastefulness, their arrogance, almost anything but their sexuality. As one example of this, early in the play, still holding out hope that the King will mature and become a good king, Mortimer Senior dispenses some advice to his nephew:

> Nephew, I must to Scotland; thou stayest here.
> Leave now to oppose thyself against the King;
> Thou seest by nature he is mild and calm,
> And seeing his mind so dotes on Gaveston,
> Let him without controlment have his will.
> The mightiest kings have had their minions:
> Great Alexander loved Hephaestion;
> And conquering Hercules for Hylas wept;
> And for Patroclus stern Achilles drooped.
> And not kings only, but the wisest men:
> The Roman Tully loved Octavius,
> Grave Socrates, wild Alcibiades.
> Then let his grace, whose youth is flexible
> And promiseth as much as we can wish,
> Freely enjoy that vain light-headed Earl,
> For riper years will wean him from such toys. (4.387–402)

Mortimer Senior sees precedent for Edward's love of Gaveston among the 'mightiest kings' and the 'wisest men', suggesting both that there is no particular problem with it and that the king will, with luck, grow out of it and into as good a king 'as we can wish'. It is certainly no justification for treason or usurpation, at least in Mortimer Senior's view. His expectation that Edward will outgrow his enjoyment of 'minions' is, to be sure, not exactly an endorsement of same-sex relationships, but it is nuanced and complicated in ways that can provoke interesting conversations among students.

Speeches like this and others (such as Gaveston's opening speech on his joy at returning to England and Edward) represent opportunities in the classroom for introducing questions about gender and sexuality that underscore how the play is far from unambiguous about same-sex relationships. Instead, the play treats Gaveston and Edward's relationship in ways that are both complicated and in need of historical context. The lack of any kind of blanket condemnation or endorsement has been a reliable question raised by students in class discussions. The extensive scholarship on homosexuality in the play and Renaissance literature in general can help provide that context and enrich classroom discussion of Marlowe's deliberately non-judgemental approach to gender and sexuality. The work of Alan Bray, Jonathan Goldberg and Gregory Bredbeck (among many others) is essential in locating the play's representation of homoerotic relationships in context and students have profited from reading this body of scholarship in tandem with the play.

Film and adaptation

Unlike Shakespeare's drama, which can be found in a range of versions on television and in the cinema, Marlowe's work has generally been under-produced for the small and big screens.[16] There have been three TV adaptations of *Edward II* (one in French): Stephen Harrison produced a televised version of the play for the BBC in 1947, Richard Marquand and Toby Robertson's production of the play starring Ian McKellen was aired on the BBC in 1970 (and is available on DVD) and a French version aired in 1982. Derek Jarman's 1991 film is the most recent, and it remains the only cinematic treatment of Marlowe's play. It offers a fairly free adaptation of the text. With it, Jarman explicitly set out to make a 'gay love-story' in the political context of the late 1980s and early 1990s.[17] It also remains the only readily available filmed production of the play. The film's topicality, in a sense, echoes the play's even if the topical references of the 1590s were quite different. The film's intervention in the sexual politics of the 1980s and 1990s can be used to raise similar questions about how Marlowe's play might have intervened in its own historical moment. Students are generally engaged by questions about adaptation and Jarman's film is an opportunity to encourage students to consider questions about adaptation, about topicality in general and about reception.[18] As one example, Jarman's willingness to move away from the text of the play allows students to consider a writer's relationship to sources in ways that can reflect back on what Marlowe does in adapting chronicle material to the stage.

One other important version of the play, if again under-produced and to my knowledge never filmed for English-speaking audiences, merits some discussion as a teaching resource. Bertolt Brecht's *Life of Edward II of England* (1924) adapts Marlowe's play and is one of the originary texts of Brecht's epic theatre. Both plays speak to political questions as much as to ones about gender and sexuality or historiography. Students could productively consider the plays in relation to their moments of initial production, or how they respond to their historical and literary antecedents, or what their production history has to say about reception. Because Brecht's historical drama often turns to the early modern period, it offers a way to discuss more recent drama's use of historical subjects in relation to Marlowe's play and those of his contemporaries.[19] Students might also consider connections between Brecht's epic theatre and early modern drama, particularly in terms of what Brecht calls 'alienation effects'.

Bibliography

This bibliography does not pretend to be comprehensive and that is especially true of the annotated section. The chapters by Farabee and by Haber in this volume demonstrate the range and complexity of the scholarship on *Edward II* and Marlowe's work more generally. There are few texts that focus primarily on teaching *Edward II*. For example, there is no volume in the MLA Approaches to Teaching series dedicated to Marlowe's work, only scattered references in the volume on early modern drama and on Elizabethan poetry. In fact, editions of the play are often the most helpful resources for teaching the play. Of single-text editions, I have preferred texts edited after 1990 for reasons of accessibility and the currency of their bibliographies. Ribner's 1970 text is an exception because it offers an overview of the play's critical history that serves as an introduction to earlier criticism.

Texts

Select individual editions

Beer, Anna ed., *Christopher Marlowe: Edward II* (Oxford: Oxford University Press, 2013).

Beer's edition is part of the Oxford Student Texts series and is aimed at A-level study of the play. As a consequence, it has extensive notes, sections on contexts and themes and contains exercises and sample essay questions. While specifically designed for A-level study, the text's apparatus makes it a valuable tool for all students.

Forker, Charles ed., *Edward II* (Manchester: Manchester University Press, 1994).

Forker's *Edward II*, like those in the Revels Plays in general, is a full scholarly edition with an extensive introduction, a detailed discussion of the text of the play, and a full bibliography. The introduction provides a scholarly account of the play, a discussion of the play's critical history and an overview of the play in performance. An appendix contains extensive quotes from Marlowe's sources, allowing students to see how Marlowe transformed those materials into the play.

Guy-Bray, Stephen ed., *Edward II* (London: Bloomsbury, 2014).

This is a revised edition of the play designed for students, featuring a new introduction but retaining the text and notes from Wiggins and Lindsey's previous edition in the series. The new introduction emphasizes the way that the play's representation of 'sodomy' (a term Guy-Bray prefers to homosexuality or homoeroticism) affects the politics of the play. Its apparatus includes extensive explanatory footnotes and a bibliography for further reading.

Ribner, Irving ed., *Edward II: Text and Major Criticism* (New York: Odyssey, 1970).

Ribner's edition presents the text and representative criticism to 1970. While this edition predates others I have included here, it remains an important resource because it offers an overview of the reception of the play in criticism, showing the changing critical fortunes of the play in a succinct way.

Rowland, Richard ed., *The Complete Works of Christopher Marlowe: Edward II* (Oxford: Oxford University Press, 1994).

The Oxford *Works* prints *Edward II* (like most of the other plays in the series) in a stand-alone volume. Offering an old-spelling text with a general and textual introduction and extensive endnotes, the edition does not offer in-page glosses and the apparatus, while excellent, is not as immediately accessible as in other editions. Rowland prints relevant sections of Holinshed.

Wiggins, Martin and Robert Lindsey eds, *Edward II* (London: A&C Black, 1997).

The second edition of the play in the New Mermaids series has an excellent introduction by Martin Wiggins that carefully locates the play in both its original context and its reception history. It has extensive notes and a bibliography.

Concordances

Crawford, Charles, *The Marlowe Concordance* (New York: B. Franklin, 1964).

Fehrenbach, Robert et al., *A Concordance to the Plays, Poems, and Translations of Christopher Marlowe* (Ithaca: Cornell University Press, 1982).

Ule, Louis, *A Concordance to the Works of Christopher Marlowe* (New York: Olms, 1979).

Select anthologies

Bevington, David et al. eds, *English Renaissance Drama* (New York: W. W. Norton & Co., 2002).

The anthology prints four of Marlowe's plays (*1 Tamburlaine*, *Doctor Faustus*, *The Jew of Malta* and *Edward II*) with solid introductions to each play that help orient students to the plays, glosses and notes, along with a general bibliography.

Bevington, David and Eric Rasmussen eds, *Doctor Faustus and Other Plays* (Oxford: Oxford University Press, 1995).

This collection from the Oxford World's Classics series prints *Edward II* with both parts of *Tamburlaine*, *The Jew of Malta* and *Doctor Faustus*. It contains a general introduction, endnotes to the plays and a bibliography of further reading.

Gibbons, Brian ed., *Christopher Marlowe: Four Plays* (London: Methuen, 2001).

Gibbons' edition collects *Edward II* with *Tamburlaine 1 and 2*, *The Jew of Malta* and *Doctor Faustus*. Gibbons' collection prints the texts from New Mermaids stand-alone editions with a new introduction and a short and flawed bibliography. Students looking for more in-depth commentary and bibliographies may be better served by the New Mermaids edition described above.

Kinney, Arthur ed., *Renaissance Drama: An Anthology of Plays and Entertainments* (New York: Wiley-Blackwell, 2005).

Kinney's collection prints *Edward II* and *Doctor Faustus*. The volume has an excellent general introduction, and the introduction to *Edward II* is very good in that it contextualizes the play and raises questions about its major issues for students. Kinney includes a bibliography for each play in the volume.

Romany, Frank and Robert Lindsey eds, *The Complete Plays* (London: Penguin, 2003).

The Penguin collection of Marlowe's plays is both complete, and its annotations, while light, are illuminating. The introduction is brief but informative. It has the additional and not unimportant virtue of being affordable.

Select criticism

Bartels, Emily and Emma Smith eds, *Marlowe in Context* (Cambridge: Cambridge University Press, 2013).

The volume contains many provocative, relatively short and accessible essays on subjects from individual plays to Marlowe's place in the literary culture of early modern England and, as the title suggests, is designed to put Marlowe's life and works into context. It includes an essay about Marlowe in film as well. Several essays are discussed below, but the whole book is a major resource for undergraduate and graduate students alike.

Bray, Alan, 'Homosexuality and the Signs of Male Friendship', *History Workshop* 29 (1990): 1–19.

Bray's important essay offers an historical discussion of attitudes to both male friendship and sodomy in early modern England, suggesting that these attitudes are ambiguous and that texts like Marlowe's *Edward II* bring out tensions between the discourses of friendship and sodomy. It offers an effective and accessible introduction to these questions for students.

Belt, Debra, 'Anti-Theatricalism and Rhetoric in Marlowe's *Edward II*', *English Literary Renaissance* 21.2 (1991): 134–60.

Belt places Marlowe's play in the context of anti-theatrical discourses, arguing that the play needs to be read as a kind of 'concessio – that is, it takes anti-theatrical claims to their logical conclusion and in so doing demonstrates their inadequacy' (159). But, at the same time, the play also recognizes that anti-theatricalist worries about the persuasive force of theatre are rooted in real effects, effects toward which Marlowe displays a complicated and ambivalent attitude. Belt's placing of the play into controversies about the theatre reminds students how Marlowe's work is part of complex system of production and reception.

Bredbeck, Gregory, *Sodomy and Interpretation: Marlowe to Milton* (Ithaca: Cornell University Press, 1991).

Bredbeck's book examines how discourses of sodomy undercut or subvert dominant political or social discourses. His chapter on *Edward II* argues that Mortimer's attention to Edward's sodomy and the danger represented by Gaveston allows him to both advance himself and to conceal that desire. The book's range and its theoretical sophistication make it especially valuable for graduate students.

Cheney, Patrick ed., *The Cambridge Companion to Christopher Marlowe* (Cambridge: Cambridge University Press, 2004).

Cheney's volume is a valuable resource for graduate and advanced undergraduate courses on Marlowe. Its contents offer a comprehensive overview of Marlowe's work and can guide students in developing their own work.

Cheney, Patrick, *Marlowe's Counterfeit Profession: Ovid, Spenser, Counter-Nationhood* (Toronto: University of Toronto Press, 1997).

Cheney's book reads Marlowe's work in terms of 'the idea of a literary career; the practice of professional rivalry; and the writing of nationhood' (3). He describes Marlowe as following the pattern of Ovid's career rather than Virgil's, a different model than that followed by Spenser or Milton.

Dooley, Mark, 'Queer Teaching/Teaching Queer: Renaissance Masculinities and the Seminar', in *Masculinities in Text and Teaching*, ed. Ben Knights (New York: Palgrave, 2008), 59–74.

Dooley's chapter offers a detailed and provocative account of his teaching of *Edward II* in a class on 'Early Modern Sex and Sexualities: Lyly to Milton' and of responses to the play. It is less a guide to teaching the play than a meditation on how *Edward II*'s questioning of identities prompted Dooley to reflect on his own teaching.

Forker, Charles R., 'Marlowe's *Edward II* and Its Shakespearean Relatives: The Emergence of a Genre', in *Shakespeare's English Histories: A Quest for Form and Genre*, ed. John W. Velz (Binghamton: Medieval & Renaissance Texts & Studies, 1996), 55–90.

This essay discusses Marlowe's play in relation to Shakespeare's historical drama, introducing questions about genre and of relations between Marlowe and Shakespeare's work. Much of the text of this essay was subsumed into Forker's introduction to his Revels edition of the play.

Goldberg, Jonathan, *Sodometries: Renaissance Texts, Modern Sexualities* (Stanford: Stanford University Press, 1992).

Goldberg's book contains an extended consideration of Marlowe's *Edward II* that points out that the relationship between Gaveston and Edward cannot be placed easily into either gender or class systems and reads it in terms of alliance rather than hierarchies of difference. More focused on the play than Bray's essay, Goldberg's book is an important text for students interested in questions about gender and sexuality.

Haber, Judith, 'Submitting to History: Marlowe's *Edward II*', in *Enclosure Acts: Sexuality, Property, and Culture in Early Modern England*, ed. Richard Burt and John Michael Archer (Ithaca: Cornell University Press, 1994), 170–84.

In her chapter, Haber argues that the play represents 'a submission to history' (179) figured by Edward's death at the end of the play – Edward (and the play) submits to the force of the historical narrative about his death. The story, in Haber's account, is both fictional and inescapable and thus represents the play's consistent emphasis on contradiction. The essay helps students think about the complicated interactions between fiction and history in the play.

Helgerson, Richard, *The Elizabethan Prodigals* (Berkeley: University of California Press, 1976), *Self-Crowned Laureates: Spenser, Jonson, Milton and the Literary System* (Berkeley: University of California Press, 1983).

Taken together, these two books give an overview of ideas about authorship and the literary system in the period. While not focused on Marlowe, they do represent a compelling account of the system in which Marlowe composed his works and in which ideas about his career developed.

Kewes, Paulina, 'Marlowe, History, and Politics', in Bartels and Smith, 138–54.

Kewes' chapter puts Marlowe's play into the context of broad political issues of importance to his original audiences, arguing that *Edward II* and *The Massacre at Paris* engage with questions of sovereignty, confessional divisions and the dramatization of history. She points out ways that Marlowe's take on history is distinct from Shakespeare's and that that take is linked to Marlowe's interest in non-English histories.

Knowles, Ronald, 'The Political Contexts of Deposition and Election in *Edward II*', *Medieval and Renaissance Drama in England: An Annual Gathering of Research, Criticism and Reviews* 14 (2001): 105–21.

Knowles places Marlowe's work into the context of resistance theory, arguing that the play introduces 'major political questions of the later Middle Ages and early modern Europe' (107) and while it raises unsettling questions about election and succession, they are contained both by the play's tragic form and by closing with the succession of 'the hero-king, Edward III' (117).

Parks, Joan, 'History, Tragedy, and Truth in Christopher Marlowe's *Edward II*', *Studies in English Literature* 39.2 (1999): 275–90.

Parks' essay offers a detailed and compelling argument about how Marlowe's play turns his historical materials into a stage tragedy. Her essay shows how Marlowe's play innovatively places historical narrative into a tragic structure that avoids the episodic structure of chronicle plays. This essay can productively introduce the issue of genre into class discussion.

Pendergraft, Stacy, 'Marlowe Mee: Constructing the Marlowe Project', *Shakespeare Bulletin* 27.1 (2009): 51–62.

Pendergraft's essay discusses the process of producing a

student performance for the Sixth International Marlowe Conference in 2006. While *Edward II* is only mentioned in passing, she describes a very interesting approach to teaching Marlowe's work through performances rooted in a close reading of the text.

Rutter, Tom, *The Cambridge Introduction to Christopher Marlowe* (Cambridge: Cambridge University Press, 2012).

Rutter's volume offers, as its title suggests, an introduction to Marlowe's work that can give students a convenient and provocative overview of Marlowe's life and work. The book includes chapters on Marlowe's biography, on *Edward II* and on Marlowe's afterlives on stage and in other media.

Semler, Liam E., *Teaching Shakespeare and Marlowe: Learning vs. the System* (Bloomsbury: London, 2013).

Semler's short book narrates his teaching of Shakespeare and Marlowe within 'the system' of schools and universities. The Marlowe discussion treats Marlowe as a counter to this system and an opportunity to challenge habits of thought inculcated in a test-driven secondary education system. His teaching exercises may be of use to other teachers of Marlowe.

Syme, Holger Schott, 'Marlowe in his Moment' in Bartels and Smith, 275–84.

Syme questions the prevailing narrative about the advent and triumph of Marlowe's kind of drama – represented by the 'mighty line'. The essay provocatively recontextualizes Marlowe's work in the 1580s and 90s and suggests that the usual narrative ignores just how little we know about the theatrical field and privileges the extant texts as representative when we cannot be certain that they are. It can help students rethink conventional narratives about literary and theatre history.

White, Paul Whitfield, ed., *Marlowe, History, and Sexuality: New Critical Essays on Christopher Marlowe* (New York: AMS Press, 1998).

An important volume on the various connections between Marlowe, history and sexuality, this collection introduces students to the range of Marlowe scholarship and includes seminal essays by Mark Thornton Burnett on the politics of *Edward II,* by Patrick Cheney on authorship, by Mario DiGangi on Renaissance homoeroticism and by Tom Cartelli on Derek Jarman's film of the play.

Select electronic resources (Public access)

Database of Early English Playbooks (DEEP): http://deep.sas.upenn.edu/

Enormously useful resource on surviving printed plays, DEEP includes publisher and printer details, references to the Stationers' Register and information about first performances (where available). Searchable by date of publication or performance, modern title, original print title, text on title page, by period generic designation, and by genres given in the Harbage-Schoenbaum *Annals*, printers or publishers, etc.

English Short Title Catalogue (ESTC): http://estc.bl.uk

The ESTC catalogues books printed in English from 1473 to 1800 and contains about 460,000 titles. Searchable, if not the most user-friendly interface.

Henslowe Alleyn Digitisation Project: http://www.henslowe-alleyn.org.uk/index.html

The Project offers free access to digitized materials from the Henslowe-Alleyn archive at Dulwich College, including correspondence between Henslowe and Alleyn as well as Henslowe's *Diary* which remains one of the most important sources we have about early modern drama. The *Diary* includes records related to early performances of many of Marlowe's plays.

Lost Plays Database: http://www.lostplays.org/index.php/Main_Page

Developing online resource on 'lost plays' – plays that either did not get printed or which were lost once printed. Helpful in discussion of context and chronology as well as an example of an ongoing research project.

Luminarium: http://www.luminarium.org/

A digital library focused on English literature from the Middle Ages through the eighteenth century. It contains both links to online texts and to a selection of Marlowe criticism organized by work. As the site editor writes, the site was designed to 'provide a starting point for students and enthusiasts of English Literature'.

Marlowe Bibliography Online: http://www.marlowebibliography.org/

A collaborative project of the Marlowe Society of America and the University of Melbourne that provides a searchable annotated bibliography of the scholarship. It is updated every six months. Its searchability makes it especially useful for focused research.

Marlowe Society: http://www.marlowe-society.org/index.html

A scholarly organization focused on Marlowe's work. The Society's website contains information about the works, Marlowe's biography and about Marlowe-related events.

Marlowe Society of America: http://users.ipfw.edu/stapletm/msa/MSANavi.html#

The Society's homepage offers an extensive set of resources including *The MSA Newsletter*, facsimile texts, editions and studies to 1952, along with links to the Lost Plays Database and more recent scholarship.

The Perseus Digital Library: http://perseus.mpiwg-berlin.mpg.de/cache/perscoll_Renaissance.html

The Renaissance collection at the Perseus Digital Library contains searchable texts of Marlowe's works (drama and poetry) as well as the English Faust Book. It links to the Latin for Marlowe's translations of Ovid's *Amores* and Lucan's *Pharsalia*.

Select electronic resources (Subscription)

Early English Books Online (EEBO).

Generally available through university libraries. Contains scans of the microfilm of ESTC titles for the period. Its value cannot be overstated.

Early English Books Online – Text Creation Partnership.

Available through subscription. The project is creating SGML/XML encoded electronic versions of the materials in the EEBO archive. The texts created are fully searchable. As of this writing, 25,000 texts are freely available and the rest are only available to TCP partner libraries. Eventually all the texts will be freely accessible.

JSTOR.

Online collection of journals containing many of the articles listed in the bibliography. It is available through many libraries.

NOTES

Introduction

1   All quotations from the play are taken from the New Mermaids 2014 revised edition of *Edward II*, eds Martin Wiggins and Robert Lindsey with a new introduction by Stephen Guy-Bray.

2   Charles R. Forker, in his New Revels edition of *Edward II* (Manchester: Manchester University Press, 1994), argues for 1591 as the 'likeliest' date of composition; he admits, though, that his primary evidence of verbal borrowing 'is slippery ground' (14–16). See also David Riggs, *The World of Christopher Marlowe* (New York: Henry Holt and Co., 2004), 284. Alternatively, Guy-Bray (2014) has suggested that 1587, the publication date of Holinshed's second edition, could be the play's *terminus ad quo*.

3   Edward Arber, *A Transcript of the Registers of the Company of Stationers of London, 1554–1640 A.D.*, 5 vols (London, 1875–94), 2.634. William Jones worked as a bookseller in London between 1587 and 1618. For Jones's immediate family, see William E. Miller, 'Printers and Stationers in the Parish of St Giles Cripplegate 1561–1640', *Studies in Bibliography* 19 (1966): 29–30. The STC has identified Robert Robinson as the printer of the twelve-sheet quarto.

4   Two copies of Jones's 1594 edition exist, one in Zürich and another recently discovered in Germany (see Jeffrey Masten, 'Bound for Germany: Heresy, Sodomy, and a New Copy of Marlowe's *Edward II*', *Times Literary Supplement* [21/28 December, 2012], 17–19).

5   The first edition of *Edward II* is, bibliographically speaking, an octavo but is routinely referred to as a quarto. Published in 1594 by the London bookseller Thomas Woodstock, *Dido*

Queen of Carthage may have been distributed months before *Edward II*. Its title page advertises that the play was 'Written by Christopher Marlowe, and *Thomas Nash. Gent.*'

6   Figures in this paragraph are derived from the DEEP database, http://deep.sas.upenn.edu/index.html.

7   All of these were new print titles except for *The Spanish Tragedy*.

8   According to Zachary Lesser, in 'Playbooks', in *The Oxford History of Popular Print Culture*, vol. 1 (Oxford: Oxford University Press, 2011), 520–34, during this period 'an average of thirteen professional plays were published per year' (526).

9   For 'boomlets' and 'booms' in professional playbook publication, see Alan Farmer and Zachary Lesser, 'The Popularity of Playbooks Revisited', *Shakespeare Quarterly* 56.1 (2005): 1–32.

10 *Edward II* was transferred again in 1638, this time as part of a lot of over a dozen titles from Henry and Moses Bell to John Haviland and John Wright (Arber, 4.434).

11 Peter W. M. Blayney, in 'The Publication of Playbooks', in *A New History of Early English Drama*, eds John D. Cox and David Scott Kastan (New York: Columbia University Pres, 1997), 389, has estimated that only around one in five of the play titles printed between 1583 and 1642 were reprinted within nine years.

12 See Holger Schott Syme, 'Marlowe in his Moment', in *Marlowe in Context*, eds Emily Bartels and Emma Smith (Cambridge: Cambridge University Press, 2013), 274–84.

13 A number of other late-Elizabethan professional plays like *Edward I* and *Edward III* were also familiarizing audiences with this period of English history. For these offerings, see Knutson's chapter in this volume.

14 For a detailed overview of *Edward II*'s main sources, see Forker, 41–65. Further confirmation of what W. Moelwyn Merchant has described, in his 1967 New Mermaids edition of *Edward II* (London: A&C Black), as the 'remarkable Elizabethan and Jacobean interest in a turbulent period that

Shakespeare chose not to handle' (xviii) can be found in George Peele's *Honor of the Garter* (1593); Thomas Talbot's *A Book Containing the True Portraiture ... of the Kings of England* (1597); Thomas Dekker's *Seven Deadly Sins of London* (1606); Thomas Heywood's *Troia Britanica* (1609); William Martyn's *Youth's Instruction* (1612); John Taylor's *A Brief Remembrance of all the English Monarchs* (1618); Elizabeth Cary's 1626 manuscript poem *The History of the Life, Reign, and Death of Edward II*; and Ben Jonson's fragmentary *Mortimer his Fall* (printed in 1640, composition date unknown). Cf. Curtis Perry, *Literature and Favouritism in Early Modern England* (Cambridge: Cambridge University Press, 2009).

15 Each of these three titles was revised by Drayton in the early seventeenth century and republished numerous times before 1640.

16 Ben Jonson coined the phrase in his short First-Folio encomium to Shakespeare: 'if I thought my judgment were of years, / I should commit thee surely with thy peers, / And tell how far thou didst our Lyly outshine, / Or sporting Kyd, or Marlowe's mighty line'. For further discussion of Marlowe's language in *Edward II*, see Gieskes's chapter in this volume.

17 Less generously, Muriel Bradbrook, in *Themes and Conventions of Elizabethan Tragedy* [New York: Macmillan, 1935], complained of *Edward II*, 'how it is possible to fail as poetry and succeed as drama is not easy to understand'. In the introduction to his 1997 New Mermaid edition of the play, Wiggins complained, 'Marlowe never wrote drabber verse than that spoken by most of the people in *Edward II*' (xxii).

18 Cf. Catherine Nicholson, 'Marlowe and the Limits of Rhetoric', in *Marlowe in Context*, eds Emily Bartels and Emma Smith (Cambridge: Cambridge University Press, 2013), 27–38.

19 For *Tamburlaine* as inspiration for a host of lesser imitations, see Peter Berek, 'Tamburlaine's Weak Sons: Imitation as Interpretation before 1593', *Renaissance Drama* 13 (1982): 55–82.

20 Most commentators, citing the play's substitution of 'Killingworth Castle' for Kenilworth Castle and other small

details, believe that Marlowe worked mainly from the 1587 expanded edition of Holinshed. Much of the work below on source material is indebted to the notes and appendices of Forker.

21 For Marlowe's particular engagement with Holinshed, see Joan Parks, 'History, Tragedy, and Truth in Christopher Marlowe's *Edward II*', *Studies in English Literature* 39 (1999): 275–90; and Georgia E. Brown, 'Tampering with the Records: Engendering the Political Community and Marlowe's Appropriation of the Past in *Edward II*', in *Marlowe's Empery: Expanding his Critical Contexts*, eds Sara Munson Deats and Robert A. Logan (Newark, DL: University of Delaware Press, 2002), 164–87.

22 All quotations from Holinshed (1587) are taken from *The Holinshed Project*, http://www.english.ox.ac.uk/holinshed/

23 For a broader discussion of ambiguity in the play, see Robert A. Logan, '*Edward II*', in *Christopher Marlowe at 450*, eds Sara Munson Deats and Robert A. Logan (Aldershot: Ashgate), 125–44. Cf. Wilbur Sanders, *The Dramatist and the Received Idea: Studies in the Plays of Marlowe and Shakespeare* (Cambridge: Cambridge University Press, 1968).

24 Cf. Alan Shepard, *Marlowe's Soldiers: Rhetorics of Masculinity in the Age of the Armada* (Aldershot: Ashgate, 2002).

25 Cf. Wiggins (1997) who argues that 'Effeminacy rules … in a court where taste in clothes is considered more important than such manly pursuits as warfare' (xxv); and Guy-Bray (2014) who suggests that Edward II 'would rather spend the country's money on culture than on killing' (xxiii).

26 The 1587 edition of Holinshed does at one point describe Gaveston as 'so scornefull and contemptuous a merchant' (6.321), this likely an addition by Abraham Fleming.

27 Cf. Claude J. Summers, 'Sex, Politics, and Self-Realization in *Edward II*', in '*A Poet and a filthy Play-maker': New Essays on Christopher Marlowe*, eds Kenneth Friedenreich, Roma Gill and Constance Brown Kuriyama (New York: AMS Press, 1988), 221–40, esp. 224–7.

28 For overviews of critical approaches to sex and sexuality in the play, see Haber's chapter in this volume.

29 See Merchant, xxi–xxii and Summers, n.3 and n.17.

30 For readings in this vein, see Judith Weil, *Christopher Marlowe: Merlin's Prophet* (Cambridge: Cambridge University Press, 1977); Stephen Greenblatt, 'Marlowe and Renaissance Self Fashioning', in *Two Renaissance Mythmakers: Christopher Marlowe and Ben Jonson*, ed. Alvin Kernan (Baltimore: Johns Hopkins University Press, 1977), 41–69; and Purvis Boyette, 'Wanton Humour and Wanton Poets: Homosexuality in Marlowe's *Edward II*', *Tulane Studies in English* 22 (1977): 33–50.

31 See especially Gregory W. Bredbeck, *Sodomy and Interpretation: Marlowe to Milton* (Ithaca: Cornell University Press, 1991).

32 Jonathan Goldberg, in *Sodometries: Renaissance Texts, Modern Sexualities* (Stanford: Stanford University Press, 1992); Mario DiGangi, in *The Homoerotics of Early Modern Drama* (Cambridge: Cambridge University Press, 1997); and Guy-Bray (2014) have each argued that homosexuality is not wholly equated with sodomy in *Edward II*.

33 As Stephen Orgel, in *Impersonations* (Cambridge: Cambridge University Press, 1996), has pointed out, Marlowe does not actually give us the graphic method as described in Holinshed (e.g. '[T]hey kept him down, and withall put into his fundament an horne, and through the same they thrust vp into his bodie an hot spit, ... the which passing vp into his intrailes, and being rolled to and fro, burnt the same, but so as no appearance of any wound or hurt outwardlie might be once perceiued' [6.341]). Taken literally, the play has Lightborne and company crush Edward II to death.

34 Wiggins, in his introduction to his 1997 New Mermaid edition, reproduces an early seventeenth century epigram about Lightborne (xvi).

35 See Irving Ribner, *The English History Play in the Age of Shakespeare* (Princeton: Princeton University Press, 1957).

36 In scene 4, Edward II asks, 'wherefore walks young Mortimer aside?' (4.354); in the same scene, Mortimer Senior advises

his nephew to 'let his grace, whose youth is flexible / And promiseth as much as we can wish, / Freely enjoy that vain light-headed Earl, / For riper years will wean him from such toys' (4.399–402). Wiggins calls *Edward II* 'a young man's play' (xix).

37 In what is his short seven-stanza account of Mortimer Junior in *The Mirror for Magistrates* (1578), Thomas Churchyard writes, 'With love of [Mortimer Junior], Queene so much was stird, / As for his sake from honour she did scale' (sig. B3ʳ).

38 For a range of perspectives on Marlowe's Isabella, see Sara Munson Deats, *Sex, Gender, and Desire in the Plays of Christopher Marlowe* (Newark: University of Delaware Press, 1997); Simon Shepherd, 'Representing "Women" and Males: Gender Relations in Marlowe', in *Christopher Marlowe*, ed. Richard Wilson (London: Longman, 1999), 62–82; Johanna Gibbs, 'Marlowe's Politic Women', in *Constructing Christopher Marlowe*, eds J. A. Downie and J. T. Parnell (Cambridge: Cambridge University Press, 2000), 164–76; and Dympna Callaghan, 'The Terms of Gender: "Gay" and "Feminist" *Edward II*', in *Feminist Readings of Early Modern Culture: Emerging Subjects*, eds Valerie Traub, M. Lindsay Kaplan, and Dympna Callaghan (Cambridge: Cambridge University Press, 1996), 275–301. It is to Gibbs and Callaghan that much of this paragraph is indebted.

39 Marlowe moved Isabella's castigation years forward from 1330 for dramatic effect.

40 Mortimer Junior would not be executed until 1330, the fourth year of Edward III's reign. As Callaghan has pointed out, this tableau is also patently Freudian, Edward III pledging allegiance to his dead father with a symbol of castration after renouncing his mother (288).

41 Cf. Sullivan's reading of this scene in his contribution to this volume. In suggesting that Edward III's closing actions recall his father's private affections, I am echoing Marie Rutkoski in 'Breeching the Boy in Marlowe's *Edward II*', *Studies in English Literature, 1500–1900* 46 (2006): 281–304.

42 *Tamburlaine, Parts One and Two*, ed. Anthony B. Dawson (London: Methuen, 1997), 2.7.28–9.

43 *King Richard III*, ed. James R. Siemon (London: Bloomsbury, 2009), 5.5.19–21.

Chapter 1

1 Frederick S. Boas, *Christopher Marlowe: A Biographical and Critical Study* (Oxford: Clarendon Press, 1940), qtd in vii–viii. Germany invaded Poland in 1939. The first air raid siren went off in London in September of 1939 and this quickly led to blackouts and evacuations of children.

2 In 2012, another copy of the 1594 printing of the play was brought to scholarly attention; it was bound in a collection of texts in Universitätsbibliotek, Erlangen-Nürnberg, Germany. See Jeffrey Masten, 'Bound for Germany; Heresy, Sodomy, and a New Copy of Marlowe's *Edward II*', *Times Literary Supplement*, 21 December 2012, 17–19.

3 Charles Forker, ed. *King Richard II* (London: Thomson, 2002), 159.

4 James Bednarz, in 'Marlowe and the English Literary Scene', in *The Cambridge Companion to Marlowe*, ed. Patrick Cheney (Cambridge: Cambridge University Press, 2004), 90–105, writes, 'Marlowe, in turn was so intrigued by Shakespeare's challenging reinterpretation [of *Tamburlaine*] that he used 2 and *3 Henry VI* as models for *Edward II*, his own experiment in dramatizing English chronicle history' (100).

5 Robert Greene and Thomas Nashe may have reframed their writing careers and projects in response to Marlowe's (and Shakespeare's) successes on the stage (Bednarz, 95–100).

6 Michael Hattaway, *Elizabethan Popular Theatre: Plays in Performance* (London: Routledge & Kegan Paul, 1982), 144. Charles R. Forker, 'Introduction', in *Edward the Second by Christopher Marlowe*, ed. Charles Forker (Manchester: Manchester University Press, 1994), 99. For more on Pembroke's Men, see Knutson's chapter in this volume.

7 Siobhan Keenan, 'Reading Christopher Marlowe's *Edward II*:

The Example of John Newdigate in 1601', *Notes and Queries* 53.4 (2006): 452–8. These quotations are from p. 457.

8   Lois Potter, 'Marlowe in the Civil War and Commonwealth: Some Allusions and Parodies' in *'A Poet and a filthy Play-maker': New Essays on Christopher Marlowe*, eds Kenneth Friedenreich, Roma Gill and Constance B. Kuriyama (New York: AMS Press, 1988), 75.

9   Edward Phillips, *Theatrum Poetarum, or, A compleat collection of the poets* (London: Charles Smith, 1675), sig. Aa12ᵛ. In 1830, James Broughton sorted out the biographical error of calling Marlowe an actor.

10 William Winstanley, *The Lives of the Most Famous English Poets* (London: H. Clark, 1687), introduction by William Riley Parker (Gainsville: Scholars' Facimiles & Reprints, 1963), sig. K3ᵛ.

11 Judith O'Neill, Introduction, *Critics on Marlowe: Readings in Literary Criticism* (Coral Gables: University of Miami Press, 1970), 6.

12 Jeremy Lopez, *Constructing the Canon of Early Modern Drama* (Cambridge: Cambridge University Press, 2014), 59.

13 See Lopez's discussion of Dodsley's manuscript notes (60–2).

14 Thomas Warton, *The History of English Poetry, from the Close of the Eleventh to the Commencement of the Eighteenth Century*, Volume III (London: J. Dodsley, 1781).

15 Unless otherwise noted, all in-text quotations from *Edward II* are taken from the New Mermaids 2014 revised edition of *Edward II*, eds Martin Wiggins and Robert Lindsey with a new introduction by Stephen Guy-Bray.

16 See Hugh Reid, in 'Warton, Thomas (1728–90)', *Oxford Dictionary of National Biography* (Oxford: Oxford University Press, 2004), for a description of the wide appeal and impact of Warton's book.

17 Joseph Ritson, *Observations on The Three First Volumes of the History of English Poetry in a Familiar Letter to the Author* (London: J. Stockdale and R. Faulder, 1782).

18 Transcriptions of the Baines letter are widely available; the passages here are quoted from *Critics on Marlowe: Readings*

in Literary Criticism, ed. Judith O'Neill (Coral Gables: University of Miami Press, 1970), 10.

19 An example may serve to illustrate the tone of Ritson's project: 'You have, Mr. Warton, in the course of this idle controversy acquitted yourself with uncommon adroitness, and gained every advantage you could wish for over your numerous adversaries. And while you thus artfully fabricate your own facts, how should it be otherwise?' (28–9).

20 Charles Lamb, *Specimens of English Dramatic Poets Who Lived About the Time of Shakespeare,* 1808 (London: Henry G. Bohn, 1854).

21 George Saintsbury, *A History of English Criticism: Being the English Chapters of A History of Criticism and Literary Taste in Europe,* 1911 (Edinburgh: Blackwood, 1930), 350.

22 The octavo printing of the play has neither act nor scene divisions. In Forker's edition, these passages have the following lineation: 1.1.50–70; 1.4.385–418; 2.2.140–98; 5.1.1–111; and 5.5.41–108.

23 This passage is quoted from Lamb's version; in Forker, the last line appears as: 'The murmuring commons overstrechèd hath' (2.2.156–9).

24 Lopez has pointed out that, in some instances, Lamb's 'excerpts show a strong preference for passages of voluptuous description whose context, were it known, would ironize the poetic pleasure they provide' (*Constructing*, 38).

25 This entry, dated as 1809–10, comes from Notebook 18 and appears as entry 3,654 in Volume III of Kathleen Coburn's edition of Coleridge's notebooks (Princeton: Princeton University Press, 1973).

26 Susan Valladarus, in *Staging the Peninsular War: English Theatres 1807–1815* (Aldershot: Ashgate, 2015), has shown that Coleridge, through his lectures on Shakespeare and engagement with the theatre of his time, developed a connection between dramatic literature and the contemporaneous politics of the Peninsular War of 1807–14.

27 William Hazlitt, *Lectures on the Dramatic Literature of the*

Age of Elizabeth (1820), in *The Complete Works of William Hazlitt in Twenty-One Volumes,* Volume Six, ed. P. P. Howe (London: J. M. Dent, 1931), 178–9, 179. Hazlitt comments: 'Dr. Johnson said of these writers generally, that "they were sought after because they were scarce, and would not have been scarce, had they been much esteemed." His decision is neither true history nor sound criticism. They were esteemed, and they deserved to be so' (*Lectures*, 179).

28 Hazlitt's literary criticism fell out of favour in the early twentieth century, but in the nineteenth century his influential voice helped to bring early-modern dramatists back into print.

29 A. C. Bradley, 'Christopher Marlowe', in *The English Poets: Selected with Critical Introductions by Various Authors*, ed. T. H. Ward (London: Macmillan, 1881), 413.

30 G. Gregory Smith, 'Marlowe and Kyd: Chronicle Histories', in *The Drama to 1642, Part One, The Cambridge History of English Literature,* Volume Five, eds A. W. Ward and A. R. Waller (Cambridge: Cambridge University Press, 1911), 172–3.

31 Felix Schelling, *English Drama* (London: J. M. Dent, 1914), 69.

32 Given Eliot's useful and interesting commentary on *Dido Queene of Carthage*, in 'Christopher Marlowe' (1919), in *Essays on Elizabethan Drama* (New York: Harcourt, Brace & World, 1960), 62, one wishes he had commented on *Edward II*.

33 See Andrea Stevens's chapter on the theatrical history of *Edward II* in this volume. See also Louise J. Laboulle, 'A Note on Bertolt Brecht's Adaptation of Marlowe's *Edward II*', *The Modern Language Review* 54.2 (1959): 214–20.

34 Quotation from Bertolt Brecht's *Leben Eduards des Zweiten von England* from Eric Bentley's translation (New York: Grove Press, 1966), 4–5.

35 James Broughton, 'Life and Writings of Christopher Marlowe', *Gentlemen's Magazine* 100 (1830): 593.

36 J. Leslie Hotson, *The Death of Christopher Marlowe* (Cambridge: Harvard University Press, 1925). Marlowe

biographies of the earlier twentieth century include C. G. Tucker Brooke's *The Life of Marlowe, and the Tragedy of Dido, Queen of Carthage* (London: Methuen, 1930), Mark Eccles' *Christopher Marlowe in London* (Cambridge: Harvard University Press, 1934), and John Bakeless' *The Tragicall History of Christopher Marlowe* (Cambridge: Harvard University Press, 1942).

37 Paul H. Kocher, *Christopher Marlowe: A Study of his Thought, Learning, and Character* (Chapel Hill: University of North Carolina Press, 1946), 205 n.43.

38 Harry Levin, Jr., *The Overreacher: A Study of Christopher Marlowe* (Cambridge: Harvard University Press, 1952), 82.

39 Michael Hattaway, *Elizabethan Popular Theatre: Plays in Performance* (London: Routledge & Kegan Paul, 1982), 141.

40 Sara Munson Deats, 'Marlowe's Fearful Symmetry in *Edward II*' in *'A Poet and a filthy Play-maker': New Essays on Christopher Marlowe,* eds Kenneth Friedenreich, Roma Gill, and Constance B. Kuriyama (New York: AMS Press, 1988), 241.

41 J. B. Steane, *Marlowe: A Critical Study* (Cambridge: Cambridge University Press, 1964).

42 Clifford Leech, 'Marlowe's *Edward II*: Power and Suffering', *Critical Quarterly* 1.3 (1959): 196.

43 Stephen Greenblatt, 'Marlowe and Renaissance Self-Fashioning', in *Two Renaissance Mythmakers: Christopher Marlowe and Ben Jonson*, ed. Alvin Kernan (Baltimore: Johns Hopkins University Press, 1977), 52.

44 Claude J. Summers' 'Sex, Politics, and Self-Realization in *Edward II*', in *'A Poet and a filthy Play-maker': New Essays on Christopher Marlowe,* eds Kenneth Friedenreich, Roma Gill, and Constance B. Kuriyama (New York: AMS Press, 1988), 223.

45 *Hart Crane: The Life of an American Poet* (New York: Viking Press, 1937), 145.

46 Paul Mariani, *The Broken Tower: A Life of Hart Crane* (New York: Norton, 1999), 368.

Chapter 2

1. All references taken from the revised New Mermaids edition, eds Martin Wiggins and Robert Lindsey, with a new introduction by Stephen Guy-Bray (London: Bloomsbury Press, 2014).

2. 'Reviewing What We Think We Know about Christopher Marlowe, Again', in *Christopher Marlowe the Craftsman*, eds Sarah K. Scott and M. L. Stapleton (Aldershot: Ashgate Press, 2010), 39.

3. Clifford Leech, '*Exeunt to the cave*: Notes on the Staging of Marlowe's Plays', *Tulane Drama Review* 8 (Summer 1964): 192; see also Gordon Geckle, *Tamburlaine and Edward II: Text and Performance* (London: Macmillan Press, 1988), 33–4.

4. Ibid.

5. Tiffany Stern, *Making Shakespeare from Stage to Page* (New York: Routledge Press, 2004), 26–7.

6. Patrick Ryan, 'Marlowe's *Edward II* and the Medieval Passion Play', *Comparative Drama* 32.4 (Winter 1989–9): 465–95.

7. David Fuller, 'Love or Politics: The Man or the King? *Edward II* in Modern Performance', *Shakespeare Bulletin* 27.1 (2009): 84.

8. See Alan Bray, *Homosexuality in Renaissance England* (New York: Columbia University Press, 1995); see also Jonathan Goldberg, *Sodometries: Renaissance Texts, Modern Sexualities* (Stanford: Stanford University Press, 1992).

9. See Curtis Perry, 'The Politics of Access and Representations of the Sodomite King in Early Modern England', *Renaissance Quarterly* 53.4 (2000): 1054–83.

10. David Moore Bergeron, *King James & Letters of Homoerotic Desire* (Iowa City: University of Iowa Press, 1999), 175.

11. David H. Horne, *The Life and Minor Works of George Peele*, vol. 1 (New Haven: Yale University Press, 1952), 253; see also Charles Forker's mention of this poem in his Revels edition of *Edward II* (Manchester: Manchester University Press, 1994), 99.

12 Qtd in David Bevington's 'Introduction to *Edward II*' in *English Renaissance Drama* (New York: W. W. Norton & Co., 2002), 356.

13 For his compelling account of the 'phobic' element in Edward's murder, see Jonathan V. Crewe, 'Disorderly Love: Sodomy Revisited in Marlowe's *Edward II*', *Criticism* 51.3 (2009): 393.

14 Peter Womack, 'Notes on the "Elizabethan" Avant-Garde', in *Shakespeare and the Twentieth Century: The Selected Proceedings of the International Shakespeare Association World Congress*, eds Jonathan Bate, Jill Levenson, and Dieter L. Mehl (Newark: University of Delaware Press, 1998), 75.

15 Geckle quotes from an anonymous review of the play lauding the fact that 'the terrible close to the death scene was rightly curtailed' (79); see also Forker, 100.

16 Rima Hakim, *Marlowe on the English Stage, 1588–1988: A Stage History of Three Marlowe Plays*, PhD Thesis (University of Leeds, 1990), 133.

17 Brecht quoted in Edward Braun, *The Director & The Stage: From Naturalism to Grotowski* (London: Methuen, 1982), 163. All references to Brecht's adaptation come from Eric Bentley's translation *Edward II, A Chronicle Play* (New York: Grove Press, 1966).

18 See John Fuegi's discussion of Brecht's rehearsal processes, including especially the influence of Soviet actress and director Asja Lazis, in *Brecht and Company: Sex, Politics, and the Making of the Modern Drama* (New York: Grove Press, 1994), 132.

19 Eric Bentley, *Bentley on Brecht* (Evanston: Northwestern University Press, 2008), 167–8.

20 For Bentley, 'Brecht's tragedy has a puritanic aspect. His hero has been a heterosexual before the play opens; becomes a homosexual later; and, later still, withdraws, through friendship, and, even more, through friendship betrayed, into heroic solitude' (176).

21 See also Bentley's headnote to his chapter on *Edward II*, 158.

22 Deborah Willis, 'Marlowe Our Contemporary: *Edward II* on Stage and Screen', *Criticism* 40.4 (1998): 599–622.
23 Loren Kruger, '*Edward II* by Bertolt Brecht' (Review), *Theatre Journal* 40.3 (October 1988): 413.
24 Nick Curtis, 'The king, in his gold skirt and platform boots, is dead' (Review), *The Evening Standard* (7 January 1999), 52.
25 Charles McNulty, 'Marlowe and Shakespeare Get the Treatment' (Review), *Village Voice* (2–8 February 2000), 73.
26 Sarah Boxer, 'The King Says No. That's Trouble, No?' (Review), the *New York Times* (25 February 2000, Late Edition), 3.
27 Marilyn Stasio, '*Edward II*' (Review), *Variety* (19–25 September 2005), 78.
28 See Guy-Bray, xviii; and Goldberg.
29 Toby Robertson, 'Directing "Edwards II"', *Tulane Drama Review* 8.4 (1964): 183.
30 Clifford Leech, 'Marlowe's "*Edward II*": Power and Suffering', *Critical Quarterly* 1 (1959): 181–96.
31 'A Double Crown' (Review), *Time* 94.12 (19 September 1969), 77.
32 Sebastian Buckle, *The Way Out: A History of Homosexuality in Britain* (London: I. B. Tauris & Co., 2015), 17.
33 This production is accessible through youtube.com.
34 Angela K. Ahlgren, 'Christopher Marlowe's "Unholy Fascination": Performing Queer *Edward II* in the 1990s', *Journal of Dramatic Theory and Criticism* 25.2 (2011): 12; McKellen is quoted in the programme notes to the 1990 RSC production directed by Gerard Murphy (Ahlgren discusses how these notes 'rehearse the play's own allegedly queer past' and thus refer to the 1969 production).
35 Robertson said that 'the performance with Ian made the earlier part of the play more histrionic' (89).
36 The anonymous *Time* reviewer cited above describes the scene as follows: 'It ends with a death scene in which Marlowe dredges the most profound pity up from the most nightmarish sensationalism: the deposed king dragged from the castle

cesspool, half mad and dripping with muck, washed and soothed and kissed by his murderer in the lingering tender dialogue with which a frightened lover is put to sleep. Then smothered with a feather blanket, crushed beneath an upturned table. Then legs up, and the flaming retribution for pederasty, a cauterization evidenced by the chronicles Marlowe knew but made into a myth beyond history, as searing as an image by Hieronymus Bosch' (77).

37 Anne Donaldson (Review), *Herald Scotland* (12 July 1990); Peter Hepple (Review), *The Stage* (9 May 1991).

38 Hepple, 9 May 1991.

39 Paul Taylor, 'The boy who would be king' (Review), *The Independent* (12 July 1990), 16. Taylor also mentions, 'the deranged hang of the curtains at the back and the rusting ironmongery which lies in bleak heaps to the side of the stage. The world of this play is a cheerless, vicious place, where, in the absence of any more dynamic virtue, the passive ability to withstand cruelty and degradation warrants a disproportionate respect. Aptly bracketed here by two grim funeral corteges, Murphy's production emphasizes this point by largely deterring audience sympathy until the king and his crowd are sundered and Edward's gruesome prison ordeal begins'.

40 Benedict Nightingale, 'Rushing, roaring Marlowe' (review), *The Times* (11 July 1990).

41 Jack Tinker (Review), *Daily Mail* (13 May 1991).

42 Michael Billington, 'The King is smothered' (Review), *Guardian Weekly* (22 July 1990), 23.

43 Robert Hewison, 'Madness, fatal passion, and a war of the poses' (Review), *London Sunday Times* (15 July 1990).

44 Nightingale, 11 July 1990.

45 Ibid.

46 *London Theatre Record* (2–15 July 1990), 924.

47 Derek Jarman, *Queer Edward II* (London: BFI, 1991), ii.

48 Bert Cardullo, 'Outing Edward, Outfitting Marlowe: Derek Jarman's Film', *Literature/Film Quarterly* 37.2 (2009): 88.

49 'Ian said afterwards she's a cross between Joan Crawford and Christine Keeler … . It's strange how the echo of period in her costumes has everyone remembering movie history. Someone else said Hepburn. Tilda said as long as they don't all agree on the reference – she's happy' (Jarman, 148).

50 Susan Bennett, *Performing Nostalgia: Shifting Shakespeare and the Contemporary Past* (London: Routledge, 1996), 110; Niall Richardson, 'The Queer Performance of Tilda Swinton in Derek Jarman's *Edward II*: Gay Male Misogyny Reconsidered', *Sexualities: Studies in Culture and Society* 6.3–4 (November 2003): 429.

51 Lois Potter, 'What Happened to the Mighty Line?: Recent Marlowe Productions', *Shakespeare Bulletin* 27.1 (Spring 2009): 65.

52 Irene Backalenick, '*Edward II*' (Review), *Back Stage* 45.45 (2004): 35.

53 Justin Shaltz, '*Edward II* and *Measure for Measure*' (Review), *Shakespeare Bulletin* 24.1 (Spring 2006): 92.

54 Rachel Evans, '*Edward II*' (Review), *Theatre Journal* 60.3 (October 2008): 482.

55 Tim Treanor, '*Edward II*', *DC Theatre Scene* (12 November 2007), Web, 5 March 2014.

56 Andrea Stevens, '*Edward II*' (Review), *Shakespeare Bulletin* 27.1 (Spring 2009): 118. Gale Edwards's production came in at three hours and fifteen minutes; Graney's clocked eighty minutes without a break.

57 Nicholas Hamilton, '*Edward II*' (Review), *The Stage* (24 February 2011), 20.

58 Glen Meads, '*Edward II*' (Review), *The Stage* (15 September 2011), 18.

59 *Edward II* at The National Theatre' (Review), the *Telegraph* (5 September 2013).

60 Michael Billington, '*Edward II*' (Review), the *Guardian* (5 September 2013); Kirk Melnikoff, '*Edward II*' (Review), *Marlowe Society of America Newsletter* 33.1 (Fall 2013): 4–5.

61 Johann Persson, '*Edward II* at The National Theatre' (Review), *The Independent* (6 September 2013); Charles

Spencer, '*Edward II*, National Theatre' (Review), the *Telegraph* (5 September 2013).

62 Andrzej Lukowski, '*Edward II*' (Review), *Time Out*, London (5 September 2013).

Chapter 3

1 Bruce Brandt, in the introduction to his extremely helpful annotated bibliography ('Christopher Marlowe Studies: Bibliography, 2000–2009', *Marlowe Studies: An Annual* 1 (2011): 193–277), concludes from comparing records for Marlowe's plays in the 1980s and the 2000s that 'Marlowe studies continue at a remarkably even pace' (194); in the case of *Edward II*, at least, that seems in large part because he is not considering the 1990s. In addition to Brandt, I was aided by the following useful bibliographies and studies: Patrick Cheney, 'Recent Studies in Marlowe (1987–1998)', *English Literary Renaissance* 31(2001): 288–328; Valerie Traub, 'Recent Studies in Homoeroticism', *English Literary Renaissance* 30 (2000): 284–320; 'Marlowe Bibliography Online', eds David McInnis and Gayle Allan, http://www.marlowebibliography.org/; and Stephen Guy-Bray, 'Introduction', in *Edward II* by Christopher Marlowe, rev. edn (London: Bloomsbury, 2014), vii–xxxiv.

2 Alan Stewart, '*Edward II* and Male Same-Sex Desire', in *Early Modern English Drama: A Critical Companion*, eds Garrett A. Sullivan, Patrick Cheney and Andrew Hadfield (Oxford: Oxford University Press, 2009), 82.

3 Michel Foucault, *The History of Sexuality, vol. I, An Introduction*, trans. Robert Hurley (New York: Pantheon, 1978), 101; quoted by Jonathan Goldberg in 'Introduction: "That Utterly Confused Category"', *Sodometries: Renaissance Texts, Modern Sexualities* (Stanford: Stanford University Press, 1992), 3.

4 Gregory W. Bredbeck, *Sodomy and Interpretation: Marlowe to Milton* (Ithaca: Cornell University Press, 1991), 76, 77.

5 Alan Bray, 'Sodomy and the Signs of Male Friendship

in Elizabethan England', in *Queering the Renaissance*, ed. Jonathan Goldberg (Durham: Duke University Press, 1994), 40–61. Bray's ideas here are further developed and contextualized in his posthumously published book *The Friend* (Chicago: University of Chicago Press, 2003).

6 Stephen Orgel, *Impersonations: The Performance of Gender in Shakespeare's England* (Cambridge: Cambridge University Press, 1996), 46.

7 Bruce Smith, 'Master and Minion', in *Homosexual Desire in Shakespeare's England: A Cultural Poetics* (Chicago: University of Chicago Press, 1991), 223.

8 Emily Carroll Bartels, *Spectacles of Strangeness: Imperialism, Alienation, and Marlowe* (Philadelphia: University of Pennsylvania Press, 1993), 147, 156. Bartels (147–56) presents a useful discussion of Marlowe's alteration of his source material in Holinshed's *Chronicles*.

9 Mario DiGangi, 'Marlowe, Queer Studies, and Renaissance Homoeroticism', in *Marlowe, History, and Sexuality: New Critical Essays on Christopher Marlowe*, ed. Paul Whitfield White (New York: AMS Press, 1998), 204; DiGangi develops in this essay, with particular reference to *Edward II*, the position put forth in his earlier book, *The Homoerotics of Early Modern Drama* (Cambridge: Cambridge University Press, 1997).

10 Claude J. Summers, 'Marlowe and Constructions of Renaissance Homosexuality', *Canadian Review of Comparative Literature* 21 (1994): 27.

11 Jennifer Brady, 'Fear and Loathing in Marlowe's *Edward II*', in *Sexuality and Politics in Renaissance Drama*, eds Carole Levin and Karen Robertson (1991), 177, 183, 187.

12 Stephen Guy-Bray, 'Homophobia and the Depoliticizing of *Edward II*', *English Studies in Canada* 17 (1991): 132, 126.

13 Viviana Comensoli, 'Homophobia and the Regulation of Desire: A Psychoanalytic Reading of Marlowe's *Edward II*', *Journal of the History of Sexuality* 4 (1993): 175–200.

14 Dympna Callaghan, 'The Terms of Gender: "Gay" and

"Feminist" *Edward II*', in *Feminist Readings of Early Modern Culture: Emerging Subjects*, eds Valerie Traub, Lindsay M. Kaplan and Dympna Callaghan (Cambridge: Cambridge University Press, 1996), 290, 292.

15 Kathleen Anderson, '"Stab as Occasion Serves": the Real Isabella in Marlowe's *Edward II*', *Renaissance Papers* (1992): 39.

16 Sara Munson Deats, *Sex, Gender, and Desire in the Plays of Christopher Marlowe* (Newark: University of Delaware Press, 1997), 186.

17 Thomas Healy, *Christopher Marlowe* (Plymouth: Northcote House), 80.

18 Ian McAdam, '*Edward II* and the Illusion of Integrity', *Studies in Philology* 92 (1995): 204, 203, 221, 228. McAdam develops his ideas, discussing all Marlowe's plays, in *Christopher Marlowe and the Irony of Identity: Self and Imagination in the Drama of Christopher Marlowe* (Newark: University of Delaware Press, 1999).

19 Derek Jarman, *Queer Edward II* (London: British Film Institute, 1991).

20 Thomas Cartelli, '*Queer Edward II*: Postmodern Sexualities and the Early Modern Subject', in *Marlowe, History, and Sexuality: New Critical Essays on Christopher Marlowe*, ed. Paul Whitfield White (New York: AMS Press, 1998), 122.

21 Deborah Willis, 'Marlowe Our Contemporary: *Edward II* on Stage and Screen', *Criticism* 40 (1998): 600.

22 John Michael Archer, *Sovereignty and Intelligence: Spying and Court Culture in the English Renaissance* (Stanford: Stanford University Press, 1993), 76–7.

23 Lawrence Normand, '"What Passions Call You These?": *Edward II* and James VI', in *Christopher Marlowe and English Renaissance Culture,* eds Darryll Grantley and Peter Roberts (Aldershot: Scolar, 1996), 174.

24 Mark Thornton Burnett, '*Edward II* and Elizabethan Politics', in *Marlowe, History, and Sexuality*, 81.

25 Curtis Perry, 'The Politics of Access and Representations of

the Sodomite King in Early Modern England', *Renaissance Quarterly* 53 (2000): 1054.

26 Dennis Kay, 'Marlowe, *Edward II*, and the Cult of Elizabeth', *Early Modern Literary Studies* 3 (1997): 1.1–30, http://purl.oclc.org/emls/03-2/kaymarl.html (accessed 1 March 2015).

27 Curtis C. Breight, *Surveillance, Militarism and Drama in the Elizabethan Era* (Basingstoke: Palgrave, 1996), 134.

28 William Zunder, *Elizabethan Marlowe: Writing and Culture in the English Renaissance* (Cottingham: Unity, 1994), 57, 61.

29 Carla Coleman Prichard, '"Learn Then to Rule Us Better and the Realm": Restoration of Order and the Boy King in Marlowe's *Edward II*', *Renaissance Papers* (1998): 33.

30 David H. Thurn, 'Sovereignty, Disorder, and Fetishism in Marlowe's *Edward II*', *Renaissance Drama* 21 (1990): 119.

31 Judith Haber, 'Submitting to History: Marlowe's *Edward II*', in *Enclosure Acts: Property and Culture in Early Modern England*, eds Richard Burt and John Michael Archer (Ithaca: Cornell University Press, 1994), 179; I contextualize my ideas in my later book, *Desire and Dramatic Form in Early Modern England* (Cambridge: Cambridge University Press, 2009).

32 Fred B. Tromly, *Playing with Desire: Christopher Marlowe and the Art of Tantalization* (Toronto: University of Toronto Press, 1998), 113–32.

33 Catherine Belsey, 'Desire's Excess and the English Renaissance Theatre: *Edward II, Troilus and Cressida, Othello*', in *Erotic Politics: Desire on the Renaissance Stage*, ed. Susan Zimmerman (London: Routledge, 1992), 84, 88.

34 Matthew N. Proser, *The Gift of Fire: Aggression and the Plays of Christopher Marlowe* (New York: Peter Lang, 1995), 2.

35 Katherine A. Sirluck, 'Marlowe's *Edward II* and the Pleasure of Outrage', *Modern Language Studies* 22 (1992): 22.

36 William B. Kelly, 'Mapping Subjects in Marlowe's *Edward II*', *South Atlantic Review* 62 (1998): 1.

37 Roger Sales, *Christopher Marlowe* (Basingstoke: Macmillan, 1991), 117.

38 Douglas Cole, *Christopher Marlowe and the Renaissance of Tragedy* (Westport: Praeger: 1995), 103, 104.

39 Joan Parks, 'History, Tragedy and Truth in Christopher Marlowe's *Edward II*', *Studies in English Literature* 39 (1999): 290.

40 Patrick Ryan, 'Marlowe's *Edward II* and the Medieval Passion Play', *Comparative Drama* 32 (1999): 466.

41 Debra Belt, 'Anti-Theatricalism and Rhetoric in Marlowe's *Edward II*', *English Literary Renaissance* 21 (1991): 135.

42 Thomas Cartelli, *Marlowe, Shakespeare, and the Economy of Theatrical Experience* (Philadelphia: University of Pennsylvania Press, 1991), 121.

43 Patrick Cheney, *Marlowe's Counterfeit Profession: Ovid, Spenser, Counter-Nationhood* (Toronto: University of Toronto Press, 1997), 158–9.

44 Robert P. Merrix and Carole Levin, '*Richard II* and *Edward II*: The Structure of Deposition', *Shakespeare Yearbook* 1 (1990): 7.

45 Maurice Charney, 'Marlowe's *Edward II* as Model for Shakespeare's *Richard II*', *Research Opportunities in Renaissance Drama* 33 (1994): 40, 32.

46 Charles R. Forker, '*Edward II* and its Shakespearean Relatives: The Emergence of Genre', in *Shakespeare's English Histories: A Quest for Form and Genre*, ed. John W. Velz (Binghamton: Medieval and Renaissance Texts and Studies, 1996), 65–6.

47 Meredith Skura, 'Marlowe's *Edward II*: Penetrating Language in Shakespeare's *Richard II*', *Shakespeare Survey* 50 (1997): 42.

48 Thomas Cartelli, '*Edward II*', in *The Cambridge Companion to Christopher Marlowe,* ed. Patrick Cheney (Cambridge: Cambridge University Press, 2004), 139.

49 Jonathan Crewe, 'Disorderly Love: Sodomy Revisited in Marlowe's *Edward II*', *Criticism* 31 (2009): 389.

50 David Clark, 'Marlowe and Queer Theory', in *Christopher Marlowe in Context,* eds Emily Bartels and Emma Smith (Cambridge: Cambridge University Press, 2013), 240.

51 H. David Brumble, 'Personal, Paternal, and Kingly Control in

Marlowe's *Edward II*', *Explorations in Renaissance Culture* 34 (2009): 56.

52   David Stymeist, 'Status, Sodomy, and the Theater in Marlowe's *Edward II*', *Studies in English Literature* 44 (2004): 237–8.

53   Alan Stewart, '*Edward II* and Male Same-Sex Desire', in *Early Modern English Drama,* 93.

54   Lawrence Normand, '*Edward II,* Derek Jarman, and the State of England', in *Constructing Christopher Marlowe*, eds J. A. Downie and J. T. Parnell (Cambridge: Cambridge University Press, 2000), 184, 189.

55   Amanda Bailey, 'The Italian Vice and Bad Taste in *Edward II*', in *Flaunting: Style and the Subversive Male Body in Renaissance England* (Toronto: University of Toronto Press, 2007), 78.

56   Bailey quotes from Robert Greene, *The Life and Complete Works in Prose and Verse*, ed. Alexander B. Grossart (New York: Russell and Russell, 1964), II, 226.

57   Joanna Gibbs, 'Marlowe's Politic Women', in *Constructing Christopher Marlowe*, 166, 170.

58   Jennifer L. Sheckter, 'Perform to Power: Isabella's Performative Self-Creation in *Edward II'*, *Marlowe Studies: An Annual* 3 (2013): 131.

59   Kate Chedgzoy, 'Marlowe's Men and Women: Gender and Sexuality', in *The Cambridge Companion to Christopher Marlowe,* 250–1; Chedgzoy also discusses homoeroticism and its relation to marriage and political power in the play.

60   Claire Hansen, '"Who taught thee this?": Female Agency and Experiential Learning in Marlowe's *Tamburlaine, The Jew of Malta, and Edward II*', *Journal of Language, Literature and Culture* 60 (2013): 170.

61   Doris Feldman, 'Construction and Deconstruction of Gendered Bodies in Selected Plays of Christopher Marlowe', in *The Body in Late Medieval and Early Modern Culture*, eds Darryll Grantley and Nina Taunton (Aldershot: Ashgate, 2000), 29.

62   Alan Shepard, *Marlowe's Soldiers: Rhetorics of Masculinity in the Age of the Armada* (Aldershot: Ashgate, 2002), 83, 85.
63   Merry G. Perry, 'Masculinity, Performance, and Identity: Father/Son Dyads in Christopher Marlowe's Plays', in *Placing the Plays of Christopher Marlowe: Fresh Cultural Contexts*, eds Sara Munson Deats and Robert A. Logan (Aldershot: Ashgate, 2008), 104.
64   Marie Rutkoswki, 'Breeching the Boy in Marlowe's *Edward II*', *Studies in English Literature* 46 (2006): 281, 296.
65   Marcie Bianco, 'To Sodomize a Nation: Edward II, Ireland, and the Threat of Penetration', *Early Modern Literary Studies* 16 (2007): 11.1–21, http://extra.shu.ac.uk/emls/si-16/bianedii.htm (accessed 1 March 2015).
66   Jeffrey Rufo, 'Marlowe's Minions: Sodomitical Politics in *Edward II* and *The Massacre of Paris*', *Marlowe Studies: An Annual* 1 (2011): 6.
67   Ronald Knowles, 'The Political Contexts of Deposition and Election in *Edward II*', *Medieval and Renaissance Drama in England* 14 (2001): 105.
68   Chloe Kathleen Preedy, *Marlowe's Literary Scepticism: Politic Religion and Post-Reformation Polemic* (London: Bloomsbury, 2012), 149.
69   Preedy notes that the rationales in the play were more usually associated with Catholic rebels than with radical Protestants, but that connections to the writings of the latter group are also present.
70   Curtis Perry, *Literature and Favoritism in Early Modern England* (Cambridge: Cambridge University Press, 2009), 185.
71   Paulina Kewes, 'Marlowe, History, and Politics', in *Christopher Marlowe in Context*, 144.
72   Laurie Shannon, *Sovereign Amity: Figures of Friendship in Shakespearean Contexts* (Chicago: University of Chicago Press, 2002), 156, 157.
73   The first phrase comes originally from Aristotle.
74   Shannon defines *mignonnerie* as 'a friendship crossing the boundaries of degree, most particularly on captivating a king' (13).

75 Jeffrey Masten, 'Toward a Queer Address: The Taste of Letters and Early Modern Male Friendship, *GLQ: A Journal of Lesbian and Gay Studies* 10 (2004): 379.

76 Peter Sillitoe, '"Where is the court but here?": Undetermined Elite Space and Marlowe's *Edward II*', *Literature Compass* 1 (2004): 1–15.

77 Emma Katherine Atwood, '"All Places Are Alike": Marlowe's *Edward II* and English Spatial Imagination', *Journal of Medieval and Early Modern Studies* 43 (Winter 2013): 51; quoting Henri Lefebvre, *The Production of Space*, trans. Donald Nicholson-Smith (Oxford: Blackwell 1993), 3.

78 Patrick Cheney, *Marlowe's Republican Authorship: Lucan, Liberty, and the Sublime* (Basingstoke: Palgrave, 2009), 148.

79 Patrick Cheney, '*Edward II*: Marlowe, Tragedy, and the Sublime', in *The Cambridge Companion to English Renaissance Tragedy*, eds Emma Smith and Garrett A. Sullivan, Jr. (Cambridge: Cambridge University Press, 2010), 174.

80 Georgia Brown, 'Tampering with the Records: Engendering the Political Community and Marlowe's *Edward II*', in *Marlowe's Empery: Expanding His Critical Contexts*, eds Sara Munson Deats and Robert A. Logan (Newark: University of Delaware Press, 2002), 165.

81 Clare Harraway, *Re-citing Marlowe: Approaches to the Drama* (Aldershot: Ashgate, 2000), 60.

82 Sara Munson Deats, 'Marlowe's Interrogative Drama: *Dido, Tamburlaine, Doctor Faustus, and Edward II*', in *Marlowe's Empery*, 125.

83 Lisa Hopkins, '"Truest of the Twain": History and Poetry in *Edward II*', *Marlowe Studies: An Annual* 3 (2013): 111.

84 Alan Dessen, '*Edward II* and Residual Allegory', in *Christopher Marlowe the Craftsman: Lives, Stage, and Page*, eds Sarah K. Scott and M. L. Stapleton (Aldershot: Ashgate, 2010), 71.

85 Ruth Lunney, 'Marlowe's *Edward II* and the Early Playhouse Audience', in *Placing the Plays of Christopher* Marlowe, 28.

Lunney discusses all of Marlowe's plays in her earlier book, *Marlowe and the Popular Tradition: Innovation in the English Drama before 1595* (Manchester: Manchester University Press, 2002); her essay is a reframing of the material on *Edward II* from this book.

86   Meg F. Pearson, 'Audience as Witness in *Edward II*', in *Imagining the Audience in Early Modern Drama, 1558–1642*, eds Jennifer A. Low and Nova Myhill (New York: Palgrave, 2011), 107.

87   Thomas Page Anderson, '*Edward II* and the Aesthetics of Survival', in *Performing Early Modern Trauma from Shakespeare to Milton* (Aldershot: Ashgate, 2006), 94.

88   Evelyn Tribble, 'Marlowe's Boy Actors', *Shakespeare Bulletin* 27 (2009): 13, 14.

89   Roslyn L. Knutson, 'Marlowe, Company Ownership, and the Role of Edward II', *Medieval and Renaissance Drama in England* 18 (2005): 37–46.

90   George L. Geckle, 'Narrativity: *Edward II* and *Richard II*', *Renaissance Papers* (2000), 99.

91   Robert A. Logan, *Shakespeare's Marlowe: The Influence of Christopher Marlowe on Shakespeare's Artistry* (Aldershot: Ashgate, 2007), 84.

92   The term is Stephen Greenblatt's from *Renaissance Self-Fashioning: More to Marlowe* (Chicago: University of Chicago Press, 1980); Logan both criticizes and develops Greenblatt's seminal idea in *Shakespeare's Marlowe*, 85ff.

93   David Bevington, 'Christopher Marlowe: The Late Years', in *Placing the Plays of Christopher Marlowe*, 221, 222.

94   Jon Surgal, 'The Rebel and the Red Hot Spit: Marlowe's *Edward II* as Anal-Sadistic Protoype', *American Imago* 61 (2004): 165.

95   Christopher D. Foley, 'Marlowe's *Edward II* and "The Woeful Lamentations of Jane Shore": Tactical Engagements With Sewers in Late-Elizabethan London', *Early Modern Literary Studies* 23 (2014), https://extra.shu.ac.uk/emls/journal/index.php/emls/article/view/179, 1, 2, 3 (accessed 1 March 2015).

96   Siobhan Keenan, 'Reading Christopher Marlowe's *Edward II*:

the Example of John Newdigate in 1601', *Notes and Queries* 53 (2006): 454, 453.

97 Jeffrey Masten, *Bound for Germany, TLS* 21 December 2012, 17–19, http://www.the-tls.co.uk/tls/public/tlssearch.do?querystring=masten&sectionId=1797&p=tls (accessed 1 March 2015).

98 Jonathan Goldberg and Madhavi Menon, 'Queering History', *PMLA* 120 (2005): 1609; this essay mentions some critical texts that are doing the work its authors recommend (1608–17).

99 Valerie Traub, 'The New Unhistoricism in Queer Studies', *PMLA* 128 (2013): 33; Traub also provides a useful overview of 'unhistoricism' and related critical approaches (21–39).

Chapter 4

1 All references to *Edward II* come from *Edward II*, rev. edn, eds Martin Wiggins and Robert Lindsey (1997: London: Methuen, 2014). References to *The Massacre at Paris* come from *The Complete Works of Christopher Marlowe*, ed. Edward E. Esche, vol. 5 (Oxford: Clarendon Press, 1987–98). All titles are modernized for capitalization and spelling unless referring to a particular early modern edition.

2 Paul H. Kocher, 'François Hotman and Marlowe's *The Massacre at Paris*', *PMLA* 56 (1941): 349–68; Kocher, 'Contemporary Pamphlet Background for Marlowe's *The Massacre at Paris*', *MLQ* 8 (1947): 151–73, 309–18; Julia Briggs, 'Marlowe's *Massacre at Paris*: A Reconsideration', *Review of English Studies* 34.135 (1983): 257–78; Vivien Thomas and William Tydeman, eds, *Christopher Marlowe: The Plays and Their Sources* (London: Routledge, 1994).

3 David Potter, 'Marlowe's *Massacre at Paris* and the Reputation of Henri III of France', in *Christopher Marlowe and English Renaissance Culture*, eds Darryll Grantley and Peter Roberts (Aldershot: Scolar Press, 1996), 70–95; Andrew M. Kirk, *The Mirror of Confusion: The Representation of French History in English Renaissance Drama* (New York: Garland, 1996), 77–106; Richard Hillman, *Shakespeare,*

Marlowe, and the Politics of France (Houndmills: Palgrave, 2002), Ch. 4, esp. 75–97; Jeffrey Rufo, 'Marlowe's Minions: Sodomitical Politics in *Edward II* and *The Massacre at Paris*', *Marlowe Studies* 1 (2011): 5–23

4 J. A. Nicklin, 'Marlowe's Gaveston', *The Free Review* 5 (1895): 323–7 (324).

5 John Bakeless, *The Tragicall History of Christopher Marlowe*, 2 vols (Cambridge: Harvard University Press, 1942), 2: 88.

6 See, for example, Bruce R. Smith, *Homosexual Desire in Shakespeare's England: A Cultural Poetics* (Chicago: University Chicago Press, 1991), 209–23; Jonathan Goldberg, *Sodometries: Renaissance Texts, Modern Sexualities* (Stanford: Stanford University Press, 1992), 105–26; Mario DiGangi, *The Homoerotics of Early Modern Drama* (Cambridge: Cambridge University Press, 1997), esp. 107–15; Laurie Shannon, *Sovereign Amity: Figures of Friendship in Shakespearean Contexts* (Chicago: U of Chicago Press, 2002), 159–65. DiGangi notes that 'In *Edward II* Marlowe's depiction of favouritism resembles the lesser-known partnership between Henry III and Epernoun' (108), but does not pursue the resemblance.

7 Marlowe, *Edward II*, ed. W. Moelwyn Merchant (London: Ernest Benn, 1967); *Edward II*, ed. Charles F. Forker (Manchester: Manchester University Press, 1994); *Edward II*, ed. Rowland; *Edward II*, ed. Martin Wiggins and Robert Lindsey (London: A&C Black [New Mermaids, 2nd edn], 1997.

8 *Edward II*, ed. Rowland, discussion at xx–xxii, footnote at xxiii n.15. The resonance with James VI of Scotland is explored most fully in Lawrence Normand, '"What passions call you these?" *Edward II* and James VI', in *Christopher Marlowe and English Renaissance Culture*, eds Darryll Grantley and Peter Roberts (Aldershot: Scolar Press, 1996), 172–96; see also Rufo, 6, 14–15.

9 *Marlowe Edward II: Actes du Colloque, Université Stendhal, Grenoble, Novembre 1991*, ed. Jean Perrin (Grenoble: Ellug, 1992).

10 Hillman, 72–4 and 97–111, quoted at 73, 85. In arguing that 'audiences must have recognized that [*Edward II*] mirrored

contemporary stories and personages from the chaotic affairs that plagued the neighbouring nations of Scotland and France', Rufo mentions *Histoire tragique*, but does not pursue the connection (6, 18).

11 Stafford to Walsingham, 6 June 1588, Paris, The National Archives, Kew, State Papers 78/18, fo. 236^r.

12 Denis Pallier, *Recherches sur l'imprimerie à Paris pendant la Ligue (1585–1594)* (Geneva: Droz, 1976); Frédéric J. Baumgartner, *Radical Reactionaries: The Political Thought of the French Catholic League* (Geneva: Droz, 1975); Keith Cameron, *Henri III a Maligned or Malignant King? (Aspects of the Satirical Iconography of Henri de Valois)* (Exeter: University of Exeter, 1978).

13 On favourites, see Nicolas Le Roux, *Le Faveur du roi: Mignons et courtisans au temps des derniers Valois (vers 1547–vers 1589)* (Paris: Champ-Vallon, 2000).

14 On Épernon, see Léo Mouton, *Un Demi-roi: le Duc d'Épernon* (Paris: Perrin, 1922); Rosy Bassa, *Le Duc d'Epernon ou le dernier des chevaliers* (Paris: La Pensée Universelle, 1987).

15 Pierre de l'Estoile, *Registre-Journal du regne de Henri III*, t. VI, *1588–1589*, eds Madeleine Lezard and Gilbert Schrenck (Geneva: Droz, 2003, 64). Unless otherwise noted, all translations are my own.

16 Richard Douglas to Archibald Douglas, 3 July 1588, Hatfield House, Cecil Papers [CP] 166/29 and 10 July 1588, CP 166/28.

17 *Lettre d'vn gentil-homme Catholicque Apostolicque & Romain, & vray François & fidelle Seruiteur du Roy à vng sien Amy Sur l'histoire de Pierre de Gauerston nouuellement mis en lumiere par l'Archeuesque de Lyon à la Requeste de ceux de la ligue* ('Rheins': 'Par Iehan de Foigny auec permission de Monseigneur le Cardinal de Guise', 1588), Universal Short Title Catalogue reference no. [hereafter USTC] 12288.

18 *Responce a l'antigaverston de Nogaret; à M. l'Espernon* (n. p.: n. pub, 1588), USTC 9263 and 54848; *Repliqve à l'antigauerston, ou response faicte à l'histoire de gauerston,*

par le Duc d'Espernon (n.p.: n. pub, 1588), USTC 9305, 16362 and 19753.

19 Pierre Matthieu, *Histoire des derniers trovbles de France* (Lyon: n. pub., 1594), sigs. Q5^r–Q6^v; trans. as *An historical collection of the most memorable accidents, and tragicall massacres of France* (London: Thomas Creed, 1598), sig. 2L5^{r-v}. Jacques-Auguste de Thou, *Histoire universelle ... depuis 1543, jusqu'en 1607. Traduite sur l'edition Latine de Londres*, vol. 10, *1587–1589* (London, 1734), 239–42.

20 Pierre Victor Cayet, *Chronologie novenaire, contenant l'historire de la gverre ...,* 3 vols (Paris: Jean Richer, 1608), I, sig. K7^v.

21 Stuart Carroll, *Noble Power during the French Wars of Religion: The Guise Affinity and the Catholic Cause in Normandy* (Cambridge: Cambridge University Press, 1998), 209–10.

22 'PH[ilippe] D[esportes] T[ironensis]' or 'PH[ilippe] D[e] T[iron]' (Desportes was known as 'M. de Tiron'). Jacqueline Boucher, 'Philippe Desportes et la chute de Henri III. Un ambitieux déçu', in *Philippe Desportes (1546–1606): Un poète presque parfait entre Renaissance et classicisme*, ed. Jean Balsamo (Paris: Klincksieck, 2000), 19–36 (26–7).

23 See John D. Staines, *The Tragic Histories of Mary Queen of Scots, 1560–1690: Rhetoric, Passions, and Political Literature* (Farnham: Ashgate, 2009).

24 My research has been greatly facilitated by the work of Andrew Pettegree and his team for the Universal Short Title Catalogue (ustc.ac.uk). The editions of the *Histoire tragique* are USTC 6951, 8205, 8909, 10882, 11626, 13933, 15501, 16188, 16193, 19554, 47591, 48784, 58445, 60210, 62490, 88073, 88819 and 89587. I am also counting as a variant *L'Estrange amitie d'Edovard, second, roy d'Angleterre, à l'endroit de Pierre de Gauerston gentilhomme de Gascogne, & quelle en fut l'yssue* (n.p.: n.pub., 1588), USTC 35670.

25 *Histoire tragique*, USTC 11626. I refer to Brigham Young University Library, Provo, UT, callmark AC 901 A1 no 150, available online: http://www.lib.byu.edu/digital/fpp/

26 Thomas Walsingham, *Historia breuis .... ab Edwardo primo, ad Henricum quantum* (London: Henry Bynneman, 1574); *Repliqve a l'Antigaverston*, USTC 16362, sig. B2^r.

27 To illustrate the 'long' version, I refer to USTC 19554, Bibliothèque nationale de France, Paris [BnF], callmark LA 25 24 (1), available on Gallica (gallica.bnf.fr), G3^v.

28 Clare Sponsler, 'The King's Boyfriend: Froissart's Political Theater of 1326', in *Queering the Middle Ages*, eds Glenn Burger and Steven F. Kruger (Minneapolis: University of Minnesota Press, 2001), 143–67, at 152–3.

29 See Guy Poirier, *L'Homosexualité dans l'imaginaire de la Renaissance* (Paris: Honoré Champion, 1996); Gary B. Ferguson, *Queer (Re)Readings in the French Renaissance: Homosexuality, Gender, Culture* (Aldershot: Ashgate, 2008), 147–90; Poirier, *Henri III de France en mascarades imaginaires: Mœurs, humeurs et comportements d'un roi de la Renaissance* (Québec: Presses de l'Université Laval, 2010); Katherine Crawford, *The Sexual Culture of the French Renaissance* (Cambridge: Cambridge University Press, 2010), esp. 215–30.

30 Although the most fundamental change to the *Histoire tragique* was the addition of the address 'Au lecteur', there exist many other variations on the libel, all dated 1588. One version omits 'Au lecteur' but adds a sentence to the end of the 'Histoire' that displays a knowledge of the post-Gaverston story (USTC 8909). Another version adds a verse 'Reqveste presentee par les Estats de la France à Messieurs du Conseil' ('A request presented by the Estates of France to the Gentlemen of the Council') lamenting the economic necessity into which France has fallen, which is abruptly rebutted with a single line: 'Go away, gentlemen; we're doing our business' (this verse also circulated in print under its own title page) (USTC 48784). Another prints the epistle to Épernon and the 'Au lecteur' section but drops the 'Histoire' section altogether, despite retaining the *Histoire tragique* title (USTC 46591). Another condenses the 'Histoire' section, and renames the Gaverston/Edward story 'L'Estrange amitié' ('The strange friendship') (USTC 6951) while another drops all the material except the 'L'Estrange

amitié' précis of the 'Histoire' and 'Au lecteur' and (alone
among the dozen-plus redactions) gives a new title to the
result: *L'Estrange amitié*. A German translation printed
in Basle by Samiel Apiario under the title *Fuchschwentzer
Spiegel* (*Foxtail Mirror*, or *A mirror for Court-Flatterers*)
comprises only the letter to Épernon, omitting the English
history (USTC 658343).

31 André Rossant, *Les Mœurs, humeurs et comportemens* (Paris: Anthoine le Riche, 1589), sig. Q4^r.

32 Pierre Matthieu, *Aman. Seconde tragedie* (Lyon: Benoît Rigaud, 1589), sig. †3^r.

33 *De l'Excommunication, & censures ecclesiastiques, encourues par Henry de Valois, pour l'assassinat commis és personnes de messieurs le Cardinal & duc de Guyse* (Paris: Guillaume Bichon, 1589), sig. I4^v.

34 *L'Atheisme de Henry de Valoys* (Paris: Pierre-des-Hayes, 1589), sigs. B4^r and D3^v.

35 Miriam Yardeni, 'Henri III Sorcier', in *Henri III et Son Temps*, ed. Robert Sauzet (Paris: J. Vrin, 1992), 57–66 (59–60).

36 *Les Choses horribles continues en une lettre envoyée à Henry de Valois par un enfant de Paris, le vingthuitiesme de Janvier 1589* ([Paris]: Jacques Grégoire, 1589), 4–5.

37 They resurfaced, retooled against Cardinal Mazarin, among the Mazarinades published during the 'Fronde' of the mid-seventeenth century.

38 Thomas H. Clancy, *Papist Pamphleteers: The Allen-Persons Party and the Political Thought of the Counter-Reformation in England, 1572–1615* (Chicago: Loyola University Press, 1964), 24–5; Curtis C. Breight, *Surveillance, Militarism and Drama in the Elizabethan Era* (Houndmills: Macmillan/St Martin's Press, 1996), 134–5.

39 *By the Queene. A Declaration of Great Troubles pretended against this Realme by Seminarie Priests and Jesuists, with a Prouision for Remedy thereof* (London: deputies of Christopher Barker, [1591]).

40 *An Advertisement written to a Secretarie of my L. Treasvrers*

    of Ingland, by an Inglishe Intelligencer as he passed throughe Germanie towards Italie ([Antwerp: Joachim Trognaesius,] 1592), sig. D9ᵛ.

41 [Richard Verstegan], *A Declaration of the Trve Cavses of the Great Troubles, Presvpposed to be Intended against the Realme of England* ([Antwerp: JoachimTrognaesius?], [1592]), sig. E2ᵛ.

42 *Apologia pro rege Catholico Philippo II* (Constantiae, apud Theodorum Samium, 1592), sig. R8ᵛ; translation by Victor Houliston, *Catholic Resistance in Elizabethan England: Robert Persons's Jesuit Polemic, 1580–1610* (Aldershot: Ashgate, 2007), 51.

43 *OED*, s.v. minion.

44 Rufo suggests such a triangulation when he notes that 'Marlowe's return to the minion and his immersion in contemporary French controversies in *Massacre* is an undervalued resource in analyzing the superior *Edward*' (6); his analysis, however, mentions the *Histoire tragique* only in passing (18).

45 Michael Drayton, *Peirs Gaueston* (London: N[icholas] L[ing] and Iohn Busby, 1594), sigs. L1ʳ⁻ᵛ.

46 Oddly, the net effect of Drayton's *ad fontes* research is to produce a strangely de-historicized, almost escapist account of the Gaveston-Edward relationship – one that is unabashedly and persistently sexual and erotic.

Chapter 5

1 *DEEP: Database of Early English Playbooks*, eds Alan B. Farmer and Zachary Lesser. Created 2007. Accessed 21 April 2015, http://deep.sas.upenn.edu. Unless otherwise noted, *DEEP* is the source of stationers' information cited here.

2 The belief that Pembroke's Men were in business in the summer of 1592 is based on a misleading reading of the provincial record (see n. 23).

3   Charles R. Forker, ed. *Edward II: Christopher Marlowe* (Manchester: University of Manchester Press, 1994), 16.

4   Scott McMillin and Sally-Beth MacLean consider the dramaturgical preferences of the Queen's Men as too old-fashioned for Marlowe's action-figure characters and their mighty lines (*The Queen's Men and their Plays* [Cambridge: Cambridge University Press, 1998], 121–7, 143).

5   Lawrence Manley and Sally-Beth MacLean, *Lord Strange's Men and Their Plays* (New Haven: Yale University Press, 2014), 4, 35–6, 341.

6   Constance B. Kuriyama, *Christopher Marlowe: A Renaissance Life* (Ithaca: Cornell University Press, 2002), 117.

7   Scott McMillin, *The Elizabethan Theatre and The Book of Sir Thomas More* (Ithaca: Cornell University Press, 1987), 62.

8   T. J. King, *Casting Shakespeare's Plays: London Actors and their Roles, 1590–1642* (Cambridge: Cambridge University Press, 1992), 144–7, 152–4. I omit *Titus Andronicus* (Q1594) because it did not belong to Pembroke's company exclusively according to its title page, which advertises also Derby's Men and Sussex's Men.

9   E. K. Chambers, *The Elizabethan Stage*, 4 vols (Oxford: Clarendon Press, 1923), 2.129.

10 Lost plays are indicated by quotation marks; extant plays by italics. For additional information on lost plays discussed here, consult the *Lost Plays Database*, http://www.lostplays.org

11 A detailed account of scholarly commentary on Pembroke's birth narratives may be found in Terence Schoone-Jongen, *Shakespeare's Companies: William Shakespeare's Early Career and the Acting Companies, 1577–1594* (Aldershot: Ashgate, 2008), 128–35.

12 Andrew Gurr, *The Shakespearian Playing Companies* (Oxford: Clarendon Press, 1996), 267.

13 Kuriyama, transcript of British Library Harleian MSS 6848, F. 154, 228–9, esp. 229.

14 David Cook and F. P. Wilson, eds, 'Dramatic Records in the Declared Accounts of the Treasurer of the Chamber,

1558–1642', in *Collections VI* (Oxford: Malone Society, 1961), 28.

15   John H. Astington, *English Court Theatre, 1558–1642* (Cambridge: Cambridge University Press, 1999), 97.

16   Alfred Hart, *Stolne and Surreptitious Copies: A Comparative Study of Shakespeare's Bad Quartos* (Melbourne: Melbourne University Press, 1942), 376, 377.

17   H. B. Charlton and R. D. Waller, eds, *Edward II* (London: Methuen, 1933 [rev. by F. N. Lees, 1955]), 8.

18   Even though the playhouse is not named, a letter dated November 1587 by Philip Gawdy is taken as evidence of the Admiral's Men at the Theatre when a weapon on stage misfired into the audience and killed a child and a pregnant woman (*English Professional Theatre, 1530–1660*, eds Glynne Wickham, Herbert Berry and William Ingram [Cambridge: Cambridge University Press, 2000], 277, Item #172). Chambers claims the 1591 date (2.135–6).

19   This is the entry for Leicester misleadingly dated by Murray (1.72). The record occurs in the Chamberlains' Accounts, Leicestershire Record Office: BRIII/2/62, mb 2. It is entered in the account year of 1592–3 between entries for 24 April and 11 June. The Leicester account years run from Michaelmas (29 September) to Michaelmas; therefore, a payment entered between 24 April and 11 June of 1592–3 falls in 1593, not 1592 (email, Sally-Beth MacLean, 1 May 2014). The entry – 'It{e}m geven vnto the Earle of Penbrucke his players more than was gaythered xiiij s.' – will be published in *Leicestershire*, ed. Alice B. Hamilton, forthcoming in the REED series.

20   MacLean plotted the circuits in 'Players on Tour: New Evidence From Records of Early English Drama', in *The Elizabethan Theatre X*, ed. C. E. McGee (Port Credit: P. D. Meany, 1988), 55–72. The following volumes provide the entries reported here on Pembroke's provincial stops in 1593: Ipswich (E. K. Chambers, ed. 'Players at Ipswich', in *Collections II.3* [Oxford: Malone Society, 1931], 136); King's Lynn (David Galloway and John M. Wasson, eds, 'Records of Plays and Players in Norfolk and Suffolk, 1330–1642', in

Collections XI (Oxford: Malone Society, 1980/1), 65; Rye (*Sussex*, ed. Cameron Louis [Toronto: University of Toronto Press, 2001], 136); Bath (*Somerset, including Bath*, ed. James Stokes with Robert J. Alexander, 2 vols [Toronto: University of Toronto Press, 1996], I.15); Coventry (*Coventry*, ed. R. W. Ingram [Toronto: University of Toronto Press, 1981], 338); Ludlow and Shrewsbury (*Shropshire*, ed. J. A. B. Somerset, 2 vols [Toronto: University of Toronto Press, 1994], I.89, 277); Bewdley (*Herefordshire/Worcestershire*, ed. David Klausner [Toronto: University of Toronto Press, 1990], 362); Leicester (ed. Alice B. Hamilton, *Leicestershire* [Toronto: University of Toronto Press, forthcoming]); and York (*York*, eds Alexandra Johnston and Margaret Rogerson, 2 vols [Toronto: University of Toronto Press, 1979]), I.455. For the most recent information publically available on touring, consult *REED Patrons and Performances*, https://reed.library.utoronto.ca.

21   Peter H. Greenfield, 'Entertainments of Henry, Lord Berkeley, 1593–4 and 1600–5', *REED Newsletter* 8.1 (1983): 12–24, esp. 12.

22   R. A. Foakes, ed. *Henslowe's Diary*, 2nd edn (Cambridge: Cambridge University Press, 2002), 280.

23   J. A. B. Somerset, 'The Lords President, Their Activities and Companies: Evidence from Shropshire', in *The Elizabethan Theatre X*, ed. C. E. McGee (Port Credit: P. D. Meany, 1988), 93–111, esp. 110.

24   Roslyn L. Knutson, 'Pembroke's Men in 1592–3, Their Repertory and Touring Schedule', *Early Theatre* 4 (2001): 129–38.

25   REED scholarship has replaced the dyspeptic view of touring offered by Tucca, Ben Jonson's blowhard captain in which players walked with their 'pumps full of gravel ... after a blind jade and a hamper, and [stalked] upon boards and barrel heads to an old cracked trumpet' (*Poetaster*, ed. Tom Cain. [Manchester: Manchester University Press, 1995]. 3.3.170–4).

26   Peter H. Greenfield, 'Touring', in *The New History of Early English Drama*, eds John D. Cox and David Scott Kastan (New York: Columbia University Press, 1997), 251–68, esp. 264.

27 Photographs (most by Sally-Beth MacLean) of early modern guildhalls may be found online at *REED Patrons and Performances*. The photographs reproduced widely of St Mary's, Coventry are by Andrew Paterson.

28 C. J. Sisson, 'Shakespeare Quartos as Prompt-Copies', *The Review of English Studies* 18.70 (1942): 129–43, esp. 138–9. Scholars incline to assume that the 'Lere' play was Shakespeare's, but the anonymous *King Leir* had also been printed by 1609.

29 Leslie Thomson, 'Staging on the Road, 1586–1594: A New Look at Some Old Assumptions', *Shakespeare Quarterly* 61.4 (2010): 526–50, esp. 533.

30 The play is lost, but the summary of Cornwall's story provided by Manley and MacLean suggests a complex historical-political narrative (135–8).

31 David M. Bevington, *From Mankind to Marlowe: Growth of Structure in the Popular Drama of Tudor England* (Cambridge, MA: Harvard University Press, 1962), 236. Bevington calls for 'additional hired actors' who appear not to be counted among the cast number of eleven men. As if to illustrate the vagaries of casting studies, David Bradley assigns *Edward II* to twenty men and five boys (*From Text to Performance in the Elizabethan Theatre: Preparing the Play for the Stage* [Cambridge: Cambridge University Press, 1992], 233).

32 Currently, textual scholars prefer 'based on an authorial draft' (which implies 'unabridged') to the simplistic tag 'good'.

33 Leslie Thomson, 'Marlowe's Staging of Meaning', *Medieval and Renaissance Drama in England* 18 (2005): 19–36, esp. 20, 26; Thomson, 'Staging on the Road', 544.

34 Manley and MacLean qualify these numbers by observing that the plays, both in their 1594/1595 and 1623 versions, have 'grand fifth-act battles' calling for additional players, a requirement 'even more evident in the Pembroke's versions' (360).

35 Scott McMillin, 'The Plots of *The Dead Man's Fortune* and *2 Seven Deadly Sins:* Inferences for Theatre Historians', *Studies in Bibliography* 26 (1973): 235–43, esp. 243. The players with

Pembroke's is a vexed question beyond the scope of this study; for an overview of scholarly opinion, see Schoone-Jongen, 124–8.

36 Hart gave the title 'Inter-Play Borrowings' to his chapter on the Pembroke Group (352). The term implies that any given play can be a borrower or borrowee or both.

37 A. S. Cairncross, 'Pembroke's Men and Some Shakespearian Piracies', *Shakespeare Quarterly* 11 (1960): 344–9, esp. 345.

38 MacDonald P. Jackson, '"Edward III", Shakespeare and Pembroke's Men', *Notes and Queries* N. S. 12 (1965): 329–31.

39 See Karl P. Wentersdorf, '*Arden of Faversham* and the Repertory of Pembroke's Men', *Theatre Annual* 31 (1975): 57–71; 'The Repertory and Size of Pembroke's Company', *Theatre Annual* 33 (1977): 71–85, esp. 83–5; and '*Romeo and Juliet* (Q1) and the Pembroke Repertory', *Theatre Annual* 34 (1979): 87–104. W. W. Greg suggested the assignment of the A-text in *Marlowe's 'Doctor Faustus' 1604–1616* (Oxford: Oxford University Press, 1950), 60–2.

40 Richard Proudfoot, '*The Reign of King Edward the Third* (1596) and Shakespeare', in *Proceedings of the British Academy*, vol. LXXI (1985), 159–85, esp. 182.

41 Scholars have addressed the authorship and textual quality of Shakespeare's history plays in Pembroke's repertory but not their repertorial dynamics with *Edward II*.

42 For the narrative behind the lost play, see Manley and MacLean, 135–8.

43 As the authors point out, Dante took Henry of Cornwall's part in *The Inferno* by punishing De Montfort's son, Guy, in the flaming river, Phlegethon (seventh circle).

44 Frank S. Hook, ed. *Edward I* in *The Dramatic Works of George Peele* (New Haven: Yale University Press, 1961), 124.

45 Manley and MacLean identify 'mvlomvrco' as George Peele's *The Battle of Alcazar* (75–8).

46 Even though the text of *The Massacre at Paris* is short, the casting is not noticeably streamlined. Bradley counts parts for thirteen to sixteen men and five to six boys (233).

47 Peter W. M. Blayney, 'The Publication of Playbooks', in *A New History of Early English Drama*, eds John D. Cox and David Scott Kastan (New York: Columbia University Press, 1997), 383–440, esp. 396.

48 Cf. Forker, 3. Nevertheless, the old assumption hangs on that *Edward II* was sold to mitigate Pembroke's losses from touring (see Kuriyama, 117).

49 The assumption here is that Pembroke's did not sell their only copy of *Edward II*.

50 Holger Schott Syme, 'Three's Company: Alternative Histories of London's Theatres in the 1590s', *Shakespeare Survey* 65 (2012): 269–89, esp. 281. The phrase, 'a break-up', is Syme's; the others quoted here are Henslowe's.

51 Some configuration of a company under the Earl of Pembroke's patronage stayed in business after the turmoil in the playhouse world, 1597–8; a Pembroke's company leased the Rose in October 1600 for two performances, neither of which was of *Edward II*.

52 Beeston is listed among the players in the cast list for the Chamberlain's *Every Man in His Humour*, 1598; he might also be the 'Kit' named in the theatrical plot of '2 Seven Deadly Sins', now dated 1597–8 and reassigned to the Chamberlain's Men (David Kathman, 'Reconsidering *The Seven Deadly Sins*', *Early Theatre* 7.1 [2004]: 13–44, esp. 26).

53 Herbert Berry, *The Boar's Head Playhouse*, illus. by C. Walter Hodges (Washington, DC: Folger Shakespeare Library, 1986), 51.

54 William Lloyd, noting that the assignment on the 1622 title page is to the 'late Queenes *Maiesties Seruants*', thinks the company may be the Children of the Revels to the Late Queen Anne, also known as the Red Bull Revels company (email, 5 February 2015).

55 A tomb for Dido is in Henslowe's inventory dated 10 March 1598/9, as is 'Dides robe' on the list dated 13 March 1598/9 (319, 323).

56 Not without qualms, most theatre historians consider 'ne' to be usually a sign of a new play.

57 Martin Wiggins, in association with Catherine Richardson, *British Drama 1533–1642: A Catalogue*, 10 vols (Oxford: Oxford University Press, 2012), III (1590–7), #1091.

58 Roslyn L. Knutson, 'The History Play, *Richard II*, and Repertorial Commerce', in *Richard II: New Critical Essays*, ed. Jeremy Lopez (New York: Routledge, 2012), 74–94, esp. 86.

59 Another play, *Thomas of Woodstock*, often called 'part one' of *Richard II*, belongs in the sequence of dramatic narratives that connects the chronicles of Edward II, Richard II and Henry VI. *Woodstock* was in performance in the early 1590s, but it is not possible to be more specific than that about its owners or stage runs.

60 *Richard II* was first published in 1597, the year that Pembroke's Men arrived at the Swan playhouse, perhaps with *Edward II* in repertory.

61 Wiggins notes that a piece of the narrative of Alice Perrers is that 'a friar helps her to secure the king's infatuation through witchcraft' (III, #1091). This detail suggests one narrative tentacle of the 1597–8 play that might have reached out to *The Contention*.

62 The two suits alike in the lost 'Mortimer' beg to be read as apparelling for twins. Could the play have mocked Marlowe's *Edward II* through matching suits for Edward and Gaveston?

63 Wiggins does not connect this 'Mortimer' with Ben Jonson's 'Mortimer His Fall'.

64 Holger Schott Syme, 'The Meaning of Success: Stories of 1594 and its Aftermath', *Shakespeare Quarterly* 61.4 (2010): 490–525, esp. 494.

65 Syme's statistics contradict Andrew Gurr's claim that such plays as Marlowe's were 'the beating heart' of the repertory of the Admiral's Men (*Shakespeare's Opposites: The Admiral's Company 1594–1625* [Cambridge: Cambridge University Press, 2009], 171).

66 Often dated c. 1594, the edition has been shown by R. Carter Hailey to be a 1596 printing ('The Publication Date of

Marlowe's *Massacre at Paris*, with a Note on the Collier Leaf', *Marlowe Studies: An Annual* 1 (2011): 25–40, esp. 323.

67 The play did continue to be offered (or some version of it) on the continent (*Doctor Faustus A- and B-Texts [1604, 1616]: Christopher Marlowe and His Collaborator and Revisers*, eds David Bevington and Eric Rasmussen [Manchester: Manchester University Press, 1993], 49–50).

68 Jeremy Lopez, 'Alleyn Resurrected', *Marlowe Studies: An Annual* 1 (2011): 167–80, esp. 170.

69 G. E. Bentley declared that Queen Anna's Men 'had gone completely to pieces as a London dramatic company by the summer of 1623' (*The Jacobean and Caroline Stage*, 7 vols [Oxford: Clarendon Press, 1941–68], 1.170). For the players of the two Queen's companies, see Bentley, 1.158–75 and 218–59.

70 E. K. Chambers, ed., 'Dramatic Records: The Lord Chamberlain's Office', in *Collections II.3* (Oxford: The Malone Society, 1931), 389–90.

71 Karen Britland, ed., 'Mortimer His Fall', in *The Cambridge Edition of the Works of Ben Jonson*, 7 vols (Cambridge: Cambridge University Press, 2012), 7.403–16, esp. 405–6. When printed in the 1640 folio, the fragment carried the notation, 'He died and left it unfinished'.

Chapter 6

1 Pierre Bourdieu, 'Social Space and Symbolic Power', *Sociological Theory* 7.1 (1989): 14–25, 19.

2 Sir William Wentworth, 'Advice to his Son' (1604), in *Wentworth Papers*, ed. J. P. Cooper, Camden 4th series, 12 (London: Royal Historical Society, 1973), 11.

3 Unless noted, quotations from *Edward II* are from the New Mermaids 2014 rev. edn, eds Martin Wiggins and Robert Lindsey, with a new introduction by Stephen Guy-Bray. Marlowe's other plays are quoted from *Christopher Marlowe Four Plays*, eds William C. Carroll, Brian Gibbons and Tiffany Stern (London: Methuen Drama, 2011).

4   'Base' and cognates occur nineteen times in *Edward II*;
    the two *Tamburlaine* plays together total twenty instances.
    On 'socially dismissive' vocabulary, see William Zunder,
    Elizabethan Marlowe (Hull: Unity Press, 1994), 47.

5   For example: Mortimer Junior (1.120; 2.26; 21.78); Gaveston
    (1.41–2; 4.134; 4.148; 4.162); Edward (4.63; 18.8–9; 20.1;
    20.49; 20.91–3); Isabella (4.145; 8.31; 17.14–15; 18.75);
    Lancaster (9.19); Leicester (19.55); Baldock (19.112–14); and
    Kent (1.159; 18.20–1).

6   See Claude J. Summers, 'Sex, Politics, and Self-Realization
    in *Edward II*', in *'A Poet and a filthy Play-maker': New
    Essays on Christopher Marlowe*, eds Kenneth Friedenreich,
    Roma Gill, and Constance Brown Kuriyama (New York:
    AMS Press, 1988), 221–40. For adaptation, see Georgia
    E. Brown, 'Tampering with the Records: Engendering the
    Political Community and Marlowe's Appropriation of the Past
    in *Edward II*', in *Marlowe's Empery: Expanding his Critical
    Contexts*, eds Sara Munson Deats and Robert A. Logan
    (Newark, DL: University of Delaware Press, 2002), 164–87;
    cf. Emily C. Bartels, *Spectacles of Strangeness: Imperialism,
    Alienation, and Marlowe* (Philadelphia: University of
    Pennsylvania Press, 1993), 142–56.

7   *Edward II* ignores Gaveston's baronial descent as an 'esquire
    of Gascoine' (Holinshed 6:313; 1587 edn from *The Holinshed
    Project* [www.cems.ox.ac.uk/holinshed]) or 'Gentlemans sonne
    of Wasconie'(John Foxe *Acts and Monuments* [1583], 390;
    from *John Foxe's The Actes and Monuments Online* [http://
    www.johnfoxe.org/]), or his being a 'goodlie gentleman'
    (Holinshed 6:319). Nor is there mention that Edward I for
    'good seruice his father had done hym in hys warres …
    receiued [Gaveston] to his Court, and placed [Gaveston]
    with hys sonne Edwarde' among the Prince's household
    squires (Foxe [1583], 390); cf. J. S. Hamilton, *Piers Gaveston
    Earl of Cornwall 1307–1312: Politics and Patronage in the
    Reign of Edward II* (Detroit: Wayne State University Press,
    1988), 19–30. Marlowe ignores Spencer Senior's renown as
    counsellor and 'knight of great vertue' (John Stowe, *Annales*
    [London: 1580], 332), the family's vast land-holdings and
    Spencer Junior's appointment by prelates and nobles to be

Edward's Chamberlain (Stowe, *Annales*, 332; Holinshed, 6:321). Marlowe makes Robert Baldock a household tutor despite his degree in Civil Law and Holinshed's styling him 'master' – i.e. gentleman – even before advancement to high office.

8   See Table 1. I thank Alex Macconochie for helping with data. Basing his argument in part on the Latin in Stage Directions, Charles R. Forker believes 'Q1' (actually a quarto-form octavo) *Edward II* was printed from Marlowe's fair copy or a transcript of that manuscript (*Edward II* [1994; rpt. New York: St Martin's Press, 1999], 11).

9   William Harrison divides 'gentlemen' into 'the baronie or estate of lords (which conteineith barons and all aboue that degree)' and 'those that be no lords, as knights, esquiers, & simple gentlemen' (Holinshed 1:165); cf. *The Oxford Handbook of Holinshed's Chronicles*, eds Paulina Kewes, Ian W. Archer and Felicity Heal (Oxford: Oxford University Press, 2013), 394. William Segar defines gentlemen and noblemen as overlapping categories: 'Of Gentlemen, the first and principal is the King, Prince, Dukes, Marquesses, Earls, Vicounts, and Barons. These are the Nobilitie, and be called Lords, or Noblemen. Next to these be Knights, Esquiers, and simple Gentlemen, which last number may be called *Nobilitas minor*: for they in Parliament haue no place among the Lords' (*Honor Military and Ciuill* [London, 1602], 51).

10 Jonathan Goldberg, *Sodometries: Renaissance Texts, Modern Sexualities* (Stanford: Stanford University Press, 1992), 271; cf. Summers, 'Sex, Politics, and Self-Realization in *Edward II*'; James Voss, '*Edward II*: Marlowe's Historical Tragedy', *English Studies* 63 (1982): 517–30; for Edward's 'violation of class structure' in 'patronage of his lowborn minions', see David H. Thurn, 'Sovereignty, Disorder, and Fetishism in Marlowe's *Edward II*', *Renaissance Drama* 21 (1990): 115–41, 116.

11 Pierre Bourdieu, *On the State: Lectures at the Collège de France 1989–1992*, eds Patrick Champagne et al., trans. David Fernbach (Cambridge: Polity Press, 2014), 47. There are parallels with Formalism's de-familiarization, but the Marlovian specifics may recall Judith Weil on Marlowe's

'teasing, elliptical analogies' and strategic 'obscurity' (*Christopher Marlowe: Merlin's Prophet* [Cambridge: Cambridge University Press, 1977] 16, 171).

12 Lawrence Stone, 'Social Mobility in England, 1500–1700', in *Seventeenth Century England: Society in an Age of Revolution*, ed. Paul S. Seaver (New York: Franklin Watts, 1976), 38, 42. On the opposition of nobles and gentry, see D. M. Palliser, *The Age of Elizabeth* (2nd edn; London: Routledge, 2014), who claims an 'expansion of the gentry, within which the nobles formed a small proportion' between the mid-sixteenth and mid-seventeenth centuries (103–5). On the sixteenth-century shift in parlance by which 'gentry, once synonymous with nobility, came to be used of the lesser nobility' (i.e. knights, esquires and gentlemen) and 'nobility' restricted to the peerage (barons and above), see Peter Coss, *Origins of the English Gentry* (Cambridge: Cambridge University Press, 2003), 2; see also Ruth Kelso, *The Doctrine of the Gentleman in the Sixteenth Century* (1929; rpt. Urbana: University of Illinois Press, 1964), 19–20. Cf. Janet Dickinson, 'Nobility and Gentry', in *The Elizabethan World*, eds Susan Doran and Norman Jones (2011; rpt. New York: Routledge, 2014), 285–300, 287. For earlier eras, see Michael Jones, ed., *Gentry and Lesser Nobility in Late Medieval Europe* (Gloucester: Sutton, 1986); for later evolution, see Keith Wrightson, 'Estates, Degrees, and Sorts: Changing perceptions of Society in Tudor and Stuart England', in *Language, History and Class*, ed. P. J. Corfield (Oxford: Oxford University Press, 1991), 30–52, esp. 37–40 on the 'gentleman'.

13 Felicity Heal and Clive Holmes, *The Gentry in England and Wales 1500–1700* (Stanford: Stanford University Press, 1994), 15–16.

14 M. L. Bush, *The English Aristocracy: A Comparative Synthesis* (Manchester: Manchester University Press, 1984), 3.

15 Humfrey Braham, *The Institucion of a Gentleman* (London: 1555), prologue. Compare Thomas Milles' timeless division: '[N]othing is euery where, and in all places so sincerely obserued and kept, as is that old and general diuision of *people*, into *Noble,* and *Vnnoble*, with a certaine difference of the *Vnnoble* sort among themselues, as of the *Nobler* sort

among themselues also' (*The Catalogue of Honor* [London: 1610], 23).

16 Lawrence Stone, *The Crisis of the Aristocracy 1558–1641* (1965; corrected edn, Oxford: Clarendon Press, 1966), 185–6.

17 On Gaveston's manipulative intent and lyrical power, see Judith Haber, *Desire and Dramatic Form in Early Modern England* (Cambridge: Cambridge University Press, 2009), esp. 31.

18 On English 'apishness', see Hilary M. Larkin, *The Making of Englishmen: Debates on National Identity 1550–1650* (Leiden: Brill, 2014), Ch. 3.

19 Samuel Daniel, *Collection of the History of England* (London: 1621), 172–5. On the favourite, see Curtis Perry, *Literature and Favouritism in Early Modern England* (Cambridge: Cambridge University Press, 2006) and 'The Politics of Access and Representations of the Sodomite King in Early Modern England', *Renaissance Quarterly* 53. 4 (2000): 1054–83.

20 On Gaveston's 'Italian' style, see Amanda Bailey, *Flaunting: Style and the Subversive Male Body in Renaissance England* (Toronto: University of Toronto Press, 2007), Chapter Four; cf. Gregory Woods, 'Body, Costume, and Desire in Christopher Marlowe', in *Homosexuality in Renaissance and Enlightenment England*, ed. Joseph A. Summers (1992; New York: Routledge, 2013), 69–84.

21 Michael Drayton, *Peirs Gaueston Earle of Cornwall* (London: 1594); Thomas Dekker, *The Seuen Deadly Sinnes of London* (London: 1606).

22 I use *avatar* in David Crouch's sense as a 'giant' embodiment of a 'habitus' ('Chivalry and Courtliness: Colliding Constructs', in *Soldiers, Nobles and Gentlemen*, eds Peter Coss and Christopher Tyerman [Woodbridge: Boydell Press, 2009], 42).

23 Cf. Hilary M. Larkin on the 'host of vectors from class to gender, and religion to politics' that criss-crossed 'normative values about Englishness' (*The Making of Englishmen: Debates on National Identity* [Leiden: E. J. Brill, 2013], 122).

24 Pierre Bourdieu, *Distinction: A Social Critique of the*

Judgement of Taste, trans. Richard Nice (1979; Cambridge, MA: Harvard University Press, 1984), 110–11; on 1590's youth culture, see Alexandra Shepard, *Meanings of Manhood in Early Modern England* (Oxford: Oxford University Press, 2006), esp. 211–13.

25 *Annales rerum Anglicarum et Hibernicarum regnante Elizabetha* in *The Historie of the Life and Reigne of the most Renowned and Victorious Princesse Elizabeth*, trans. R. N. (London: 1630), 2:68.

26 Camden's 'villae elegantia, laxitate, et cultu' ['houses striking for their elegance, spaciousness, and splendor'], employs 'cultu', recalling the 'cultus' of our national 'habite' in the 'cultivation' of the new. On banqueting and 'overhospitality', see Chris Meads, *Banquets Set Forth: Banqueting in English Renaissance Drama* (Manchester: Manchester University Press, 2001), esp. Ch. 1. Aaron Shapiro generously helped with Camden's Latin.

27 We never see a 'wanton poet' either, though Holinshed mentions and Fabian prints Edward's own verses (Holinshed 6:342; Robert Fabian, *The Chronicle of Fabian* (London: 1559), 7:185–6).

28 Bruce Smith suggests this remark implies a 'conspiracy of sodomites' (*Homosexual Desire in Shakespeare's England* [Chicago: University of Chicago Press, 1991], 217).

29 Costume expense might have mattered, but the play includes undermotivated characters with costumes, e.g. '*HERALD ... with his coat of arms*' (11.150 sd), or the armed 'Champion' (23.70 sd).

30 'I was better when a king' (*R2*, 5.5.35); 'Was never subject long'd to be a king / As I do long and wish to be a subject' (*2H6*, 4.9.4–5); 'Art thou King, and wilt be forc'd?' (*3H6*, 1.1.237). Shakespeare citations from *The Arden Shakespeare Complete Works*, eds Richard Proudfoot et al. (London: Thomas Nelson, 1998).

31 See Table 1. The title of Duke did not exist during Edward II's reign; see Milles, *The Catalogue of Honor* (London: 1610), 27.

32 Jaques terms the soldier 'Jealous in honour, sudden,

and quick in quarrel' (2.7.151); cf. John Norden, *The Mirror of Honor* (London: 1597), 22; on honour and noble resistance to Edward II, see Mervyn James, *Society, Politics, Culture* (Cambridge: Cambridge University Press, 1986), 343.

33 See Autolycus and the Clown (*WT*, 4.4.724–8), Edmund and the anonymous Edgar (*Lear*, 5.3.139–52); also Cloten on derogation (*Cym*, 2.1.14–22). For duelists' self-restrictions, see Keith Thomas, *The Ends of Life* (Oxford: Oxford University Press, 2009), 157.

34 Mortimer Senior, a baron, is first to exclaim against Gaveston's creation as 'an earl', urging the earls to identify with himself and his baronial nephew: 'An earl! ... We may not, nor we will not suffer this' (2.12–15). Mortimer Junior would become Earl of March, but Marlowe ignores this, despite contemporary emphasis on Mortimer's promotion: 'hee too loftye was before, / His new degree ... made him now much more' (*The Last Part of the Mirour for Magistrates* [London: 1578], sig. 4^v; cf. Ben Jonson's *Mortimer his Fall*).

35 *The Cambridge Companion to Christopher Marlowe*, ed. Patrick Cheney (Cambridge: Cambridge University Press, 2004), 167.

36 For this distinction, see Holinshed 1:184. Some Elizabethans decried the 'naughtie ways' of Lancaster and the barons, lumping them together as 'hanged and decollate'; see Wilfrid Holme, *The fall and euill successe of rebellion* (London: 1572), sig. B4^v.

37 See Holinshed, 6:349.

38 The play's punning 'over-peered' is noted by William D. Briggs, ed., in *Marlowe's Edward II* (London: David Nutt, 1914); James Voss cites it to emphasize that Gaveston and Spencer 'represent a challenge to the traditional hierarchy of birth which is the basis of the peers' social position and the backbone of the entire English state' (520).

39 I borrow *chrono-normativity* from Elizabeth Freeman, *Time Binds: Queer Temporalities, Queer Histories* (Durham: Duke University Press, 2010).

40 For Braham promise-keeping defines 'a Gentleman a soldier or man of warre' (*Institucion*, sig. E3ᵛ).

41 On policy, see Howard S. Babb, 'Policy in Marlowe's *The Jew of Malta*', *ELH* 24 (1957): 85–94.

42 James discusses faithfulness to 'friends', meaning equals, among men of honour (330). For friendship, rank and sodomitical relationships, see Alan Bray, 'Homosexuality and the Signs of Male Friendship in Elizabethan England', *History Workshop* 29 (1990), 1–19. Cf. Karen Cunningham on male friendship offering 'new social and patriotic practices' ('"Forsake thy king and do but follow me": Marlowe and Treason', in *Marlowe's Empery: Expanding His Critical Horizons*, eds Sara Munson Deats and Robert A. Logan (Newark: University of Delaware Press, 2002), 133–49; 144). See also, Mario DiGangi, 'Marlowe, Queer Studies, and Renaissance Homoeroticism', in *Marlowe, History and Sexuality: New Critical Essays*, ed. Paul Whitfield White (New York: AMS Press, 1998), 195–212, 209.

43 See Forker, 1.3.1n., 5n.

44 Cf. Richard II: 'I bear a burthen like an ass' (*R2*, 5.5.93).

45 Marlowe uses 'goodly' ironically to refer to Ithamore's rags (*Jew of Malta*, 4.2.104–5); cf. *1Tamburlaine*, 2.4.11; 4.4.56. Holinshed calls Gaveston 'a goodlie gentleman and a stout' because he 'would not once yeeld an inch to any of [the lords], which worthilie procured him great enuie amongst the cheefest peeres of all the realme' (Holinshed 6:319).

46 Plural designation that Gaveston shares with Edward (1.77; 1.148; 11.54; 18.5) and with Marlowe's text: '*Enter both the MORTIMERS*' (2.0sd); '*Manent both Mortimers*' (4.386sd). Mortimer himself refers to 'We', 'the family of the Mortimers' (6.147–50).

47 Spenser, *Faerie Queene* 1.1.53; cf. 1.7.46, 2.7.25. Cf. Patrick Cheney, *Marlowe's Counterfeit Profession: Ovid, Spenser, Nationhood* (Toronto: University of Toronto Press, 1997), 312–13.

48 Compare Wilson's feckless heir who 'lyves att home like a mome and knowes the sound of no other bell but his own'

(Thomas Wilson, *The State of England, Anno Dom. 1600*, ed. F. J. Fisher, *Camden Miscellany* 16 [1936]: 24).

49 Gaveston's glance at old-fashioned style recalls his 'all your beards' (9.5), mocking them by Elizabethan fashion standards, but perhaps also suggesting aging; see Will Fisher, *Materializing Gender in Early Modern English Literature and Culture* (Cambridge: Cambridge University Press, 2006), 83–129; esp. 88–9. For 'beefe' and hospitality, see Thomas Nashe, *Quaternio or A fourefold vvay to a happie life* (London: 1633), 9. On beef-eating signifying conventionality, see Bailey, 87.

50 Dennis Kay, 'Marlowe, *Edward II*, and the Cult of Elizabeth', *EMLS* 3.2 (September 1997): 1.1–30, http://purl.oclc.org/emls/03-2/kaymarl.html (accessed 1 March 2015).

51 The play represents behaviour later associated with the court of James I. Francis Osborn attacks Sir Philip Herbert as 'caressed by King James for his hansome face' and claims that James 'made him a *Knight*, a *Baron*, a *Viscount*, and an *Earl* in one day' (*The Works of Francis Osborn* [7th edn, London, 1673], 505).

52 Compare the charge that 'wanton Spencer' Junior 'Revelled in England's wealth and treasury' (18.59–61).

53 Cf. Perry (in 'Politics of Access') opposing 'public and orderly' to 'private and disorderly' royal patronage in the play.

54 Marlowe's Gaveston gets honours, not jewels (Woods, 83). Holinshed's Gaveston loots Edward's 'iewell-house' (6:320; cf. Hamilton, *Piers Gaveston*).

55 Milles refers to those under the degree of barons who are neither knights nor esquires as 'plaine tearmed Gentlemen'; 'above the common and vulgar sort of men' but differing from 'named nobility' in 'honour and dignitie much' (24).

56 'Base' and its cognates appear nine times previously in reference to Gaveston; 'upstart' is used twice previously for Gaveston.

57 For civil law concerning levying war and treason, see M. H. Keen, 'Treason Trials under the Law of Arms', *Transactions of*

the Royal Historical Society, 5th series, 12 (1962): 85–103. For debate about nobility 'native' or 'dative', see Milles, 12–13.

58 Cf. Harrison in Stowe; Forker, 2.2.243n.; Holinshed calls Baldock 'Master' (6:322). John Ferne counts a Doctor of Civil or Canon Law as a 'Gentleman of Blood' (*The Blazon of Gentrie* [London: 1586], 88).

59 Marlowe knew from Thomas Watson, a 'gentlem[a]n of good account', that 'read[ing] unto' a noble's child, rendering 'service' to 'our lady' (5.30, 80) need not compromise a university man's gentility; see Charles Nicholl, *The Reckoning* (1992; rpt. Chicago: University of Chicago Press, 1996), 189–90, 341; cf. Ibrahim Alhiyari, 'The Papists' and the Davie Jones' Lists: Who is Watson the Poet?', *N&Q* 61 (2014), 223–5. Baldock's clothing evokes the 'Meer Scholler' (W. J. Paylor, ed., *The Overburian Characters* [Oxford: Basil Blackwell, 1936], 33–4). On economic prospects, see Mark H. Curtis, 'The Alienated Intellectuals of Early Stuart England', *Past & Present* 23 (1962): 25–43.

60 The contemptuousness of this omission is emphasized by its occurring immediately following Leicester's empathizing with Edward. On the Chancellor's precedence and 'right Honourable' title, see Segar, 236–7; on his right to a coat of arms and on the affront of omitting his 'addition of worship', see Ferne, 60, 77.

61 For nature's debt, see M. P. Tilley, *Dictionary of Proverbs in the Sixteenth and Seventeenth Centuries* (Ann Arbor: University of Michigan Press, 1950), D 168; for *Mirror* as source, see Forker, 5.2.22n.

62 Ironically, Spencer Junior mentions 'lessons' and 'preachments' when jesting about the heads of the 'nobility' that will 'preach on poles' (11.20–2).

63 Spencer Junior lectures Baldock against saying 'an't may please your honour' (5.40) but employs 'an it like your grace' to Edward with apparent sincerity (11.43), underlining the role of social context in utterances; cf. 4.2.

64 That is, they are seen not as having followers, as would any noble or royal officer, but as associated with a group apishly constituted by mere likeness: a rhetorical move important

in the case of Gaveston (see Holinshed, 6:319 on likes attracting one another). The multi-valent term 'servant', which might include gentlemen or the offspring of noblemen attending on lords, complicates Spencer's designation as a 'servant'. Cf. Lancaster's use of 'his lordship' to mock 'My lord of Cornwall' (2.21, 17) and Mortimer Junior's similarly mock-formal usage (4.266, 285).

65 *Edward II* Q1 (1594) had been entered posthumously in the *Stationers' Register* on 6 July 1593. The 1619 title page of *The Whole Contention Between the Two Famous Houses of Lancaster and York* names Shakespeare 'gent'. I rely here on DEEP ('gent', http://deep.sas.upenn.edu/advancedsearch.php).

66 Cf. Ferne's formula: 'I.S. of D … Gentle-man, of the Innes of Court' (92).

67 See Ferne, 91–2, 60 and Squibb, 47–8.

68 See Constance Brown Kuriyama, *Christopher Marlowe: A Renaissance Life* (Ithaca: Cornell University Press, 2002), 203.

69 For Jonson's arrest as 'yoman', see 'Middlesex Sessions Rolls: 1598', http://www.british-history.ac.uk/middx-county-records/vol1/pp242-251 (accessed 27 June 2015). On 20 October 1623 he appears as '*Beniamin Johnson* of Gresham Colledge in London gent. aged fifty. yeares and vpwards' (Ian Donaldson, 'Jonson, Benjamin (1572–1637)', *Oxford Dictionary of National Biography*, Oxford University Press, 2004; online edn, September 2013, http://www.oxforddnb.com/view/article/15116 (accessed 27 June 2015).

70 Kuriyama guesses that Watson was 'more elegantly outfitted' or known personally to Sir Owen Hopton, the presiding official (83).

71 David Riggs, *The World of Christopher Marlowe* (New York: Henry Holt, 2004), 255.

72 R. B. Wernham, 'Christopher Marlowe at Flushing in 1592', *EHR* 91 (1976): 344–5.

73 Translation from Mark Eccles, *Christopher Marlowe in London* (1934; rpt. New York: Octagon Books, 1967), 166.

74 On this generational narrative, see Lawrence Manley and Sally Beth Maclean, *Lord Strange's Men and Their Plays*

(New Haven: Yale University Press, 2014), 165. The Countess of Pembroke attracted dedications between 1590 and 1593 from Marlowe, Spenser, Nashe, Watson, Nicholas Breton and Samuel Daniel (Eccles, 166–7).

75 Some recent studies have emphasized that the quest for patronage did not demand unmixed flattery; in fact, some poets seem to have woven critiques of hereditary aristocracy among their praises. For example, analyses of Spenser's dedicatory sonnets to the *Faerie Queene* (1590), of Marlowe's Latin epitaph lauding Sir Roger Manwood (1592–3) and of George Chapman's response to *Nennio, or A Treatise of Nobility* (1595) have detected 'edgy independence', risky presumption that a potential patron might appreciate 'the linguistic dexterity required to subvert political authority while seeming, at the same time, to submit to it'; some accounts have found writers enlisting opacity and triviality to register resentment at 'the public structure of rank by birth'. See William A. Oram, 'Seventeen Ways of Looking at Nobility: Spenser's Shorter Sonnet Sequence', in *Renaissance Historicisms: Essays in Honor of Arthur F. Kinney*, eds James M. Dutcher and Anne Lake Prescott (Cranbury, NJ: Associated University Presses, 2008), 103–19; Dympna Callaghan, 'Elegiac Aesthetics and the Epitaph on Sir Roger Manwood', in *Christopher Marlowe, the Craftsman*, eds Sarah K. Scott and M. L. Stapleton (Aldershot: Ashgate, 2010), 159–78; John Huntington, *Ambition, Rank, and Poetry in 1590s England* (Urbana: University of Illinois Press, 2001), 13–14, 69–74.

76 Urry calls John Marlowe 'indigent' (Urry, 42); Huntington refers to Marlowe's 'poor upbringing' (Huntington, 55).

77 See Eric Carlson 'The Origins, Function, and Status of the Office of the Churchwarden, with Particular Reference to the Diocese of Ely', in *The World of Rural Dissenters, 1520–1725*, ed. Margaret Spufford (Cambridge: Cambridge University Press, 1995), 164–207, esp. 170, 189.

78 Amanda Flather, *Gender and Space in Early Modern England* (Woodbridge: Boydell & Brewer, 2007), 147.

79 For disputes, see F. G. Emmison, *Elizabethan Life: Morals and the Church Courts* (Chelmsford: Essex Record Office, 1973),

130–6; for bibliography see Andy Wood, *The Memory of the People* (Cambridge: Cambridge University Press, 2013), 214.
80 Mary Dewar, ed., *De Republica Anglorum by Sir Thomas Smith* (Cambridge: Cambridge University Press, 1990), 76–7; Carlson, 190; Geoffrey Goodman, *Fall of Man* (London: 1616), 139–40.
81 See Catherine Wright, 'The Spatial Ordering of Community in English Church Seating, c. 1550–1700' (PhD thesis, University of Warwick, Department of History, 2002), 127–8.
82 'George Badcock of Great Bentley, co. Essex, gent v Abraham Comyns of the same', http://arts itsee.bham.ac.uk/AnaServer?chivalry+0+start.anv+case=20 (accessed 1 March 2015). On under- and over-performance, see John Walter, 'Gesturing at Authority: Deciphering the Gestural Code of Early Modern England', *Past & Present* 203, Supplement 4 (2009): 96–127.
83 See Dave Postles, 'The Politics of Address in Early-Modern England', *Journal of Historical Sociology* 18.1–2 (2005): 99–121, 114.

Chapter 7

1 See especially *Political Theology and Early Modernity*, eds Graham Hammill and Julia Reinhard Lupton (Chicago: University of Chicago Press, 2012).
2 Henry S. Turner, 'Life Science: Rude Mechanicals, Human Mortals, Posthuman Shakespeare', *South Central Review* 26 (2009): 197–217; Julian Yates, 'More Life: Shakespeare's Sonnet Machines', in *Shakesqueer: A Queer Companion to the Complete Works of Shakespeare*, ed. Mahdavi Menon (Durham: Duke University Press, 2011), 333–42.
3 *The Indistinct Human in Renaissance Literature*, eds Jean E. Feerick and Vin Nardizzi (Palgrave Macmillan, 2012); Garrett A. Sullivan Jr., *Sleep, Romance and Human Embodiment: Vitality from Spenser to Milton* (Cambridge: Cambridge University Press, 2012).

4   Graham Hammill, 'Time for Marlowe', *ELH* 75 (2008): 291–314; Nichole Miller, *Violence and Grace: Exceptional Life between Shakespeare and Modernity* (Evanston: Northwestern University Press, 2014).

5   This trend is exemplified by a 2015 MLA panel entitled 'Marlowe's Queer Futurity', which featured papers by Judith Haber ('Marlowe's Queer Jew'), Jeffrey Masten ('Edward's Futures') and Stephen Guy-Bray ('First Thing We Do, Let's Kill All the Children'). To varying degrees, all three papers consider relations among queerness, vitality and futurity.

6   Ferris Jabr, 'Why Nothing Is Truly Alive', *New York Times*, 12 March 2014, http://nyti.ms/1fTmn4m (accessed 8 February 2015).

7   John Milton, *Areopagitica*, in *The Complete Prose Works of John Milton*, 8 vols, ed. Don M. Wolfe (New Haven: Yale University Press, 1953), 2: 492.

8   This analysis obviously resonates with Lee Edelman's *No Future: Queer Theory and the Death Drive* (Durham: Duke University Press, 2004). Edelman's concept of 'reproductive futurism' concerns a contemporary politics that, in its devotion to the figure of the Child, aligns homosexuality with the death drive. In contrast, my essay is part of a larger project, centred upon Marlowe and Shakespeare, that examines how life is constituted in a range of early modern discourses, including religious, natural philosophical and literary critical ones. For a rich examination of *Edward II* in relation to Edelman's groundbreaking work, see Masten, 'Edward's Futures', an essay to which this chapter is also indebted.

9   Christopher Marlowe, *Edward II*, rev. edn, eds Martin Wiggins and Robert Lindsey (1997: London: Methuen, 2014), 19.95, 98. Henceforth cited in the text.

10 Regiment here means 'Rule or government over a person, group, or country; governance; *esp.* royal authority' (*OED*, regiment, *n.*, 1.a.). The crucial point for this argument is that Edward understands royal authority, 'company' and vitality all to be bound up in one another.

11 Laurie Shannon notes that the play focuses on 'moments in monarchical construction – and … uses the question of the

king's company, his friendships, to do it' (*Sovereign Amity: Figures of Friendship in Shakespearean Contexts* [Chicago: University of Chicago Press, 2002], 157).

12 Marlowe later references the end of bliss for both Gaveston and Edward. At the moment of his capture by Warwick, Gaveston bemoans, 'O, must this day be period of my life, / Centre of all my bliss?' (10.4–5), which, in the Revels edition of the play, Charles Forker persuasively glosses as follows: 'must this day (centre of all my bliss because I was appointed to see Edward today) ironically mark the end of my life?' (*Edward II,* ed. Forker [Manchester: Manchester University Press, 1994], 2.6.45 note). When he is arrested, Edward strongly echoes Gaveston's earlier declaration, which he could not have heard: 'O day! The last of all my bliss on earth, / Centre of all misfortune' (19.61–2). The effect of these verbal repetitions is to suggest rhetorically the interwoven nature of the lives they are both to lose.

13 Jonathan Goldberg, *Sodometries: Renaissance Texts, Modern Sexualities* (Stanford: Stanford University Press, 1992), 122. Goldberg alludes to sodomy's status as 'categorical confusion itself ... a denial of those socially constructed hierarchies that are taken to be natural ...' (122).

14 On the imbrication of politics and sexuality in early modern literature, see Melissa Sanchez, *Erotic Subjects: The Sexuality of Politics in Early Modern English Literature* (Oxford: Oxford University Press, 2013).

15 For recent work on male friendship and *Edward II*, see, among others, Shannon, *Sovereign Amity*; Alan Bray, 'Homosexuality and the Signs of Male Friendship in Elizabethan England', in *Queering the Renaissance*, ed. Jonathan Goldberg (Durham: Duke University Press, 1994), 40–61; Alan Bray, *The Friend* (Chicago: University of Chicago Press, 2003); Jeffrey Masten, 'Toward a Queer Address: The Taste of Letters and Early Modern Male Friendship', *GLQ* 10 (2004): 367–84; and Alan Stewart, '*Edward II* and Male Same-Sex Desire', in *Early Modern English Drama: A Critical Companion*, eds Garrett A. Sullivan, Jr., Patrick Cheney and Andrew Hadfield (New York: Oxford University Press, 2006), 82–95. On the relationship between the king and his

favourites, see especially Mario DiGangi, *The Homoerotics of Early Modern Drama* (Cambridge: Cambridge University Press, 1997), 100–33; and Curtis Perry, 'The Politics of Access and Representations of the Sodomite King in Early Modern England', *Renaissance Quarterly* 53 (2000): 1054–83.

16 Quoted in Shannon, *Sovereign Amity,* 4. As Shannon demonstrates, this formulation derives from Aristotle. Shannon also observes that the notion that a true friend is worth more than a kingdom is a cliché that pits friendship against the monarch's responsibility to the commonwealth.

17 Ernst H. Kantorowicz, *The King's Two Bodies: A Study in Mediaeval Political Theology* (Princeton: Princeton University Press, 1957), 171. The interpolated material is from Henry of Bracton.

18 For a critique of this approach, see Lorna Hutson, 'Imagining Justice: Kantorowicz and Shakespeare', *Representations* 106 (2009): 118–42. Hutson's essay appears in a special issue of *Representations* devoted to Kantorowicz's work.

19 See, e.g., Julia Reinhard Lupton, *Citizen-Saints: Shakespeare and Political Theology* (Chicago: University of Chicago Press, 2005).

20 See, e.g., Lorna Hutson, 'Not the King's Two Bodies: Reading the "Body Politic" in Shakespeare's *Henry IV*, Parts 1 and 2', in *Rhetoric and Law in Early Modern Europe*, eds Victoria Kahn and Lorna Hutson (New Haven: Yale University Press, 2001), 166–98.

21 In this regard, it is worth noticing how Gaveston's reference to 'living and being' is echoed in the opening line of 'The Passionate Shepherd', 'Come live with me and be my love'. Moreover, the invitation extended by Marlowe's poem is to an immediate future in which life is lived in the present tense.

22 Helkiah Crooke, *Mikrokosmographia* (London: W. Iaggard, 1616), sig. S3^r, S3^v.

23 'The dissolution of created things is but a resolution of one thing into another; hence comes the perpetuity of all things though subiect to alteration, a perpetuity I say, not of the same particular thing distinguished by one and the

same forme, but of the Elementary parts whereof it was compounded' (Crooke, sig. S3^v).

24 Fred B. Tromly, *Fathers and Sons in Shakespeare: The Debt Never Promised* (Toronto: University of Toronto Press, 2010), x.

25 William Shakespeare, *Shakespeare's Sonnets*, ed. Katherine Duncan-Jones (1997; London: Thomson Learning, 2007).

26 Shakespeare extends the replicative model of parenthood to father-daughter relations in *Lucrece* when Lucretius, bemoaning the suicide of his daughter, asserts 'That life was mine which thou hast here deprived; / If in the child the father's image lies, / Where shall I live now Lucrece is unlived?' (*The Poems*, ed. F. T. Prince [1960; London and New York: Routledge, 1990], 1752–4).

27 Patrick Cheney argues that Edward's passionate, kingly discourse during the prison scenes provides evidence of a Marlovian model of the tragic sublime. See *Marlowe's Republican Authorship: Lucan, Liberty, and the Sublime* (Basingstoke, Hampshire: Palgrave Macmillan, 2009); and '*Edward II*: Marlowe, Tragedy and the Sublime', in *The Cambridge Companion to English Renaissance Tragedy*, eds Emma Smith and Garrett A. Sullivan, Jr. (Cambridge: Cambridge University Press, 2010), 174–87.

28 For more on Edward's deposition, see Ronald Knowles, 'The Political Contexts of Deposition and Election in *Edward II*', *Medieval and Renaissance Drama in England* 14 (2001): 105–21; and Robert P. Merrix and Carole Levin, '*Richard II* and *Edward II*: The Structure of Deposition', *Shakespeare Yearbook* 1 (1990): 1–13.

29 Marie Rutkoski, 'Breeching the Boy in Marlowe's *Edward II*', *Studies in English Literature, 1500–1900* 46 (2006): 281–304, esp. 297 n.1. Rutkoski here surveys criticism in support of this view.

30 For more on Isabella, see, among others, Dympna Callaghan, 'The Terms of Gender: "Gay" and "Feminist" *Edward II*', in *Feminist Readings of Early Modern Culture: Emerging Subjects*, eds Valerie Traub, Lindsay M. Kaplan and Callaghan (Cambridge: Cambridge University Press, 1996),

275–301; Joanna Gibbs, 'Marlowe's Politic Women', in *Constructing Christopher Marlowe*, eds J. A. Downie and J. T. Parnell (Cambridge: Cambridge University Press, 2000), 164–76; Kate Chedgzoy, 'Marlowe's Men and Women: Gender and Sexuality', in *The Cambridge Companion to Christopher Marlowe,* ed. Patrick Cheney (Cambridge: Cambridge University Press, 2004), 245–61; and Alison Findlay, 'Marlowe and Women', in *Christopher Marlowe in Context* (Cambridge: Cambridge University Press, 2013), 242–51.

31 This in spite of the fact that Edward and Gaveston inpugn Isabella's integrity from very early on, as when the king alludes to her as a 'French strumpet' (4.145). Here, Isabella's putative inconstancy records her status as a perceived obstacle to the relationship between king and favourite. Of course, Edward's insult could be taken to suggest the queen has had a longer history of infidelity than is usually thought, but this interpretation is at odds with the play's unironic depiction of her initial loyalty to her husband.

32 Rutkoski, 281; Masten, 'Edward's Futures'.

33 Judith Haber, *Desire and Dramatic Form in Early Modern England* (Cambridge: Cambridge University Press, 2009), 1.

Chapter 8

1 Jeremy Lopez, *Constructing the Canon of Early Modern Drama* (Cambridge: Cambridge University Press, 2014), 59. Unless otherwise indicated, full citations for most titles quoted in this chapter are available in the Annotated Bibliography. All quotations from the play are taken from the New Mermaids 2014 revised edition of *Edward II*, edited by Martin Wiggins and Robert Lindsey with a new introduction by Stephen Guy-Bray.

2 This is primarily an effect of the lack of other examples in the most commonly used text for these courses. For example, the widely used Norton *English Renaissance Drama* does not include any other play on English history (John Ford's *Perkin*

Warbeck would be a logical choice, but the Norton uses *'Tis Pity She's a Whore* to represent Ford's work).

3   *Piers Gaveston* was printed in 1594 and was revised and expanded in 1596. *Mortimeriados* was printed in 1596. Together, the two poems run to about 600 stanzas. The Gaveston poem closes with Gaveston's funeral and Edward's threats of revenge. *Mortimeriados*, interestingly, centres on the 'tragicke' fate of Mortimer rather than Edward's story. It is difficult to make any arguments about direct connections between these works, but the fact that a number of literary treatments of Edward II's reign found their way into the public eye in the same few years is worth noting.

4   Michael Drayton, *Peirs Gaueston Earle of Cornvvall His life, death, and fortune* (London: Nicholas Ling and John Busby, 1594), sig. K3^v.

5   Thomas Kyd, *The Spanish Tragedie, Containing the lamentable end of Don Horatio, and Bel-Imperia: With the pittifull death of olde Hieronimo* (London: Edward White, 1592): sig. E1^v-E2^r.

6   The early stanzas are filled with references that at least have an affinity to Kyd's version of a classical underworld.

7   George Peele's *Edward the First* (1593, first performed between 1590 and 1593) dramatizes an earlier part of the history of this period, indicating interest in the history of the decades preceding those chronicled by Shakespeare's historical drama which focus on Edward III's descendants.

8   Mortimer Junior, the play's closest analogue to a Machiavellian schemer, remains invested in traditional lines of authority and even his fantasies of usurpation do not carry the kinds of disruptive associations that, say, Bolingbroke's do. This is not to mention that he fails in those ambitions and the dead king's son takes the throne and assumes the reins of power without question.

9   This passage, as well as the speech of Mortimer Senior that precedes it, is important in thinking about how the play represents attitudes toward sexuality.

10 Ronald Knowles' essay 'The Political Contexts of Deposition

and Election in *Edward II*' gives a helpful overview of many of the political issues at stake in the play.
11 The play was not ascribed to Marlowe until much later, and it is interesting to speculate about why Richard Jones did not put Marlowe's name on the play. On Marlowe's notoriety, see Syme, 2013.
12 See Michael Stapleton's *Marlowe's Ovid: The Elegies in the Marlowe Canon* (Aldershot: Ashgate, 2014) and his 'Marlowe's First Ovid: *Certaine of Ovids Elegies*' in *Christopher Marlowe the Craftsman: Lives, Stage, and Page*, eds Sarah K. Scott and M. L. Stapleton (Aldershot: Ashgate, 2010), 137–48.
13 Guy-Bray's introduction to the New Mermaids third edition of the play seems to me to make precisely the error Wiggins cautions against. Marlowe ought not to be reduced to a single thematic in this play or any of his work.
14 Gaveston's relatively low status is more of problem than the fact that he's a man.
15 In the play, it also appears to be Lightborne's invention – there is no instruction about it from anyone. Lightborne calls it only a 'braver way' (23.36) to murder someone.
16 His plays are staged regularly, just not filmed.
17 Derek Jarman, *Queer Edward II* (British Film Institute: London, 1991), iii.
18 Wiggins' introduction to the second edition New Mermaids text offers a good overview of Jarman's film. See also this volume's chapter on performance history.
19 To name only a few examples, *The Life of Galileo, Coriolanus, The Duchess of Malfi* and *The Threepenny Opera* are either adaptations of early modern plays or are set in the period.

SELECT BIBLIOGRAPHY

Ahlgren, Angela K., 'Christopher Marlowe's "Unholy Fascination": Performing Queer *Edward II* in the 1990s', *Journal of Dramatic Theory and Criticism* 25.2 (2011): 5–22.

Archer, John, *Sovereignty and Intelligence: Spying and Court Culture in the English Renaissance* (Stanford: Stanford University Press, 1993).

Bailey, Amanda, *Flaunting: Style and the Subversive Male Body in Renaissance England* (Toronto: University of Toronto Press, 2007).

Bartels, Emily C., *Spectacles of Strangeness: Imperialism, Alienation, and Marlowe* (Philadelphia: University of Pennsylvania Press, 1993).

Bevington, David, *From Mankind to Marlowe: Growth of Structure in the Popular Drama of Tudor England* (Cambridge: Harvard University Press, 1962).

Boyette, Purvis, 'Wanton Humour and Wanton Poets: Homosexuality in Marlowe's *Edward II*', *Tulane Studies in English* 22 (1977): 33–50.

Bray, Alan, 'Homosexuality and the Signs of Male Friendship in Elizabethan England', in *Queering the Renaissance*, ed. Jonathan Goldberg (Durham: Duke University Press, 1994), 40–61.

Bray, Alan, *Homosexuality in Renaissance England* (New York: Columbia University Press, 1995).

Bray, Alan, *The Friend* (Chicago: University Chicago Press, 2003).

Bredbeck, Gregory W., *Sodomy and Interpretation: Marlowe to Milton* (Ithaca: Cornell University Press, 1991).

Brown, Georgia E., 'Tampering with the Records: Engendering the Political Community and Marlowe's Appropriation of the Past in *Edward II*', in *Marlowe's Empery: Expanding his Critical Contexts*, eds Sara Munson Deats and Robert A. Logan (Newark: University of Delaware Press, 2002), 164–87.

Callaghan, Dympna, 'The Terms of Gender: "Gay" and "Feminist" *Edward II*', in *Feminist Readings of Early Modern Culture: Emerging Subjects*, eds Valerie Traub, M. Lindsay Kaplan, and Dympna Callaghan (Cambridge: Cambridge University Press, 1996), 275–301.

Cartelli, Thomas, '*Edward II*', in *The Cambridge Companion to Christopher Marlowe*, ed. Patrick Cheney (Cambridge: Cambridge University Press, 2004), 158–73.

Cheney, Patrick, *Marlowe's Counterfeit Profession: Ovid, Spenser, Nationhood* (Toronto: University of Toronto Press, 1997).

Cheney, Patrick ed., *The Cambridge Companion to Marlowe* (Cambridge: Cambridge University Press, 2004).

Cheney, Patrick, *Marlowe's Republican Authorship: Lucan, Liberty, and the Sublime* (Basingstoke: Palgrave Macmillan, 2009).

Crewe, Jonathan V., 'Disorderly Love: Sodomy Revisited in Marlowe's *Edward II*', *Criticism* 51.3 (2009): 385–99.

DiGangi, Mario, *The Homoerotics of Early Modern Drama* (Cambridge: Cambridge University Press, 1997).

Forker, Charles R. ed., *Edward II by Christopher Marlowe* (Manchester: Manchester University Press, 1994).

Friedenreich, Kenneth, Roma Gill and Constance B. Kuriyama, eds, '*A Poet and a filthy Play-maker': New Essays on Christopher Marlowe* (New York: AMS Press, 1988).

Fuller, David, 'Love or Politics: The Man or the King? *Edward II* in Modern Performance', *Shakespeare Bulletin* 27.1 (2009): 81–115.

Gibbs, Johanna, 'Marlowe's Politic Women', in *Constructing Christopher Marlowe*, eds J. A. Downie and J. T. Parnell (Cambridge: Cambridge University Press, 2000), 164–76.

Goldberg, Jonathan, *Sodometries: Renaissance Texts, Modern Sexualities* (Stanford: Stanford University Press, 1992).

Greenblatt, Stephen, 'Marlowe and Renaissance Self-Fashioning', in *Two Renaissance Mythmakers: Christopher Marlowe and Ben Jonson*, ed. Alvin Kernan (Baltimore: Johns Hopkins University Press, 1977), 41–69.

Guy-Bray, Stephen, 'Homophobia and the Depoliticizing of *Edward II*', *English Studies in Canada* 17 (1991): 125–33.

Haber, Judith, 'Submitting to History: Marlowe's *Edward II*', in *Enclosure Acts: Sexuality, Property and Culture in Early*

Modern England, eds Richard Burt and John Michael Archer (Ithaca: Cornell University Press, 1994), 170–84.

Haber, Judith, *Desire and Dramatic Form in Early Modern England* (Cambridge: Cambridge University Press, 2009).

Harraway, Clare, *Re-citing Marlowe: Approaches to the Drama* (Aldershot: Ashgate, 2000).

Hattaway, Michael, *Elizabethan Popular Theatre: Plays in Performance* (London: Routledge & Kegan Paul, 1982).

Hillman, Richard, *Shakespeare, Marlowe, and the Politics of France* (Basingstoke: Palgrave, 2002).

Knowles, Ronald, 'The Political Contexts of Deposition and Election in *Edward II*', *Medieval and Renaissance Drama in England* 14 (2001): 105–21.

Knutson, Roslyn L., 'Marlowe, Company Ownership, and the Role of Edward II', *Medieval and Renaissance Drama in England* 18 (2005): 37–46.

Leech, Clifford, 'Marlowe's "*Edward II*": Power and Suffering', *Critical Quarterly* 1 (1959): 181–96.

Levin Jr., Harry, *The Overreacher: A Study of Christopher Marlowe* (Cambridge: Harvard University Press, 1952).

Manley, Lawrence and Sally-Beth Maclean, *Lord Strange's Men and Their Plays* (New Haven: Yale University Press, 2014).

Masten, Jeffrey, 'Toward a Queer Address: The Taste of Letters and Early Modern Male Friendship', *GLQ* 10 (2004): 367–84.

Masten, Jeffrey, 'Bound for Germany: Heresy, Sodomy, and a New Copy of Marlowe's *Edward II*', *Times Literary Supplement* (21/28 December 2012): 17–19.

Orgel, Stephen, *Impersonations* (Cambridge: Cambridge University Press, 1996).

Parks, Joan, 'History, Tragedy, and Truth in Christopher Marlowe's *Edward II*', *Studies in English Literature* 39 (1999): 275–90.

Perry, Curtis, 'The Politics of Access and Representations of the Sodomite King in Early Modern England', *Renaissance Quarterly* 53. 4 (2000): 1054–83.

Perry, Curtis, *Literature and Favoritism in Early Modern England* (Cambridge: Cambridge University Press, 2009).

Preedy, Chloe Kathleen, *Marlowe's Literary Scepticism: Politic Religion and Post-Reformation Polemic* (London: Bloomsbury, 2012).

Rufo, Jeffrey, 'Marlowe's Minions: Sodomitical Politics in *Edward II* and *The Massacre at Paris*', *Marlowe Studies* 1 (2011): 5–23.

Rutkoski, Marie, 'Breeching the Boy in Marlowe's *Edward II*', *Studies in English Literature* 46 (2006): 281–304.

Ryan, Patrick, 'Marlowe's Edward II and the Medieval Passion Play', *Comparative Drama* 32.4 (Winter 1998–9): 465–95.

Shannon, Laurie, *Sovereign Amity: Figures of Friendship in Shakespearean Contexts* (Chicago: Univerity of Chicago Press, 2002).

Smith, Bruce, *Homosexual Desire in Shakespeare's England: A Cultural Poetics* (Chicago: University of Chicago Press, 1991).

Stewart, Alan, '*Edward II* and Male Same-Sex Desire', in *Early Modern English Drama: A Critical Companion*, eds Garrett A. Sullivan, Jr., Patrick Cheney and Andrew Hadfield (New York: Oxford University Press, 2006), 82–95.

Summers, Claude J., 'Sex, Politics, and Self-Realization in *Edward II*', in *'A Poet and a Filthy Play-maker': New Essays on Christopher Marlowe*, eds Kenneth Friedenreich, Roma Gill, and Constance Brown Kuriyama (New York: AMS Press, 1988), 221–40.

Syme, Holger Schott, 'Three's Company: Alternative Histories of London's Theatres in the 1590s', *Shakespeare Survey* 65 (2012): 269–89.

Syme, Holger Schott, 'Marlowe in his Moment', in *Christopher Marlowe in Context,* eds Emily Bartels and Emma Smith (Cambridge: Cambridge University Press, 2014), 275–84.

Thurn, David H., 'Sovereignty, Disorder, and Fetishism in Marlowe's *Edward II*,' *Renaissance Drama* 21 (1990): 115–41.

Tribble, Evelyn, 'Marlowe's Boy Actors', *Shakespeare Bulletin* 27 (2009): 5–17.

Voss, James, '*Edward II*: Marlowe's Historical Tragedy,' *English Studies* 63 (1982): 517–30.

Weil, Judith, *Christopher Marlowe: Merlin's Prophet* (Cambridge: Cambridge University Press, 1977).

White, Paul Whitfield, ed., *Marlowe, History, and Sexuality: New Critical Essays on Christopher Marlowe* (New York: AMS Press, 1998).

Willis, Deborah, 'Marlowe Our Contemporary: *Edward II* on Stage and Screen', *Criticism* 40.4 (1998): 599–622.

INDEX

'2 Seven Deadly Sins' 122
1588 ('the dangerous summer') 100–2

Acton, Wallace (as Edward II) 66
Admiral's Men, the 4, 44, 120–1, 129, 136–7, 138, 141, 143
adultery 12–13, 31, 52, 181, 191–2
Agamben, Giorgio 175
Ahlgren, Angela 57, 58, 60
AIDS crisis 57, 60–1, 70
Alleyn, Edward 93, 121–2, 125–6, 127, 134, 140, 142–3
'Alls Perce' 139
Aman 108
anachronisms 111–17
Anderson, Kathleen 77
Anderson, Thomas 92
Angels in America 67
anthologies 25–6, 29–31, 195, 211–12
antiquarians 25–7
Archer, John Michael 78–9
Arden of Faversham 2, 131, 197
aspiration 5, 12, 38, 86, 146–7, 157
Atwood, Emma 89–90

audiences 37–8, 39–40, 45, 46, 67, 92

Badcock, George 171
Bailey, Amanda 85–6
Baines, Richard xviii, 27–8, 37
Bakeless, John 98–9
Barnes, Roger xx–xxi, 3
Bartels, Emily 75, 238 n.8
Bartels, Emily and Emma Smith 212
Beale, Simon Russell (as Edward II) 1, 58–60
Bednarz, James 227 n.4
Beer, Anna 209
Beeston, Christopher 137, 143, 258 n.52
Beeston, William 143
Bell, Henry xxi, 3
Belsey, Catherine 81
Belt, Debra 82, 213
Bennett, Susan 64
Bentley, Eric 51, 233 n.20
Bentley, G. E. 260 n.69
Berry, Herbert 137, 141
Bevington, David 39, 93–4, 124, 211, 256 n.31
Bianco, Marcie 87
Billington, Michael 57, 59, 70
blank verse 5, 50, 56–7, 70
Blayney, Peter W. M. 134–5, 222 n.11

Boar's Head Theatre, the 137, 141
Boas, Frederick S. 21
book to be read 4–5, 23–4
Boucher, Jacqueline 102
Boucher, Jean 98, 102
Bourdieu, Pierre 145, 147–8
Bradbrook, Muriel 223 n.17
Bradley, A. C. 34
Brady, Jennifer 76
Braham, Humfrey 148–9
Brandt, Bruce 237 n.1
Bray, Alan 47, 74–6, 207, 213
Brecht, Bertolt 36, 49–53, 78, 208
   epic theatre, and 50–1, 69
   later productions of his *Edward II* 52
Bredbeck, Gregory 74, 207, 213
Breight, Curtis 79–80
Briggs, Julia 98
Britland, Karen 143
Broughton, James 36, 228 n.9
Brown, Georgia 90–1
Brumble, H. David 85
Burbage, James 94, 122–3, 143
Burbage, Richard 93, 122–3, 130, 143
Burnett, Mark Thornton 79
Bush, M. L. 148
Bushell, Kirsty (as Kent) 69

Cairncross, A. S. 131
Callaghan, Dympna 14, 77, 226 n.40
Camden, William 151–2, 160, 265 n.26
Campaspe 37
Cardullo, Bert 61

Carroll, Stuart 102
Cartelli, Thomas 78, 82, 84, 155
Cary, Elizabeth xxi, 77, 223 n.14
cast number 128, 256 n.31, 257 n.46
Catholic League 100, 102, 109
Cecil, William 80, 109–10
censorship 27, 55, 83
Chamberlain's Men, the 136–7, 140, 141
Chambers, E. K. 122
Charlton, H. B. and R. D. Waller 125, 129, 135
Charney, Maurice 83
Chedgzoy, Kate 86
Cheney, Patrick 82–3, 90, 204, 214, 276 n.27
Clark, David 84–5
class competition 8, 78 *see also* conforming transgression
Clement, Thomas 171
Cole, Douglas 81–2
Coleridge, Samuel Taylor 31–2
Collings, Samuel (as Gaveston and Lightborne) 68
Comensoli, Viviana 76–7
Common Conditions 3
Comyns, Abraham 171
conforming transgression 147–8, 153–63, 167, 169, 171
conspicuous consumption 149–53
corporate vitality 12, 177, 180–93
Coss, Peter 263 n.12
Crafty Cromwell 24
Crane, Hart 40–1

INDEX

Crewe, Jonathan 84
criticism, of *Edward II* 212–18, 281–4
  before the 1990s 10–11, 22–41, 50, 76
  in the 1990s 74–84
  in the twenty-first century 84–95
  psychoanalytic 76–7, 80–1, 94
Crooke, Helkiah 185–7, 191, 193, 275–6 n.23
Cunniffe, Emma (as Isabella) 68
Curtain, the 125, 137

Damon and Pithias 37
Daniel, Samuel 5, 149–50, 152, 160
Danter, John 3
Darney, Peter, dir. 68
Database of Early English Plays (DEEP) 218
date of composition 2, 120, 221 n.2
Davenant, William 25
'Dead Man's Fortune' 130
Deats, Sara Munson 39, 77, 91
Dekker, Thomas: *Seven Deadly Sins of London* 150–2
De l'Estoile, Pierre 101
Deleuze and Guattari 81
Deloney, Thomas 4
De Nogaret, Jean Louis (duc d'Épernon) 10, 98–117
Desportes, Philippe 102
Dessen, Alan 91
De Witt, Johannes 45
DiGangi, Mario 75–6, 247 n.6
Dodsley, Robert 25–6, 29

Dooley, Mark 214
doubling 11, 54, 65, 67, 68, 69
Downie, J. A. 43
Drayton, Michael
  Mortimeriados xx, 4, 198–9, 278 n.3
  Piers Gaveston xx, 4, 116–17, 150, 152, 160, 198–9, 252 n.46, 278 n.3
Duchess of Malfi, The 197

Edelman, Lee 273 n.8
editions of *Edward II*, modern 209–12
Edward II *see* corporate vitality; friendship; minion; sodomy
  leadership 8–9
  lines 121
  murder 10–11, 13, 76, 92, 97, 201, 206. *See also* Lightborne
  in performance *see* Acton; Alleyn; Beale; Brecht; Heffernan; Jacobi; Jarman; McKellen; Thornton Jr.
  sexuality 9–11, 40, 51, 74–7, 78–81, 84, 205–7
Edward II (1284–1327) xv–xvi
  representations of 4–5, 88, 98–111, 131–3, 138–41, 222–3 n.14 *see also* Daniel; Drayton; Holinshed
Edward III 14–16, 67, 69, 92–3, 191–2, 216
Edward III 131, 132–3, 139, 172–3
Edwards, Gale, dir. 66–7

Eliot, T. S. 36
Elizabeth I 14, 62, 78–80, 100, 109, 124, 151–2
Elizabethan politics 23, 79–80, 87–8, 94, 109, 200–2
Elizabethan Stage Society 43, 49
English Short Title Catalogue (ESTC) 218
Evans, Rachel 66

Fabyan, Robert 4, 82, 97, 110
Famous Victories of Henry V, The 131
Feldman, Doris 86
Ferne, John 269 n.58, 60
Feuchtwanger, Lion 50
First Part of the Contention, The 121–2, 129–30, 131–2, 140, 141, 172–3
Foley, Christopher D. 94
Forker, Charles R. 7, 22, 53, 83, 120, 209–10, 214–15, 221 n.2, 223–4 n.20
Fortune, the 140, 141
Foucault, Michel 11, 74, 95, 175
French Wars of Religion 100, 101–2
friendship 37, 47, 75, 83, 88–9, 181–3, 213, 267 n.42, 275 n.16
Froissart, Jean 106–7
Frow, Toby, dir. 68
Fuegi, John 51
Fuller, David 44, 46, 55, 57

Ganymede 10, 37
Gaveston *see* corporate vitality; friendship; minion; sodomy
as Ireland 87
opening speech 26–7, 152–3, 180–7, 198, 202–3
in performance 54, 56, 57, 59, 66, 67, 69 *see also* Brecht; doubling; Jarman
sexuality 9–10, 37, 46–8, 75–6, 79, 205–7
status 9, 40, 146, 155–65, 200–1
Gaveston, Piers (1284–1312) xv, 4, 98–111 *see also* Daniel; Dekker; Drayton; Holinshed
Geckle, George 93
gender 13–14, 64, 77, 85, 86, 151, 203, 205–7 *see also* masculinity; women
genre 1, 15–16, 22–5, 31–2, 34–8, 43, 81–2, 90–1, 93–4, 196–9
Gibbons, Brian 212
Gibbs, Joanna 86
Globe, the 137, 141
Goldberg, Jonathan 74–6, 77, 96, 181, 207, 215, 274 n.13
Goldberg, Jonathan and Madhavi Menon 96
Goodman, Godfrey 170–1
Grafton, Richard 4
Graney, Sean, dir. 67–8
Granville-Barker, Harvey 43, 50
Greenblatt, Stephen 39–40
Greene, Robert 6, 227 n.5
Greenfield, Peter 126–8
Greg, W. W. 131, 138
Gurr, Andrew 122–3

Guy-Bray, Stephen 6, 11, 46, 76, 210, 221 n.2, 224 n.25, 225 n.32

Haber, Judith 80, 192, 215
Hakim, Rima 49
Hamilton, Nicholas 68
Hampton Court 124
Hansen, Claire 86
'harey of cornwell' 127, 128, 132, 133, 134
Harraway, Clare 91
Harrison, Stephen 207
Harrison, William 262 n.9
Hart, Alfred 124, 130–1, 133, 257 n.36
Hattaway, Michael 38
Hazlitt, William 29, 32–3, 229–30 n.27
Heal, Clive and Felicity Holmes 148
Healy, Thomas 77
Heffernan, John (as Edward II) 69
Helgerson, Richard 204, 215
Henry IV (1553–1610) 100
Henry III ('Henri III') (1551–1589) xviii, 10, 79, 98–117
Henslowe Alleyn Digitization Project 218–19
Henslowe, Philip 123
  diary xviii, xix, xx, 121, 131, 132, 136, 138–9, 141–2, 143
  letter, to Alleyn 125–6, 134, 136
Herbert, Mary Sidney 168
Heywood, Thomas 142–3
Hill-Gibbins, Joe, dir. 1, 68–70

Hillman, Richard 98–9, 247–8 n.10
Hinds, Ciaran (as Mortimer Junior) 59
Histoire tragique (1588) 10, 98–117, 250–1 n.30
  'Au lecteur' 104–7, 110–11
  author 102–3
  dedicatory epistle to Épernon 103
  impact 108–9
  'Sonet av Roy' 103–4
  translator 104
history 7–9, 15, 80, 81–2, 88, 92, 95–6, 97–8, 205 *see also* Brecht; genre
Hobson, Harold 54
Holinshed's *Chronicles* 4, 7–14, 23, 47–8, 82, 85, 90–1, 146, 149, 158, 225 n.33
Holme, Wilfrid 266 n.36
Hopkins, Lisa 24, 91
Horton, Philip 40–1
Hotson, J. Leslie 36
Hytner, Nicholas, dir. 1

irony 81, 146–7, 153–64
Isabella 10–16, 31, 52, 75, 77, 86, 111–14, 191–2, 226 n.38 *see also* adultery; Cunniffe; Swinton; women
'Isle of Dogs' 136

Jabr, Ferris 176
Jackson, MacDonald 131
Jacobi, Derek (as Edward II) 53–4, 56
James I (James VI) 47, 76, 78–9, 99, 101, 268 n.51

Jarman, Derek 1, 43–4, 60–5, 69, 70, 78, 85, 207–8, 236 n.49
Jeffes, Abel 3
John a Kent and John a Cumber 128
Johnson, Samuel 32, 229–30 n.27
Jones, Bettrys (as Edward III) 69
Jones, Richard xviii, 3, 279 n.11
Jones, William xix–xx, 2, 3, 119–20, 134, 221 n.3
Jonson, Ben 168, 223 n.16
  Poetaster 255 n.25
  Mortimer His Fall 143, 223 n.14
  Tale of a Tub, A 143

Kahn, Michael 66
Kantorowicz, Ernst 183–4
Kay, Dennis 79
Kelly, William B. 81
Keenan, Siobhan 23, 94
Kewes, Paulina 88, 201–2, 216
King Leir 131
King, T. J. 122
Kinney, Arthur 212
Kirk, Andrew M. 98
Knack to Know a Knave, A 128
Knowles, Ronald 87, 216
Knutson, Roslyn L. 92–3
Kocher, Paul H. 37–8, 98
Kuriyama, Constance B. 121, 123, 142–3
Kyd, Thomas xviii, xix, 123
  Soliman and Perseda 2, 131, 133

  Spanish Tragedy, The 3, 128, 131, 133–4, 172–3, 197, 198, 199

Lamb, Charles 29–31
language 5–6, 40, 48–9, 53, 89, 147–8 *see also* blank verse
L'atheisme de Henry de Valoys 108
Leech, Clifford 39
Lefebvre, Henri 89–90
Lennox, Annie 62
Les Choses horribles 108–9
Les Moeurs, humeurs et comportemens 108
Lesser, Zachary 222 n.8
Lettre d'vn gentil-homme 101–2
Levin, Harry 38
Life and Death of Jack Straw, The 3, 172–3
Lightborne 31, 45–8, 51, 54, 57, 59–60, 66, 67, 69, 190–1 *see also* Brecht; doubling; Jarman
Lodge, Thomas: *Wounds of Civil War, The* 198
Logan, Robert 93
Longinus 90
Lopez, Jeremy 25–6, 142, 195, 229 n.24
Lord Cholmeley's players 127
Lord Strange's Men 120–1, 122–3, 125–6, 127, 128, 129, 131–2, 133–4
Lost Plays Database 219
Luminarium 219
Lunney, Ruth 92
Lust's Dominion 25

Machiavel 11, 86, 146, 160, 278 n.8
Machiavelli 82–3, 106
MacLean, Sally-Beth 125
Manley, Lawrence and Sally-Beth MacLean 123, 128, 130, 133, 256 n.34
Marlowe Bibliography Online 219
Marlowe, Christopher
  atheism 6, 27
  biography xvi–xix, 24, 36–7, 78–9, 167–71, 202
  career, conception of 82–3, 204
  Dido xx, 25, 37, 138, 142, 204, 221–2 n.5
  Doctor Faustus xx, 11, 24–5, 32–3, 43, 121, 138, 142, 172–3, 195
  Hero and Leander 25, 26, 195, 202–3
  Jew of Malta, The xviii, 11, 21, 25–6, 128, 134, 138, 140, 142, 196, 204
  Lucan translation 3–4, 90, 195, 204
  Massacre at Paris xix, 2, 87, 97–8, 112–16, 123, 131, 134, 140, 142, 172–3
  'moment' 3, 5, 217
  'Passionate Shepherd' 195, 275 n.21
  sexuality 27, 36–7, 41, 44
  Tamburlaine xvii, xviii, 5, 6, 15, 23, 30, 93, 121, 142–3, 146–7, 172–3, 203–4
Marlowe, John 169–71
  sidesman 170–1
Marlowe Society 219
Marlowe Society of America (MSA) 219–20
Martyn, William 5
Mary Queen of Scots 100, 102
masculinity 8, 86–7
Masten, Jeffrey 23–4, 89, 94–5, 192
McAdam, Ian 77–8
McKellen, Ian (as Edward II) 54–7
McMillin, Scott 121, 130
McMillin, Scott and Sally-Beth MacLean 121, 253 n.4
Medieval drama, and 11, 45–6
Melnikoff, Kirk 69–70
Merchant, W. Moelwyn 222–3 n.14
Merrix, Robert P. and Carole Levin 83
mighty line 5, 7, 217, 223 n.16
Milles, Thomas 263 n.15, 268 n.55
Milton, John 176
minion 10, 75, 87, 98, 111–15, 117
Mirror for Magistrates, The xx, 4–5, 116, 200, 226 n.37
monarchy 79, 80, 88–9, 154, 200–1
  dynastic 12, 14–15, 46, 87–8, 138–9, 176–7, 180, 183–92, 201–2
Monette, Richard, dir. 65–6
Montaigne 182
'Mortimer' 140–1
Mortimer Junior 5, 11–15, 154–7, 164, 200–1 *see also* adultery; aspiration; sodomy

Mucedorus 37
'm*v*lomvr*co*' 128, 134
Murphy, Gerald, dir. 1, 57–60, 70

Nashe, Thomas xvi–xvii, xx, 6, 25, 204, 227 n.5
Newdigate, John 23, 94
Newington Butts Theatre 136
Nicklin, J. A. 98, 111
Nightingale, Benedict 58–9
Normand, Lawrence 79, 85

Orgel, Stephen 75
Osborn, Francis 268 n.51
OutRage! 57, 61, 62, 64
Ovid 82–3, 90, 195, 204, 214
ownership, company, of *Edward II* 120–4, 135–8

Palliser, D. M. 263 n.12
Parks, Joan 82, 216
patriarchy 76–7, 176, 186–7
Patterson, Rebecca, dir. 65
Pearson, Meg 92
Peele, George
 Edward I 2, 3, 132–3, 139, 172–3, 278 n.7
 Honour of the Garter, The 48
Pembroke's Men xviii–xix, 2, 23, 44, 47, 119–20, 135–6, 143–4, 168–9, 258 n.51
 acquisition of *Edward II* 93, 123–4
 founding 122–3
 repertory 121–2, 129–35, 140
 touring 23, 125–30, 136, 143
 venues 124–7
Pendergraft, Stacy 216–17
performance history, *Edward II*
 earliest production in the US 53
 early 2, 4, 23, 38, 43–9, 92–3 *see also* Pembroke's Men; repertory
 later 49–71
Perkins, Richard 142
Perry, Curtis 79, 88
Perry, Merry 87
Perseus Digital Library 220
Persons, Robert 109
Phillips, Edward 24–5, 26
plot structure 9, 33, 38–9, 46, 83, 216
Poel, William, dir. 49, 70
Porter, Katherine Anne 41
Potter, David 98
Potter, Lois 24, 65, 67
Preedy, Chloe Kathleen 87–8, 243 n.69
Prichard, Carla 80
Proser, Matthew 81
Proudfoot, Richard 131
publication history, *Edward II*
 1594 quarto xix, 2–3, 23, 44, 119–20, 125, 135, 167, 262 n.8
 1594 quarto, copies 21–2, 94–5, 221 n.4
 1622 quarto xxi, 3–4, 44, 119, 135, 137, 138, 141
 early xix–xxi, 3–4, 12, 135, 204, 222 n.10
 eighteenth and nineteenth centuries 25–6, 29–31, 34
 Stationers' Register entry 2, 120, 132

Puckering, John 123

Queen Anna's Men xx, 44, 47, 119–20, 136, 137, 143, 260 n.69
Queen Henrietta Maria's Players 137, 142–3
Queen's Men, the 93, 120–1, 125, 127, 129, 253 n.4

Records of Early English Drama (REED) 126–7, 136, 254 n.19
Red Bull Theatre xx, xxi, 4, 44, 45, 119, 135, 137
religion 15–16, 23–4, 45–6, 77–8, 82, 87–8, 94–5, 111, 114–15, 178–9, 185 *see also* French Wars of Religion; Marlowe
repertory, *Edward II* and history plays 131–4, 138–40, 141
  1592–3 130–5
  1594–8 138–40
  1598–1612 138, 140–1
  1612–1622 138, 141–2
  1622, post 143
Replique à l'antigauerston 101, 104, 108
reputation, early 24–7, 29–33, 43
Responce a l'antigaverston de Nogaret 101
Ribner, Irving 209–10
Richardson, Niall 64
Riggs, David 168
Ritson, Joseph 27–8, 35, 229 n.19
Robertson, Tony, dir. 53–7, 59, 60, 65, 207, 234 n.35, 234–5 n.36
Robinson, Jamie (as Gaveston) 66
Romany, Frank and Robert Lindsey 212
Rose, the 121, 122–3, 125, 128, 129, 131, 133–4, 136–7, 138, 141 *see also* Darney
Rowland, Richard 99, 210
Rufo, Jeffrey 87, 98, 247–8 n.10, 252 n.44
Rutkoski, Marie 87, 192
Rutter, Tom 217
Ryan, Patrick 45–6, 82

Saintsbury, George 29
Sales, Roger 81
Schelling, Felix 35–6
Scotland xv, 7–9, 247–8 n.10
Sedgwick, Eve 11, 74
Segar, William 262 n.9
Selimus 121
Semler, Liam E. 217
sexuality 9–11, 40, 43, 73–4, 78, 84–5, 95–6, 114, 185–7, 205–7 *see also* performance history, later; sodomy
Sexual Offences Act (1967) 54–5, 57
Shakespeare, William
  King Henry IV Part 1 93–4
  King Henry VI Part 1 1, 15, 131, 172–3
  King Henry VI Part 2 1, 15, 23, 154, 172–3
  King Henry VI Part 3 23, 154, 172–3

Lucrece 276 n.26
Richard II 22–3, 30, 33, 49–50, 54, 83, 93, 139–41, 172–3, 201–2
Richard III 15–16, 131, 141, 154, 172–3
Romeo and Juliet 131
sonnets 19, 187, 191, 193
Titus Andronicus 136–7
Shaltz, Justin 66
Shannon, Laurie 88–9, 182, 273–4 n.11, 275 n.16
Shaw, George Bernard 50
Sheckter, Jennifer L. 86
Shepherd, Alan 86–7
Sidney, Philip 91
Sidney, Robert 168
Sillitoe, Peter 89
Sirluck, Katherine 81
Skura, Meredith 83
Smith, Bruce 74–5, 265 n.28
Smith, G. Gregory 34–5
Smith, Thomas 170
sodomy 11–12, 47, 52, 74–7, 79–80, 84–7, 106–7, 155, 181–4 *see also* Bray; Bredbeck; Goldberg; Guy-Bray
Soller, Kyle (as Gaveston and Lightborne) 69
Somerset, J. A. B. 126
space 89–90
spectacle 14, 70, 146
Speed, John 5
Spencer, Charles 69–70
'Spencers, The' 140–1
Stafford, Sir Edward 100–1
staging requirements 45, 129
Sponsler, Clare 106
Stapleton, Thomas 109

status, of Baldock and the Spencers 9, 146, 165–7, 261 n.7
Steane, J. B. 39
Stern, Tiffany 45
Stewart, Alan 74, 85
Stone, Lawrence 148–9
Stonewall riots 62
Stow, John 4, 82, 97, 110, 117
Stymeist, David 85
Summers, Claude J. 40, 76, 146
Surgal, Jon 94
Swan, the 45, 136, 138
Swinton, Tilda (as Isabella) 62–4
Syme, Holger 136, 140, 142, 217

'Tamar Cham', Part One 134
Taming of a Shrew, The 37, 129, 136–7, 140
Taylor, Paul 235 n.39
Thatcher, Grant (as Gaveston) 59
Theatre, the 123, 125, 129, 137, 143, 254 n.18
Theatres Act (1968) 55
Thomas of Woodstock 2, 259 n.59
Tilney, Edmund 124
Treanor, Tim 66
Thomas, Vivian and William Tydeman 98
Thomson, Leslie 128, 129
Thornton Jr., René (as Edward II) 65
Thorpe, Thomas 3–4
Thurn, David 80
tragedy 13, 33, 38–40, 77–8,

90, 98, 179, 197 *see also* genre; wheel of fortune
Traub, Valerie 96
Tribble, Evelyn 92–3
Tromly, Fred 80, 186–7
Troublesome Reign of King John, The 2, 121, 131, 154, 172–3, 201
True Tragedy of Richard Duke of York, The 121–2, 129–32, 140, 141, 172–3
tyranny 196–7, 200–1

Urry, William 170

Valladarus, Susan 229 n.26
Verstegan, Richard 109
Villiers, George 47
vitality ('life') 12, 175–93
Voss, James 266 n.38

Warton, Thomas 26–8
Watson, Thomas xviii, 168–9, 269 n.59
Wentersdorf, Karl P. 131
Wentworth, Sir William 145–6, 149

wheel of fortune 15, 50, 166, 178–9, 200
White, Paul Whitfield 218
Wickham, Glynne 44–5
Wiggins, Martin 6, 11, 139, 140–1, 196, 205, 224 n.25, 223 n.17, 224. n.25, 225–6 n.36, 259 n.61
Wiggins, Martin and Robert Lindsey 99, 178–9, 211
Willis, Deborah 51–2, 78
Wilson, Robert 3
Wilson, Thomas 267–8 n.48
Winstanley, William 25
Womack, Peter 49, 51
women, and 13–14, 63–4, 77, 86, 191–2
Worcester's Men 136–7, 141
word frequencies 172–3, 261 n.4–5, 268 n.56
WW II 21–2

youth 12, 22–3, 206, 225–6 n.36

Zunder, William 80

www.ingramcontent.com/pod-product-compliance
Ingram Content Group UK Ltd.
Pitfield, Milton Keynes, MK11 3LW, UK
UKHW021859220326
469204UK00008B/59